the consumer
and his dollars

Illustrated by Dorothy Rosenwasser

the consumer and his dollars

by David Schoenfeld
& Arthur A. Natella

Foreword by ESTHER PETERSON
Special Assistant to the President
on Consumer Affairs

1966

Oceana Publications, Inc. / Dobbs Ferry, N.Y.

FOREWORD

As consumers, all of us are called on at one time or another to be amateur accountants, mechanics, electricians, chemists, dieticians or engineers in the selection and use of products and services. Yet all to often, we don't have the information or the training for the job.

This is where consumer education comes in—or should come in. I say "should" because there is all too little education at present devoted to helping people to spend their money wisely. Traditionally, the emphasis in education has been on producer skills rather than consumer skills. Learning has been largely geared to getting a good job. Not enough emphasis has been put on what to do with the money we earn from such a job.

The result often is a person or family with adequate income but with expenditures so unplanned that all sorts of problems arise. Consumer education, by preparing both young people and adults to handle their financial responsibilities wisely, can help reduce these difficulties.

By focussing on the personal, the practical and the present, consumer education also can help make school more interesting and more useful at a time when the need has never been greater. It is a good way of increasing the relevance of school to today's young people.

I welcome this book not because it lays down a prescribed blueprint but because it doesn't. There is no one way and no one book with which to teach such a broad and flexible subject as consumer economics. The President's Committee on Consumer Interests does not pretend to have a model to follow. There are almost as many ways of teaching this subject as there are teachers themselves.

What is needed is more teaching material like this book, which treats our economy in realistic, up-to-date terms. Its greatest values, in my opinion, lie in its frank approach to today's marketplace, its ability to translate theoretical terms into reality and its usefulness as a buying guide.

I need not agree with everything that is said in these pages, nor does the teacher who may use this guide. Consumer education, if taught successfully, teaches an individual to think for himself in the marketplace.

As the authors say (page 337):

"It should be made very clear that consumer education does not have as one of its purposes that of directing consumer choices. Purely and simply, it involves the exposure of all possible alternatives and opportunities for the consideration of the consumer. The individual consumer then assumes the responsibility for making a decision after having given full consideration to his particular needs and to the product that will best meet those needs."

Esther Peterson,
Special Assistant to the
President for Consumer Affairs

PREFACE

The Consumer And His Dollars is a down-to-earth textbook designed for use on the secondary school and college levels and for adult education. It has a very immediate application these days when our national government, through implementation of the Anti-Poverty Program, is attempting to improve the economic status of low income families. It naturally follows that the acquisition of additional income is meaningless without a corresponding increase in knowledge of how to stretch the dollars earned.

Despite the fact that almost eighteen percent of the country's population has an income considered to be at or below the poverty level, the mean income per family unit is over $8,000 a year. It is no surprise, therefore, that we are considered the richest consumers in the world. We are called a nation of spenders—and spend we do—over $400 billion out of an output of some $700 billion. Americans purchase about 65 percent of the nation's goods.

Whether individuals fit into the first category mentioned or are among the more fortunate who go to make up the majority of American consumers (some 40 million families), one important fact stands out— their resources are limited and all are faced with the economic problem of scarcity. All consumers are faced with crucial decisions whether they realize it or not! Should they buy? What should they buy? How should they buy? When and where should they buy? In making their decisions they may act irrationally, emotionally, or without knowledge due to indifference, gullibility or merely because they act with implicit faith in the American marketplace. Such faith is not always justified.

The consumer will find it difficult to consistently make truly free knowledgeable choices because some of his choices will be directed partly or entirely by the producer. Unlike the government, which purchases with caution and accurate advice from the National Bureau of Standards and other agencies, the consumer is left to his own devices to wallow in a vortex of confusion and indecision.

Every phase of life today requires consumer decisions. It has been estimated that in every twenty-four hour period an average American is bombarded knowingly or otherwise with some 1,500 commercial messages. It is safe to assume that for every message there must be a response—a decision.

The objective of *The Consumer And His Dollars* is to develop an awareness and an alertness to the importance of making wise consumer decisions. Such prudent action will not only lead to increased benefits to the individual American, but will, in the final analysis, result in perpetuation and improvement of our nation's free enterprise system. Producers will become more responsive if knowledgeable choices are made, and the nation's economy will reap additional dividends through an increase of healthy competition for the consumer's dollar.

While this text is intended for use in a variety of subject matter fields, it should prove to be especially useful to teachers of consumer education and economics and to educators who have participated in university programs sponsored by the National Committee for Education in Family Finance.

We are deeply indebted to Mr. Milton P. Barnhard for his many valuable suggestions and his skillful examination of the manuscript. The authors wish also to thank Mrs. Dorothy Rosenwasser for her meaningful illustrations which add flavor throughout the book. Grateful acknowledgement is also given Mrs. Madeline Scheele for her devoted efforts in conjunction with the preparation of the manuscript. Limitation of space precludes naming all the individuals in government, industry, education and private non-profit organizations who aided in various ways in the preparation of this book. We are forever in their debt.

David Schoenfeld
Arthur A. Natella

Acknowledgements

The excerpt on page 20 is from *The Jungle* by Upton Sinclair. All Rights Reserved. Reprinted by permission of The Viking Press, Inc.

The paragraph on page 50 from "What is A Better Business Bureau Anyhow?" *Changing Times,* October 1965, is excerpted by permission from *Changing Times,* Copyright 1965 by the Kiplinger Washington Editors, Inc.

The paragraphs on pages 75 and 76 from *The Hidden Persuaders* by Vance Packard are reprinted by permission of David McKay Company. Copyright © 1957 by Vance Packard.

The automobile tests on pages 133 to 137 are reprinted by permission of Consumers Union of the U.S. Copyright © 1962 by Consumers Union of the U.S., a non-profit organization.

The chart on page 89 is reprinted from *U.S. News and World Report,* published at Washington. Copyright 1966 U.S. News and World Report, Inc.

The excerpts from the case story on pages 175 to 178 are reprinted by permission of the Center for Consumer Affairs. Copyright 1965 by the Regents of the University of Wisconsin, Madison, Wisconsin.

The illustrations on pages 292, 296, 298, 299, 301 and 303 are reprinted by permission of *The American Legion Magazine* and the artist, Bob Clarke.

The excerpts from "*The Merchants of Menace* on page 293 are reprinted by permission of the American Medical Association.

The excerpts on pages 339 to 340 are reprinted by permission of the National Association of Secondary School Principals, Washington, D.C.

CONTENTS

THE CONSUMER'S CREED

- The right to a free choice in purchasing goods and services.

- The right to buy in an environment where free competition exists.

- The right to be informed in order to be able to make wise decisions.

- The right to safety in every phase of daily living including the foods we eat, medication, the air we breathe and the water we drink.

- The right to be heard in order to create effective communication between producer and consumer.

- The right to equal rank and representation with the producer.

1. the role of
the consumer

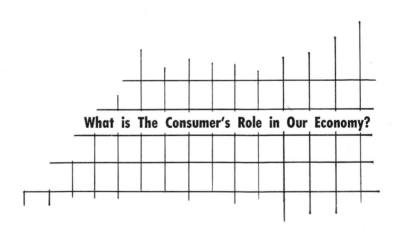

What is The Consumer's Role in Our Economy?

ARE YOU A CONSUMER?

Of course you are. Every person using goods or services of one kind or another is a consumer. As long as we live we act as consumers, even though most of us go on to become producers as well.

In order to earn money to satisfy our basic needs and the goals we may set for ourselves, we have to work. Work enables all consumers to obtain the goods and services they desire by providing purchasing power, another term for money. Whether you will work as a secretary, mechanic, store clerk, musician, electrician, lawyer or physician, you will be a producer. That means you will earn money with which you can obtain the basic necessities: food, clothing and housing. More than likely, you will be able to afford some luxuries as well. Your effectiveness as a producer will determine just how much more you will be able to obtain. You will be able to purchase an automobile, a television set, or whatever you set your sights on if you can earn the money to buy such goods. As a consumer you naturally will wish to get the most for your money. Wise use of money will permit you to enjoy a higher standard of living and to derive greater satisfaction. Effective consumer education will show you how to use your money intelligently and how to enjoy a more abundant life.

HOW IMPORTANT IS THE CONSUMER?

All the goods and services produced in our economy have one single final objective—CONSUMPTION. If there were no consumers, there would be no purpose in providing the many things that people want for the satisfaction of their needs. As a group, consumers constitute the most important element in our society. Potentially, they could direct what should be produced. In practice, however, consumers have always tended to act individually.

The producer must satisfy the consumer in order to remain in the market. The consumer exercises his economic vote every time he buys. Whenever you select a certain brand in preference to another competing brand of the same product you are casting a vote of approval for your particular choice. This vote, in our competitive economic system, means life or death for the producer.

If our economy were truly consumer directed, the above pattern would prevail. Unfortunately, such is not always the case—producers very often assume leadership by artificially creating demand for goods or services. When the producer dictates or directs the economic climate in which society operates, the economy is considered to be consumption directed. Producers' self-interest frequently tends to ignore the basic desires of the consumer for quality, economy and real value.

Examples of this are such products as: the electric back scratcher, the gold tooth pick, the electric card shuffler, the over-sized shoe horn, and the table-top egg boiler, which were certainly not produced because consumers demanded their production. There are thousands of products in this category, all produced in accordance with the usual competition for the consumer's dollar, but which do little to improve our standard of living or the overall quality of our national product.

The Consumer as the Focal Point of the Economy

Since the American consumer is so important he must learn to recognize his own power and how to utilize it for his own advantage as well as his country's. A wise, informed consumer can look forward with confidence to a life of satisfaction and well-being.

WHERE DOES THE CONSUMER PURCHASE
HIS GOODS AND SERVICES?

No matter how fine a pair of shoes a shoe company produces, no possible benefit will be derived by anyone unless (1) people learn of the existence of the shoes, (2) people find out where the shoes may be purchased, and (3) people become acquainted with the quality and value of the merchandise.

These three basic considerations apply to all goods and services. If this were not so, warehouses throughout the land would be overflowing with merchandise. In effect, without marketing and distribution the entire system would break down. Marketing and distribution form a link between the producer and the consumer.

In practice, a marketplace is created every time a buyer and a seller come together to exchange money for goods or services. A lawyer's office, a theatre box office, a supermarket and an ice-cream truck are all examples of a created market place. The marketplace is the symbol of our free competitive system with interaction between buyer and seller. Since the beginning of time, this marketplace has been dominated by the *caveat emptor* (let the buyer beware) philosophy. To a great extent, the seller has always held the advantage due to his *expertise*. An automobile salesman knows far more about his product than the prospective customer. This disadvantage can be reduced through increasing consumers' alertness and awareness.

Prices of goods and services are directly affected by consumer demand for the product and also by producer supply. Let us discover how a price is reached.

When teenagers create a demand for pocket-size transistor radios, the retail price of that product increases. In turn, manufacturers who are quick to react to any increase in demand, step up their production of radios. If the supply should begin to exceed the demand at any given time, producers might have to reduce the retail price in order to dispose of the product on hand. Price is the key factor affecting the transfer of commodities from producer to consumer. This situation will prevail if competition is perfect and complete. However, the buying and selling of commodities never take

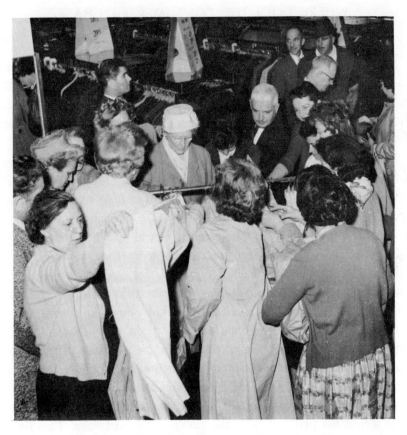

Consumers making daily decisions in the market place.

place under perfect competitive conditions. Outside influences, such as changes in taste, fashion, income, monopoly, and governmental involvement, all of which in some measure affect price, alter the delicate balance between supply and demand. So we see that the marketplace is a complex mechanism which is not as responsive as it should be to consumer demands.

WHAT IS THE AMERICAN ECONOMY?

In essence, America's economy is primarily directed by private enterprise under a modified system of governmental regulation in the public interest. A private enterprise system involves investment and assumption of risk by individuals and groups of individuals, but not by government, in order to make a profit. Thus, a reward is available to those who make investments and take the risks. Moreover, any individual enjoys the right to participate in our capitalistic system.

Any library you visit contains hundreds of thrilling accounts of individuals who rose to great heights on the American business scene by virtue of imagination, courage and strong desire to succeed. In most cases, they reaped fortunes from original investments that were very modest. The risks they took were large, however.

The basic strength of our economic system has always been illustrated by the evident eagerness to forge ahead despite tremendous odds. The prime motivation is the desire to achieve a profit.

Every economic system, capitalistic or otherwise, must provide answers to three basic questions: (a) What shall be produced?— which goods and services are demanded by the consumer? (b) How shall these be produced?—that is, what technology, labor and plant facilities are involved? (c) For whom shall these be produced? —which groups of consumers: farmer, factory worker, executive, professional, etc., and by what distribution system can these goods and services be obtained? The individual engaging in the challenging competitive struggle for profit must answer these questions in a way that will ensure satisfaction of consumer wants and needs. Failure to find correct answers will inevitably lead to failure.

In the early days of America's development our economic system was based on Adam Smith's philosophy of the *laissez faire* market— a market completely free of regulation. It was believed that this type of system would take care of society's needs provided it was left alone. Business eagerly supported this view and made every possible effort to discourage interference. As the nation progressed, however, Adam Smith's fears of business abuses (i.e., monopoly, unfair trade practices, and price discrimination leading to curtailed competition) appeared to be justified. By the end of the nineteenth century intervention by government became a necessity in order to protect the public interest. In 1887 the Interstate Commerce Act provided for regulation of railroads, and in 1890 the Sherman Anti-Trust Act was passed, thus eliminating practices that were considered to be in "restraint of trade."

As new forms of business organizations came into being and increased in power it became apparent that our nation's consumers were faced with new problems as they sought to make wise decisions. Therefore, government found itself obliged to play a larger role as a regulatory agency in order to preserve free competition.

Adam Smith's concept of *laissez faire* was predicated to a large degree on a state of perfect competition in which producers would be completely responsive to the consumption segment of the economy. This free market was the prevailing economic system in the United States until that period in our nation's history when business began to assume the power to influence the market. This power, as a consequence, offset the theoretical balance that had always characterized the market and gave rise to numerous imperfections.

In the years following the Civil War there was a clearly evident increase of instances which illustrate the attempt by business combinations to control the market by various devices. All of these resulted in price fixing, curtailment of production, and reduction of competition. These monopolistic tendencies became even more numerous as the nineteenth century drew to a close. Notable examples of combinations in this category at the time involved such commodities as beef, oil, coal, iron, steel, sugar and cotton— all commodities that offered large profit opportunities for the investor.

The first protests against the attempts by big business to curtail competition were made by the American farmer who felt the effects of the railroad companies' disregard for the "little man." In fact, the farmers' protests led to legislative action by several states (the Grange laws of the 1870's) in order to prohibit discriminatory practices by the railroads. The federal government from that period on has been thoroughly committed to its role as a regulator of the market place so that the imperfections of competition might be eliminated or at least minimized.

It should not be assumed, of course, that competition is affected solely through actions of the producer. We as consumers also do our share toward altering the competitive picture. It is no secret that certain industries have been adversely affected by the recent diet fads that have developed across the country. The cholesterol scare

To prevent excesses on the part of either consumers or producers, government has assumed the role of regulator to maintain (as far as possible) a balanced economy. This ideal is never fully realized in practice.

has reduced the demand for dairy products, certain meats, bakery products and candy. Another example of this is the change that an individual's income makes in his buying habits. A student working his way through college may favor hamburgers and frankfurters in order to make ends meet. However, after he embarks upon a career and begins to enjoy a better level of living, he probably will switch to steaks and more expensive cuts of meat. Also, is there a household that has not been shaken by the emergency that arises when ladies' fashions change? Mohair sweaters (slightly oversized) are eagerly snapped up by enthusiastic teenagers who wish to be "in." The producer has a stake in fostering these style changes which naturally result in increased sales and profits.

PRICE LEVEL

Producers constantly seek maximum return on their investments and therefore favor, as a general rule, high prices. Consumers, on the other hand, always desire maximum satisfaction at the lowest possible prices.

So we see that a real tug of war exists between all of us who are consumers and most of us who are also producers. As consumers we wish to receive top value at the lowest possible price. As producers we desire a reasonable return for our investment and the risk involved.

Production costs determine the selling price of a product and to a large degree the amount of profit that will be possible. No producer can afford to sell goods or services for any length of time at a price lower than the cost. The consumer also is limited—the price he can afford to pay for desired goods or services cannot be higher than his available purchasing power. These restrictions on the part of both producer and consumer produce a market in which each is attempting to gain advantage over the other—the consumer is always searching for the "buy of the year" (it does not exist), and the producer is engaged in a contest to get as large a share as possible of the consumer's dollar.

HOW DO ECONOMIC CONDITIONS AFFECT THE CONSUMER?

Economists have frequently referred to the actions of the economy as being similar to the ups and downs of a roller coaster ride. Even today, when we are not affected by those extreme variations in the economy which were so prevalent prior to World War II, there still exists a pattern of fluctuation which is felt directly by every consumer. It is safe to say that economic conditions are never static.

The dollars you have at your disposal do not have a fixed value. Variations in the value of the dollar (real income) reflect the changes that occur in the economy. In 1940 a dollar had a purchasing power of slightly more than twice that of a dollar in the base period of 1957-1959.[1] A man's suit which today sells for approximately $65 could be purchased in 1940 for about $25. This is how the principle of real income operates. You can see from the example just given that real income is the true value of money in terms of what goods and services you can obtain with that money.

The person who does the family shopping in your household is well aware of this principle even though he or she may not be able to explain it in economic language. How it operates is painfully clear. At one time a fixed amount of money may be able to buy four bags of meats and groceries. At another time the same amount of money may cover the cost of only three or three and a half bags of the same meats and groceries. The bags have not gotten smaller; the purchasing power of the dollar has been reduced.

The reverse situation occurs when the money at your disposal can buy more than four bags of food. In that case your money's purchasing power has increased. Unfortunately, this happy condition occurs only infrequently.

Changes in economic conditions are most quickly recognized when prices fluctuate. However, the factors basic to the changes are not always readily understood. Therefore, it is important that we examine the following listed factors:

DECREASE IN SUPPLY

A quick frost hits the citrus crops in Florida with the result that few oranges and grapefruit are in condition to be shipped to our markets. Much higher prices are charged for the remaining available supply.

INCREASE IN DEMAND

In the fall of 1965 several of the major color TV manufacturers announced price increases for their 1966 models. This was made necessary because of a tremendous demand for color TV. This de-

---

[1] *Statistical Abstract of the United States*, 1964, U. S. Department of Commerce, p. 351.

mand resulted from the fact that most television programs are being televised in color for the very first time. The manufacturers cannot keep up with this heavy demand.

INCREASED COSTS OF PRODUCTION

The 1963 strike of the New York City newspapers resulted in a wage increase for the workers. The cost of this wage increase was immediately passed along to the consumer, who had to purchase the papers at a new higher price.

FORCES OF INFLATION

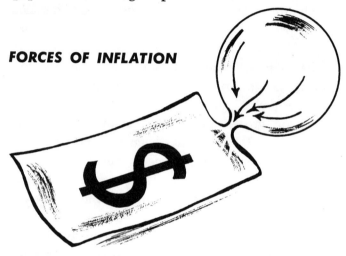

The purchasing power of the dollar is related directly to economic conditions. Where inflation exists, the dollar buys less.

INFLATION

After World War II there was a tremendous amount of money available for spending by the general public. During the war years their needs could not be met because the nation's manufacturers were busily engaged in producing for the military. However, beginning with 1946 and until 1948, when producers were able to meet the heavy demand, consumers bid up prices for such scarce or very limited items as automobiles, electric refrigerators, appliances, furniture and other household needs. An automobile that cost $850 in 1941 carried a price tag of approximately $1,750 five or six years later.

FORCES OF DEFLATION

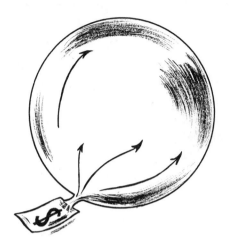

When deflation exists, the dollar increases in buying power.

DEFLATION

During a period of economic depression many people are unemployed and thus lose their purchasing power. Sellers, as a result, are faced with a decrease in the market for their goods. In order to stimulate buying, prices are reduced to attractive levels. Toward the end of the 1920's a Chevrolet automobile cost $995. Five years later the same automobile's cost had been lowered to $465.

TECHNOLOGICAL ADVANCES

With the development of assembly line methods of production prices usually reflected some of the gains realized by the producer. When Henry Ford first produced his Model T Ford it was literally assembled by hand. The first models sold for $900. As soon as Ford went into assembly line production the same model sold for $290 including the self-starter (not included in the original model which sold for $900).

In this Section you have been introduced to some important aspects of the consumer's role in our society. All of us who constitute the consumers of the nation are as important to the economy as gasoline is to an automobile—we make the wheels of the economy turn. Unless producers can sell their products to consumers they cannot remain in business.

Ideally, the economy should be balanced to the extent that producers are completely responsive to the actions of the consumer. Since such is not always the case, the consumer's status must be safeguarded and even elevated to one of equality with the producer. In the Sections that follow you will learn more about this important aspect of America's free enterprise system.

CONSUMER UNDERSTANDING CHECK

1. How does a producer go about creating a demand for his new product? Name several products for which a heavy public demand has been created in a relatively short time.

2. How many consumer-producers are there in your immediate family? How do they fit this double role?

3. Visit a local supermarket and determine how many varieties of packaged cookies and crackers are available on the shelves. Why are these different varieties available? How do these varieties affect consumer decisions?

4. How do each of the following qualify as producers?

   (a) a college professor   (e) an electrical engineer
   (b) an artist   (f) a government file clerk
   (c) a lawyer   (g) an F.B.I. agent
   (d) an assembly line worker

5. You have two dollars to spend. What factors affect your decision?

6. The family food budget is $20 for an entire week. One week you get four bags of groceries for that amount. A month later, buying the very same items, you get only three and a half bags of groceries. Why? Would this be an illustration of inflation or deflation?

7. There are approximately 8,000 items on display in an average supermarket. Every year 1,500 new items are introduced to the public. Of these only about 500 items continue to be produced after the first year. Why?

8. In **The New York Daily Tribune,** April 15, 1861, the **Tribune Almanac for 1861** was advertised at thirteen cents a copy. In 1965, the same publication was advertised at a price of one dollar a copy. What economic factors do you recognize as having caused this price change?

9. In a shopping center near your home a well-known discount house installs a shoe department. A small established shoe store close by promptly announces a special sale offering very generous price reductions. What are the motives? What benefits are there for the consumer who shops in the small neighborhood store?

10. You read in the newspaper that two supermarkets are offering a popular cereal at two different prices. The store within walking distance of your home is selling the cereal at a price two cents higher than the store which is over two miles from your home. Where would you buy the cereal? How would you defend your decision?

2. government
and the consumer

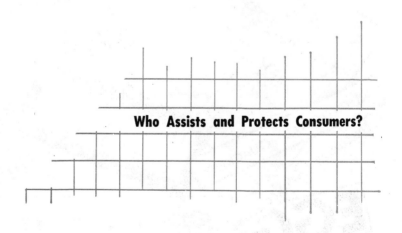

Who Assists and Protects Consumers?

DRUGS AND DRIVING

FRESH FANCY QUALITY

YOUR MONEY AND YOUR LIFE

ADVERTISING ALERT

SHOPPER'S GUIDE
To U. S. Grades for Food
U. S. DEPARTMENT OF HEALTH, EDUCATION, AND WELFARE

CHEESE BUYING GUIDE for CONSUMERS

HOUSEHOLD CHEMICALS

FAKE MEDICAL DEVICES

Read the Label

INSPECTED FOR WHOLESOMENESS U.S. DEPARTMENT OF AGRICULTURE P-00

What Consumers Should Know About FOOD STANDARDS

a guide to budgeting for the young couple

U.S. GRADES for BEEF

NUTRITIONAL QUACKERY

Consumer Service of USDA

THE CONSUMER PRICE INDEX

KNOW YOUR BUTTER GRADES

EGGS

INFORMATION service
POST OFFICE DEPARTMENT

WHY DOES THE CONSUMER NEED ASSISTANCE?

In modern society, the consumer is constantly exposed to the winds of change. Countless new products—and new forms of old products—vie for his attention and his dollar. Services take a larger and larger share of the consumer dollar. Yet they are often performed without established standards of safety or values.

Without the assistance and protection that government agencies offer, the consumer would be lost.

The American housewife—the major American consumer—cannot help but feel confused, and too often unheard, as she seeks the best value for the hard-earned dollars she spends.*

Today, making purchases is a complex and often puzzling experience because none of us is equipped to judge wisely the merits of the hundreds or perhaps even thousands of products we buy. Who can choose with assurance from thirty or forty competing brands? How can we be certain we are getting what we think we're buying? What is the actual value of a pair of slacks advertised at a bargain price of $6.95 and carrying the legend "comparable value" $13.65? What is the value received when you purchase a "first line premium grade" automobile tire? Even if you had the wisdom of Solomon and all the knowledge to be found in an encyclopedia you would not be able to answer such questions with assurance.

HOW DOES THE GOVERNMENT HELP CONSUMERS?

Toward the end of the nineteenth century the need for consumer protection was translated into legislative action by the federal government. The original efforts were directed toward maintaining fair competition. However, by the turn of the century—1900—"food processing was moving from the home kitchen and the village shop to large factories and processing plants. The housewife could no longer satisfy herself about the wholesomeness of products for her family table. Commercial food production was in its infancy. Conditions in many plants were primitive by modern standards. Homemakers were shocked by public disclosures of filthy, fraudulent, or dangerous products—foods dosed with chemical preservatives, candy colored with poisonous dyes, narcotic soothing syrup for babies, and the tragic consequences which followed when people believed in the cure-all promises of some of the 'patent' medicines."[2]

The attention of the nation was drawn to a series of scandalous conditions that menaced health and welfare, and the government was drawn into the battle that developed.

Much of the credit for emphasizing the need for reform and gov-

---

* Adapted from *The White House Message on Consumer Interests*, February 5, 1964.

[2] *FDA—What It Is and Does*, U. S. Dept. of Health, Education and Welfare, p. 10.

ernmental action went to the writings of a group of young reformers called the "Muckrakers" whose aim was to expose the evil conditions of the times. Their work was aided by the sharp rise in popularity of such inexpensive magazines as *McClure's, Cosmopolitan, Collier's* and one known as *Everybody's*. These magazines had tremendous circulation because of their sensational treatment of social evils.

The famous newspaper reporter, Lincoln Steffens, wrote a series of articles for *McClure's* which he entitled "The Shame of the Cities." He cited how business entered into corrupt dealings with dishonest politicians with resulting total disregard for the welfare of the consuming public. It was an era when "business could do no wrong."

At the same time attention was focused on the vendors of patent medicines who had for too long been selling huge quantities of adulterated or habit-forming drugs to the unsuspecting public by means of expensive advertising campaigns. *Collier's* unleashed a scathing attack on the patent medicine frauds of the era and found a staunch supporter in Dr. H. W. Wiley, chief chemist of the Department of Agriculture. In fact, Dr. Wiley joined with members of his well-known "Poison Squad" to perform experiments on themselves.

Another source of support for the activities of individuals and groups interested in eliminating adulteration of drugs and food came from the publication of a powerful novel, *The Jungle* by Upton Sinclair. It first appeared in 1906 and exposed the corruption that existed in the meat industry—how the filthy stockyards of Chicago housed diseased animals and shipped meat unfit for human consumption. The book proved to be such a sensation that many people stopped eating meat of any kind. Read the excerpt that follows and try to imagine how you would have felt as you stared at a plate of meat.

"It was only when the whole ham was spoiled that it came into the department of Elzbieta. Cut up by the two-thousand-revolutions-a-minute flyers, and mixed with a half a ton of other meat, no odor that ever was in a ham could make any difference. There was never the least attention paid to what was cut up for sausage; there would come all the way back from Europe old sausage that had been rejected, and that was mouldy and white—it would be dosed with borax and glycerine, and dumped into the hoppers, and made over again for home consumption. There would be meat that had tumbled out on the floor, in the dirt and sawdust, where the workers had tramped and spit uncounted billions of consumption germs. There would be meat stored in great piles in rooms; and the water from leaky roofs· would drip over it, and thousands of rats would race about on it. It was too dark in these storage places to see well, but a man could run his hand over these piles of meat and sweep off handfuls of the dried dung of rats. These rats were nuisances, and the packers would put poisoned bread out for them, they would die, and then rats, bread, and meat would go into the hoppers together. This is no fairy story and no joke; the meat would be shovelled into carts, and the man who did the shovelling would not trouble to lift out a rat even when he saw one—there were things that went into the sausage in comparison with which a poisoned rat was a tidbit."[3]

President Theodore Roosevelt was so shocked at the contents of *The Jungle* that he appointed a special committee to investigate the conditions described. One report submitted by this committee told how poisoned rats, ends of rope, splinters of wood and assorted garbage were gathered together and canned as potted ham.

The government could not turn a deaf ear to the angry cries of indignation and demands for correction of such abuses. So it was that Congress passed two important laws. The Meat Inspection Act of 1906 provided for the beginning of federal supervision and regulation in the meat industry. Another law, the Pure Food and Drug Act, made mandatory that labels clearly describe the ingredients of packaged foods and drugs, and prohibited the use of potentially dangerous substances in the manufacture of food and drugs. Both laws referred only to products involved in interstate commerce.

In subsequent years all levels of government, federal, state and local, have done much to protect and to assure the consumer that the food he eats and the drugs he uses are safe and fit for human consumption.

We shall now describe the operation and responsibilities of the

---

[3] *The Jungle*, Upton Sinclair.

various federal agencies that function in the interest of the consumer.

THE PRESIDENT'S COMMITTEE ON CONSUMER INTERESTS

In January, 1964, President Lyndon B. Johnson, recognizing the complexity of the consumer's lot and his ever increasing problems in the market place, established a committee. President Johnson stated that even though the American consumer was making progress, he had not yet achieved equality with the producer. Thus, his newly created committee would serve to further this aim. The President's Committee consists of two elements. One is the government branch with ten assistant secretaries from the following agencies: Department of Justice, Department of the Interior, Department of Agriculture, Department of Commerce, Department of Labor, Department of Health, Education and Welfare, Department of Housing and Urban Development, Federal Trade Commission, Post Office Department and the Council of Economic Advisors. In addition, thirteen other government agencies assist in matters relating to their area of interest and responsibility. The present chairman of the President's Committee is Mrs. Esther Peterson whose title is Special Assistant to the President for Consumer Affairs.

The other element of the President's Committee is composed of twelve private citizens; it is known as the Consumer Advisory Council. These members are appointed by the President on the basis of their special qualifications for effective consumer representation. The Council has its own chairman and can operate independently of the Committee.

The President's Committee performs the following functions:

1. Acts as the consumer voice in the Administration
2. Coordinates consumer activity of government agencies
3. Recommends legislation
4. Facilitates communication on consumer affairs between government, consumers, business, the States, and other organizations
5. Acts as an Administration ear for comments from individual consumers
6. Promotes consumer education
7. Helps disseminate information of use to the consumer

The President's Committee has no power to regulate or to enter legal proceedings in behalf of the consumer, except to give testimony in Congress. It prompts action through its recommendations to the President, government agencies and other groups.

THE FOOD AND DRUG ADMINISTRATION

The Food and Drug Administration is an agency that is part of the Department of Health, Education and Welfare. It was established as described above, in 1906, when the Pure Food and Drug Act was passed. Its scope has been expanded in subsequent years to include cosmetics, household products and all poisons. It is a scientific regulatory agency charged with enforcement of the Federal Food, Drug, and Cosmetic Act (1938) and five complementary laws passed by Congress for the protection of consumers. This agency operates in cooperation with other federal agencies such as the Public Health Service, the Bureau of Narcotics, the Post Office Department and the Federal Trade Commission.

The valuable work of the FDA was emphasized in 1962 when the efforts of Dr. Frances O. Kelsey, FDA Medical Officer, resulted in the banning of the drug thalidomide from the American drug market. Her quick action prevented this dangerous drug from reaching the nation's drug counters. Its sale in western Europe resulted in the birth of thousands of malformed babies. This is one of many instances which indicate the extreme importance of FDA's control over the introduction of new drugs. The manufacturer must prove beyond all possible doubt that a drug is absolutely safe before it may be approved for sale to the public.

This agency is of paramount importance and can be termed the leading "watch-dog" for our federal government. In carrying out its broad responsibilities for protecting the purity, quality, and labeling of foods, drugs and cosmetics, FDA does many things, including the following:

1. Makes periodic inspections of food, drug, device and cosmetic establishments and examines samples from interstate shipments of these products.

2. Assists industry in voluntary compliance with the law, and in setting up controls to prevent violations.
3. Requires manufacturers to prove the safety and effectiveness of "new" drugs before they are put on sale to the public.
4. Tests every batch (except for exemptions) of antibiotic drugs and insulin before they are sold for safe and effective human use. The manufacturers pay for such tests.
5. Enforces the law against illegal sales of prescription drugs.
6. Investigates therapeutic devices for safety and truthfulness of labeling claims.
7. Sets up standards of identity, quality, and fill of container for food products in line with the congressional mandate to "promote honesty and fair dealing in the interest of consumers."
8. Passes on the safety of food additives, and checks to see that safety rules are followed.
9. Sets safe limits on the amount of pesticide residues that may remain on food crops, and checks shipments to see that these limits are observed.
10. Passes on the safety of colors for use in foods, drugs, or cosmetics, and tests and certifies each batch manufactured, where necessary.
11. Checks imports of foods, drugs, devices, and cosmetics to make sure they comply with United States law.
12. Cooperates with State and local officials in the inspection of foods and drugs contaminated by floods, hurricanes, explosions, and fires, and assists in the removal of damaged items from the market.

FDA also enforces the Federal Hazardous Substances Labeling Act, which requires warning labels and other consumer protection information to appear on any household product that is toxic, corrosive, or flammable or that is an irritant or a strong sensitizer, or that generates dangerous pressure through decomposition, heat, or other means.

The Federal Trade Commission examines advertisements of this type very closely. One can't help wondering whether the original price was ever higher than that appearing in the ad.

THE FEDERAL TRADE COMMISSION

The Federal Trade Commission was established in 1914 in order to eliminate "unfair or deceptive acts or practices in commerce" which curtailed competition. In 1938 the Wheeler-Tea Act extended the Commission's jurisdiction to all unfair or deceptive practices whether they curtailed competition or not. This, in effect, gave the Federal Trade Commission the responsibility for protecting consumers against false advertising. This agency has enforcement powers which enable it to be effective. These days many manufacturers are anxious to check with this agency in order to find out whether they are in danger of breaking the law. Such advice often results in great savings to both business firms and the Government.

One recent advertising campaign that was exposed by the Federal Trade Commission involved a well-known professional athlete who claimed to be able to shave a section of sandpaper with the greatest of ease through the use of a certain shaving cream. The preparation was advertised as containing special softening ingredients. The Federal Trade Commission halted the television commercial by proving that the surface being shaved was not sandpaper, but a sheet of plexiglass, sprinkled with grains of loose sand. The shaving cream manufacturer was found to be in violation of the law dealing with deceptive advertising.

THE DEPARTMENT OF COMMERCE

This department has given valuable assistance to both business and consumers since 1903. The major agencies of the department are:

> The Census Bureau
> The National Bureau of Standards
> The Patent Office
> The Bureau of International Business Operations
> The Weather Bureau
> The Coast and Geodetic Survey
> The Federal Maritime Board
> The Maritime Administration

The Bureau of Public Roads
The Office of Business Economics

While the department's services are primarily designed to assist business, the information it provides is of definite benefit to consumers. The department issues statistics on population, the gross national product, corporate profits, personal income, retail sales, balance of payments, manufacturing and housing, among many others. A recent tornado warning issued by the U. S. Weather Bureau averted loss of property and life in the tornado belt of the Midwest. We are all familiar with the timely hurricane warnings issued by the same bureau—they have also prevented serious economic loss to consumers in the affected areas.

THE DEPARTMENT OF LABOR

The Department of Labor was first established in 1903 as part of the Commerce Department. Ten years later it became a separate department. Its jurisdiction covers wages and hours, labor standards, labor management relations and labor statistics. The Bureau of Labor Statistics is one of the best known divisions of the Department of Labor because of its famous *Consumer Price Index*, the yardstick of changes in the dollar's purchasing power. This Bureau also does important work in the area of surveys of employment trends and studies of commodity prices.

THE DEPARTMENT OF AGRICULTURE

In *Consumers All*, the 1965 Yearbook of Agriculture, Secretary Orville L. Freeman states: "Though a primary objective of the Department is service to United States farmers and ranchers, the real beneficiary of agricultural productivity and abundance has been, is now, and will continue to be the American consumer."

First established in 1862, the Department of Agriculture became a Cabinet department in 1889. Its prime functions relate to agriculture, but all consumers are served in a number of ways. First in importance is the service rendered by the Meat Inspection Division of the Agricultural Research Service. Food animals are examined prior to slaughter to prevent diseased meats from reaching the market. After slaughtering, each carcass is again examined. Any unsound, diseased or otherwise unwholesome meat and meat food products are destroyed at once. Along with the above, this division supervises the preparation of meat and meat food products to make sure that products are clean and wholesome and free of harmful preservatives. Approved products are marked "U. S. Inspected and Passed." Meat products offered for importation are also subject to inspection.

USDA STAMPS

Of equal importance to consumers is the Institute of Home Economics of the Agricultural Research Service. This agency disseminates information, which it has accumulated through its vast research facilities, on every conceivable area of consumer interest—from how to grow ornamental bamboo to how the U. S. Government establishes its grades for foods. It is interesting to note that it has available at the present time for consumers over one hundred bulletins to help them to acquire the most reliable information about shopping, meal planning, diet, gardening, lawn care, leisure time activities and just about any topic related to daily living. The American consumer is invited to avail himself of this valuable information so that he may benefit from the findings of the world's greatest authorities in specialized areas.

THE POST OFFICE DEPARTMENT

The Postal Fraud Statutes,[4] require the Postmaster General to prevent the Postal Establishment from being used in furtherance of schemes to defraud the public.

The passage in 1872 of the Criminal Statute marked the first official recognition by Congress of the need for consumer protection. Prior to this, the victim who was robbed by mail had little recourse. State prosecutors were without jurisdiction over swindlers from outside their state borders, and extradition procedures were costly and time consuming.

The American public is bilked of over $100 million dollars a year through mail fraud. The scope and variety of fraudulent schemes have progressed from obvious quick profit gimmicks to complex multi-million dollar promotions not easily recognized by the average citizen.

Postal inspectors have at all times representative cases under investigation covering every category of fraud schemes.

While the mails constitute a principal artery of commerce for legitimate and ethical business transactions, there are many unscrupulous mail users who seek to prey on the unsuspecting or gullible purchaser.

---

[4] 18 USC 1341, and 39 USC 4005.

The mails are too often used as a facility for offering the sale of misrepresented matter. The promoter is protected from dissatisfied customers by distance and anonymity. Add to this the hypnotic effect of misleading advertising, and it is small wonder that fraud by mail is a serious problem. Complaints from the public are the principal basis of investigation by postal inspectors.

The important work done by the Post Office Department is illustrated by the following account which appeared in *Information Service*, the Department's publication dealing with enforcement action.

In New Mexico a scheme was uncovered in September of 1965 and a man was found guilty of mail fraud in the sale of land and sentenced to three years in prison on each of sixteen counts, to run concurrently. Doing business as a land company, the man obtained $3,500,000 from victims in all 50 states and 26 foreign countries, selling 26,000 lots in Taos County, New Mexico. The land was virtually uninhabitable due to lack of water and other utilities. This scheme was operated mainly from booths set up at fairs and other public events, including the Seattle World's Fair where chances were offered to win a "free" lot, closing costs only $52.50. Everyone was a winner and every "winner" was required to purchase an additional lot for $495 after being told that county regulations did not permit a septic tank and water system on the small gift lot. U. S. Attorney John Quinn, summing up at the trial, said the lots were "wasteland in the middle of nowhere . . . nothing but piñon trees, if any, sage brush and sand . . . These people won a quarter acre on the moon for all the good they'll get out of the lots."

THE SOCIAL SECURITY ADMINISTRATION

The Social Security Adiministration was created in 1945 and is one of the principal agencies within the Department of Health, Education and Welfare. This agency administers the Old Age and Survivors Insurance Plan which is designed to provide a minimum income for all citizens who are covered by the program upon retirement or permanent disablement. The plan was never intended to be a pension, contrary to popular belief. The purpose of the plan was, on the other hand, to eliminate hardship to the aged, survivors and dependents. It sought to provide a long range solution for those problems which, during the depression period of 1929–1940, required governmental expenditures of billions of dollars for temporary relief. The program is financed by taxes levied against employers and employees. In July of 1966, this agency began administering the Medicare program, which is discussed in detail in section 11.

THE PUBLIC HEALTH SERVICE

This agency was created in 1798 and is now part of the Department of Health, Education and Welfare. All health activities of the Government are centered in this agency. It operates hospitals and also conducts research under the National Institutes of Health— Cancer, Heart, Dental Research, Mental Health, Neurological Diseases and Blindness, Arthritis and Metabolic Diseases and Allergy and Infectious Diseases.

THE SECURITIES AND EXCHANGE COMMISSION

Following the stock market collapse of 1929 much attention was drawn to the billions of dollars lost by investors who unsuspectingly had purchased fraudulent stocks. The SEC gathers comprehensive information about all listed securities so that the investor can make an accurate judgment before he buys a stock. Instead of the buyer assuming all risk, the work of the SEC has gone far toward making the security dealers and companies issuing new stock aware of their responsibilities to the investing public. The law makes it a criminal act to sell or offer to sell to the public any security that has not been registered with the SEC.

THE DEPARTMENT OF JUSTICE

The Department of Justice is headed by the Attorney General and gives legal advice to the President. It also represents the United States Government in the courts. The Antitrust Division is responsible for prosecuting violations which endanger fair and complete competition.

THE DEPARTMENT OF THE INTERIOR

The Department of the Interior is the custodian of the nation's vast natural wealth. Its jurisdiction extends to 750 million acres within the States and to islands which are possessions of the United States. Since this Department manages public lands and hydroelectric power systems, strives to increase and maintain mine safety, protects fish and wildlife and maintains national parks for use by the public, it is evident that the work of the Department directly or indirectly affects all citizens. One service of paramount importance to all consumers is the inspection and grading of fish. This service makes certain that fish offered for sale to the public is wholesome, clean and fit for eating. Always be on the alert for the Department of the Interior's grading and inspection stamp.

THE INTERSTATE COMMERCE COMMISSION

The Interstate Commerce Commission regulates all forms of transportation except air. It sets rates that are considered to be fair to both the users of transportation services and the transportation companies and enforces the maintenance of all safety systems.

THE FEDERAL COMMUNICATIONS COMMISSION

This agency oversees all telephone, telegraph and cable services to make sure that service is adequate and that rates are fair. Radio and television transmission systems also fall within the Commission's jurisdiction. Licenses are issued, and wave lengths and operating schedules are assigned to assure equitable distribution of programs in the various areas of the country.

THE FEDERAL POWER COMMISSION

This Commission has the important task of carrying out federal regulations relating to hydroelectric power and natural gas. It regulates wholesale rates for power and fuel and authorizes required construction of hydroelectric power facilities.

THE NATIONAL LABOR RELATIONS BOARD

The National Relations Board has a twofold purpose—it conducts elections among industry employees to determine which union will represent the workers as their collective bargaining agent, and it protects both employees and employers against each other's unfair labor practices.

There are many federal agencies that assist and protect us in our daily lives but space does not permit detailed elaboration of the duties and work of every one of them. The above-mentioned constitute the most powerful and most immediately effective ones that safeguard the health and welfare of the consumer. It should be noted that most of the States have agencies patterned after the federal bodies with objectives that are quite similar. To highlight special state activities that demonstrate particular emphasis on consumer problems, we will focus attention on three outstanding leaders in this movement—New York, California and Massachusetts.

NEW YORK STATE

New York State in 1957 established through the leadership of Attorney General Louis J. Lefkowitz the Bureau of Consumer Frauds and Protection under the Department of Law. No state had such a Bureau until New York initiated this action. The Bureau's results have proved to be so successful that at least 40 states have now adopted some form of consumer protection through their own attorneys general.

"The Bureau's prime interest is the protection of the consuming public of the State of New York as well as consumers all over the United States and World who deal with the business community of our State. We afford this protection through four areas of activity.

1) Mediation—mediate with the complaining party and the individual or concern being complained of;

2) Education—making known to the public the many ways they can be parted from their hard earned money by unscrupulous merchants;

3) Legislation—where activities cannot be adequately controlled by self policing or are prone to continuing fraudulent practices, legislation is drafted to protect not only the consuming public but the legitimate business community as well.

Your A B C's of Careful Buying

A GUIDE FOR THE CONSUMER

STATE OF NEW YORK

DEPARTMENT OF

LAW

NELSON A. ROCKEFELLER
Governor

LOUIS J. LEFKOWITZ
Attorney General

4) Litigation—where the fraudulent and illegal activities are such that the best interests of the public would be served through court actions, proceedings are instituted within the framework of authority."[5]

As a result of this Bureau's activities during 1964, $1,237,468.42 was recovered for the consuming public.

CALIFORNIA

The State of California has within its Department of Justice, under the Attorney General, a unit which deals with consumer frauds. This office's operation is very similar to the Bureau of Consumer Frauds and Protection of New York State.

In 1959 the Officer of Consumer Counsel was established at the request of the Governor. The creation of this Office permitted the Governor to have the benefit of advice and recommendations on all matters of concern to the consuming public of California. The combined efforts of the Consumer Counsel and the Consumer Frauds Section of the Attorney General's Office have led to the passage of important legislation that protects the consumer—for example, a limitation of interest on consumer credit charges, legislation regarding advertising, octane ratings of gasolines, exemption of prescriptions from sales taxes, and legislation increasing the amount of a home loan to be granted, thereby reducing the need for second mortgages.

MASSACHUSETTS

An act establishing a Consumer Council was adopted in 1963. This eight-man Council in the Office of the Governor conducts studies, investigation and research and advises the Executive and Legislative branches in matters affecting consumer interests, co-ordinates consumers' services carried on by departments and agencies, furthers consumer education, informs the public of such policies, decisions, or legislation as are beneficial or detrimental to consumers, informs the Governor and the Attorney General and other law enforcement agencies of such violations of laws or regulations affecting consumers as its investigations or studies may reveal,

---

[5] *Annual Report, 1964,* Bureau of Consumer Frauds and Protection, New York State Department of Law, p. i.

and studies and reports all matters referred to it by the general court or the Governor.

LOCAL PROTECTION FOR THE CONSUMER

Local governments like those on the state level are constantly on the alert to make sure that foods processed and sold within the community are safe for the public. In addition, they inspect weighing devices, commercial food establishments, multiple apartment dwellings, and render many services that in some way or other benefit every citizen in the community. Every locality whether it is a large city or a small town has a police and a fire department. Moreover, every local government is responsible for maintenance of streets, sidewalks, and highways as well as collection of garbage and sewage disposal. Thus all the citizens become the recipients of benefits from such services.

It is of vital importance that we become thoroughly informed about the many important services our governmental agencies provide for us. After all, these services are paid for from the taxes levied upon business and individuals. Informed citizens are better consumers because they are in a position to decide which services are needed, which ones require expansion and which ones are not necessary. We require assistance and protection from government and, as we have seen by the illustrations discussed in this chapter, excellent services are being rendered on all levels. The business community has cooperated well with the government, especially in recent years, and as a result of effective self-policing has succeeded in eliminating practices of the caliber mentioned earlier in this unit.

America has matured since the beginning of the twentieth century. Industry has managed to produce better products and services to satisy consumers. Undoubtedly, healthy competition and government's active interest in safeguarding the nation's consumers have been responsible for positive gains for both businessmen and those who purchase what is produced.

Government interest must always be present if we are to continue to enjoy in future years the same high level of living that has always been characteristic of our free market economy under appropriate government regulation.

CONSUMER UNDERSTANDING CHECK

1. In a large metropolitan shopping area you are very likely to encounter a number of stores that sell men's shoes. You will find prices ranging from $6.95 to over $30.00 a pair. Assuming that price is not the main consideration in your case, how would you go about determining which price range represents maximum value for dollars spent? What factors, other than price, would you consider before making your purchase of a pair of shoes?

2. A food product bears a U. S. Government stamp and sells for 59 cents; a similar product, not subject to federal regulation, sells for 47 cents in the same store. Is the lower price due to the fact that the product has not been inspected? Is it valid to assume that the cheaper product is inferior? Explain your reasoning.

3. Why wasn't the contamination of foods and drugs a matter of deep public concern until about 1900?

4. Do you consider the notorious Merkel horsemeat scandal in New York City to be proof that government regulation is ineffective? Go to your school library and get as much information as you can about this famous case. Find answers to the following questions:

   (a) Why did the federal meat inspectors permit horsemeat to be processed instead of boneless beef?
   (b) Which governmental agencies became involved in the case?
   (c) How did the public react to the scandal?

5. Explain how the legislative and judicial departments of the Government affect consumers.

6. Although taxes are paid by all citizens, the benefits resulting from government services are not distributed equally to all. Explain why this is true and how we justify such unequal participation by the public.

7. What agencies in your State exist for the purpose of protecting and assisting consumers?

8. Why do you think the inspection and grading of fish falls within the jurisdiction of the Department of the Interior rather than the Department of Agriculture?

9. The Food and Drug Administration forced a leading cosmetics company to stop the sale of a liquid which the company claimed would remove facial wrinkles within minutes. A small bottle, which sold for $2.95, was found to contain "bull's blood," among other ingredients. The case is still in court[6] and the outcome uncertain because there are phases of the case that are not clear, i.e., is the preparation a lotion or a drug? What constitutes a drug? The Government claims the company attempted to make the product look like a cosmetic yet it claimed that it could perform a therapeutic function. Do you think the product is a drug and should be marketed and regulated as such? Give specific reasons for your answer.

10. In 1958 and 1959 gullible investors were fleeced of over $2 million dollars by a ring of "boiler-room" stock salesmen, who waged a telephone pitch for worthless stocks in two companies: Lutah Uranium and The Shelton-Warren Oil Company. The stock salesmen misrepresented the stock that had never been registered with the Securities and Exchange Commission as required by law. Do you think that Government can legislate so that an individual will be prevented from acting foolishly? Use this illustration to prove your point.

---

[6] In 1966.

3. private agencies
and the consumer

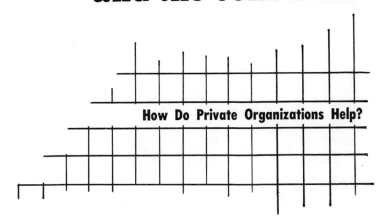

How Do Private Organizations Help?

WHAT KIND OF INFORMATION DO WE NEED?

Most people try to spend their money wisely when they shop for goods or services they need. They recognize the uncertainties involved in their decision making because of the bitter competition for their dollars and because they lack sufficient information to permit them to make value judgments among similar products. It can be said that whenever a consumer goes shopping he is haunted by two searching questions: (1) Which product will perform best for me? (2) How can I be sure that this product represents the best value for the price I am willing to pay?

While experience can be considered the most commonly used guide by the consuming public, it has very often proved to be a costly and a time-consuming technique. It would be most unwise to purchase three or four vacuum cleaners in order to determine which one best meets your individual requirements. Such experimentation would, in the first place, be prohibitive from a cost standpoint, and could, moreover, prove to be harmful if the appliances you selected actually damaged your rugs, drapes and upholstery as a result of their unsuitability.

In recognition of the great need for sources of information about the increasing quantity and variation of goods and services to which the public is exposed, a number of important nongovernmental organizations have been formed in recent years. Their main objective is to provide valid criteria for consumer decision making.

In this unit we shall discuss the valuable work done by some of the best known agencies. It is hoped that more people will avail themselves of their services and, as a result, will become more discriminating consumers.

CONSUMER-DIRECTED AGENCIES

CONSUMERS UNION

Consumers Union of the U. S. Incorporated was chartered in February, 1936 as a non-profit membership organization under the laws of the State of New York. Several months later the first issue of its now famous *Consumer Reports* went out to 3,000 charter members and subscribers. Acceptance came slowly at first—beginning first with educators and other professional people, who were quick to see the social and economic need for CU's impartial information.

SYA293

SY WWA375 GOVT PD=WUX THE WHITE HOUSE WASHINGTON DC 12
520P EST=

DR COLSTON E WARNE=
CONSUMERS UNION MT VERNON NY=1

1961 APR 12 AM 5 37

IN A PERIOD IN WHICH TOO FEW VOICES SEEM TO HAVE BEEN
RAISED IN THE INTERESTS OF THE CONSUMER, CONSUMERS UNION
HAS FOR TWENTY FIVE YEARS PROVIDED ITS UNIQUE TESTING
SERVICES ON THE QUALITY OF PRODUCTS AND GIVEN ADVICE AND
COUNSEL OF WISDOM AND FAIRNESS, NOT ONLY TO CONSUMERS
DIRECTLY, BUT TO INDUSTRY AND GOVERNMENT, ITS WORK HAS
CONTRIBUTED TO THE STRENGTH OF OUR FREE ECONOMY AND TO THE
WELL-BEING OF ALL AMERICANS. THE CONSUMERS UNION ENJOYS
BROADER SUPPORT THAN EVER BEFORE BECAUSE IT HAS ALWAYS
SOUGHT TO MEET IDEALS OF THRIFT. YOU HAVE PLAYED A
SIGNIFICANT ROLE IN EXPANDING THE HORIZONS OF AN INFORMED
PUBLIC. WITH EVERY BEST WISH=
JOHN F KENNEDY.

Then interest grew and people from all walks of life and from all parts of the nation recognized the value of CU's program; and the organization expanded. Now *Consumer Reports* is directly supported by more than 900,000 members, subscribers, and newsstand buyers. The total readership is estimated at between 4 and 5 million. Included are engineers, housewives, government employees, businessmen, trade union members, doctors, lawyers, teachers and representatives of every trade and profession in the United States. Consumers Union is the largest organization of its kind in the world, with an ever growing circulation in Canada and many foreign countries. Its income is derived solely from the sale of its magazine, *Consumer Reports,* and its publications. It has no connection with commercial interests, nor does it permit advertising of any kind in its publications.

By unbiased tests and ratings and by authoritative reports in many fields, Consumers Union has attempted and is succeeding in serving the consumer interest honestly by giving facts that people want and need to know. They have sought to find answers to these questions:

◆ Which of many competing brands is the best buy? Which offers the best quality?

◆ Which of many conflicting claims is correct?

◆ To what extent can consumers rely on brand names as a guide to quality? How meaningful is price as a guide?

◆ How can consumers tell the genuine advances in technology from the "miracles" of advertising?

◆ How do discounts or the charges of installment buying affect the real value of a given product?

◆ Is the label information accurate or misleading? Is the picture in the TV commercial or the magazine ad a fair representation?

◆ How can the consumer tell?

Consumer Reports is in reality a technical buying guide and rates thousands of brands and models each month ranging from antiperspirants and automobiles to furniture waxes, blouses, cameras, tires, TV sets, ice-cream and mattresses. It places products in categories listed as "acceptable" or "not acceptable." Moreover, within these groupings products are graded from best performing to the poorest in quality. Explanations are given for such classification.

But CU is more than a testing organization. It works for the public good in a variety of ways. In its publications it offers articles on drugs and health problems, on economic matters affecting the consumer's interests and his pocketbook, and on legislative and marketing developments which consumers ought to know about for their own protection. Consumers Union makes grants to universities, and sponsors conferences with them, to help develop solutions to prob-

lems relating to the consuming public. Members of the CU Board of Directors and staff often testify before Congressional committees and other government agencies and make technical assistance available to public officials.

Impartiality in its work has been an essential characteristic of Consumers Union's operation. The whole structure and method of operation are designed to insure that impartiality. Its strict policies keep out all sources of income except that from the sale of its publications, and have from the beginning emphasized the following:

◆ No advertising is ever accepted for *Consumer Reports* or any other CU publication.

◆ No gifts, donations, subsidies, or grants of any kind are ever accepted from any commercial source.

◆ No samples of products for testing are ever accepted (they are returned whenever they are sent).

◆ No commercial use of any of CU's test results or other material is ever knowingly permitted, nor is any commercial use of the name of Consumers Union or *Consumers Reports*. CU has successfully taken legal action against advertisers who have attempted to exploit the organization's work on several occassions, and stands ready to take legal action against others who do so.

◆ Copies of the Reports are never sold in quantity to known commercial buyers; no more than 10 copies of any issue can be purchased by anyone, except for verified educational or non-profit use.

No valid argument can be made for brand name or price being absolute guarantees of performance or value. CU demonstrated this in dramatic fashion on repeated occasions. Its work over the past years has proved to be of inestimable value to America's consumers since it has provided them with the facts needed to go to the marketplace and make the proper decisions.

While there exists wide acceptance of CU's dominant position as a resource for the American consumer, it must be placed in proper perspective. The effectiveness of its tests is limited by the fact that only leading brands are examined. Budgetary limitations also compel CU to be selective in its tests. One can readily appreciate how difficult and expensive it would be to test the hundreds or perhaps thousands of varieties of such consumer products as slippers, blouses, slacks, pipes and ties.

Another criticism that CU has encountered from time to time is the charge that its recommended selections are often unavailable in certain regions of the country. This has been true when some local brand has been judged to be a "best buy."

Consideration must also be given to the fact that CU, for the most part, tests only one sample of a given product. Exceptions to this policy are made only when extremes in performance are encountered.

All in all, however, CU has proved to be the most influential adviser to the nation's consumers. Its power can and actually does make itself felt. Unfavorable reactions from CU can doom a product to failure while approval can cause sales to leap. It must be admitted the CU has done much and is continuing to demonstrate leadership in the area of consumer assistance. Moreover, this non-profit organization has proved to be a forceful stimulator of improved product quality.

CONSUMERS' RESEARCH, INCORPORATED

This testing and research institution operates as a scientific, technical and educational service for consumers. Like CU, Consumers' Research does not have support from business or industry and does not seek such support. Its funds come from its publication *Consumer Bulletin.*

Begun in 1929 to meet the expressed needs of many citizens who were anxious to receive technical information to guide them when buying merchandise, the organization quickly grew into a research agency and a clearing house for all kinds of information to assist consumers. At the present time Consumers' Research has more than 100,000 subscribers who avidly read its monthly publication, *Consumer Bulletin.* In these bulletins popular products are test rated for quality and performance. Price ratings are sometimes included as well.

Listings of products are usually arranged in alphabetical order within A, B, or C ratings. Products receiving a rating of AA are regarded as being of the highest quality, those rated as A are considered to be of very good quality, and products rated as B are listed as being of intermediate quality. When a product is not recommended it is listed as being of C grade.

There has been criticism leveled at Consumers' Research at various times because of the stated position of its officers in the matter of social, political and economic issues. For example, CR has provided along with its evaluations of price and quality of products information related to the labor policies and working conditions in the plants of the manufacturer or jobbers who distributed the merchandise. Some hold the view that another obstacle this organization has had to battle from its beginning has been its dependence upon well-known brands. Since it cannot sample all brands, many local products that do not carry a particular brand, although they may be of very high quality, are never discovered and tested. The size of the country makes it impossible for any testing organization, not just CR, to adequately cover all sections of the country where consumer tastes vary so greatly.

However, like Consumers Union, this organization has rendered consistent service that has managed to earn consumer confidence. Though there have been frequent attempts made to question the objectivity and policies of both CU and CR, their integrity remains intact. To date even the most bitter critics of consumer agencies have been unable to prove their allegations of dishonesty and partiality. It is only logical that if evidence had existed these critics would have used it to their advantage.

THE COUNCIL ON CONSUMER INFORMATION

Although the Council on Consumer Information belongs in the ranks of private agencies that assist consumers, its organization differs from that of Consumers Union and Consumers' Research. Generally referred to as CCI, this agency serves consumers through conferences, newsletters and pamphlets. Its prime source of revenue has been grants made by Consumers Union.

The monthly *Newsletter* published by the Council on Consumer Information is a digest of pertinent information about publications on consumer information, legislation affecting the consumer, government actions against fraudulent practices, research results; in general, it serves as a clearing house for all matters relating to the nation's consumers.

Fifteen pamphlets, all costing less than 50 cents, have been published to date. They are as follows:

1. *Consumers Look at Farm Price Policies.* By Walter W. Wilcox. 38 pages. May, 1954.

2. *Consumers Look at Fair Trade.* By William Haller, Jr. 38 pages. May, 1955.

3. *What You Should Know About the Law of Estates.* By Leland J. Gordon and L. James Gordon. 20 pages. July, 1955.

4. *How to Plan a Life Insurance Program.* By Charles E. Rogers and Marguerite C. Burk. 36 pages. January, 1956.

5. *Consumers Look at Burial Practices.* By Allen Earnshaw Backman. 38 pages. April, 1956.

6. *Consumers Look at Antitrust Laws.* By Jules Joskow and Irwin M. Stelzer. 31 pages. April, 1957.

7. *Watch Your Weights and Measures.* By Leland J. Gordon. 34 pages. April, 1957.

8. *Bringing the Consumer Point of View Into Government.* By Persia Campbell. 29 pages. January, 1958.

9. *Consumers Look at Discount Houses.* By Steward M. Lee. 32 pages. October, 1958.

10. *Consumers Look at Federal Protective Services.* By Monroe W. Karmin. 40 pages. January, 1959.

11. *Consumers Can Protect Their Own Health.* By Dr. Harold Aaron. 34 pages. February, 1960.

12. *How to Choose Your Doctor, Hospital, Health Insurance.* By Dr. Harold Aaron. 32 pages. May, 1961.

13. *The Consumer Looks at Deceptive Packaging.* By Clinton L. Warne. 36 pages. August, 1961.

14. *A Guide for Family Financial Counseling.* By Choals V. Neal, Jr. 34 pages. October, 1962.

15. *Consumers Look at Labels.* By Jessie V. Coles. 55 pages. March, 1964.

CONSUMER COOPERATIVES

Consumer cooperatives are groups or organizations established by those desiring to provide themselves with goods or services at the lowest possible cost without sacrificing quality. They operate for the benefit of the members in their capacity as individual consumers. They provide such goods as food, gasoline, fuel, milk, household goods, automobiles, and they also provide services such as credit, housing, medical care, automobile repairs, and insurance.

The idea of consumer cooperatives is not a new one. As far back as 1750 cooperatives existed in England and Scotland. Most were not successful, however, as the later experiments were linked in some way with the work of the Utopian Socialists. The cooperative patterns that are now recognized as practical, economical ventures stem from the Rochdale Society of Equitable Pioneers which in 1844 began a small cooperative in Lancashire, England. The total capital amounted to 28 pounds sterling and the stock was flour, oatmeal, butter, sugar and candles.

All cooperatives, wherever they may be, subscribe to certain basic principles.

1. Membership is open to any person.
2. Each member has only one vote regardless of how much he has invested.
3. No profits are permitted—one's invested share is compensated much like the return on a loan.
4. Members should obtain the best possible product or service at the most economical price.
5. Maximum information regarding products or services should be given to all members.

In order to offer to their members products they require at the lowest net cost and representing sound value, many cooperatives produce or handle their own brands of merchandise and place grade classifications on the labels. One large co-op supermarket in the New York City area, for example, handles its own brand of automobile tires. The tires are of excellent quality and are sold at prices considerably cheaper than similar commercial makes.

THE COOPERATIVE LEAGUE OF THE U. S. A.

This organization is a national federation of cooperatives. It was organized in 1916, and its affiliated cooperatives have a membership of about 15,000,000 families. The purpose of the League is to promote cooperatives and the benefits of cooperatives. The Cooperative League of the U. S. A. maintains an effective consumers lobby in Washington. Its publication *Consumers Lobby* is available only if a person can produce concrete evidence of having communicated with his congressman or senator at least once during a three-month period. No charge is made for this publication. Contents include reports on impending legislation and advice on steps it deems appropriate on the consumer's part.

INDUSTRIAL ORGANIZATIONS

Consumers are not the only people concerned with the problem of obtaining accurate information to help them to make wise decisions. Legitimate business has recognized that consumers for too long a period of time have been deprived of the assistance and guidance that producers are uniquely qualified to give. Intelligent and successful producers have been quick to see the far-reaching benefits that will accrue to them if they do their part in presenting information regarding the proper use of products, purposes, ingredients, and standards of performance. Consumers are always pleased to be assured of the quality of products they buy. When such assurance is openly and freely provided, the producer of that product will benefit in turn, for consumers tend to be faithful to those products that can boast of certification of quality and performance. Moreover, a producer tends to encounter less price resistance from consumers who are fully informed of the merits of products.

There are many organizations that obviously serve two purposes—they inform the consumer and at the same time build confidence in products in order to increase their sales. We shall discuss briefly in the remaining portion of Unit III the work of a few of the better known associations in this category.

BETTER BUSINESS BUREAUS

"Better Business Bureaus have been on the scene in one form or another for 53 years. By and large, their reputation as foes of the schemer, the gypster, the corner-cutter has been so well earned that their basic mission has sometimes been obscured. Actually, BBB's role as defender of the public is incidental—a sort of benevolent fallout from the main task. They were created to protect business by building an environment of public confidence in which companies can operate peacefully and profitably."[7]

---

[7] *Changing Times,* October 1965, p. 17.

These bureaus are nonprofit by nature and are organized and supported by business men for their own welfare. Every bureau, while using the accepted pattern for its operation, is nevertheless independent. Their services are available to all consumers without charge and, in general, they all attempt to meet the following three objectives:

1. To encourage local businessmen to police themselves against practices which could prove to be harmful to their image.

2. To build public confidence in business.

3. To protect the community's consumers by focusing a spotlight of publicity on fraudulent operations and by providing information and protection which in the long run will benefit the ethical members of the business community.

It is estimated that in 1964 Better Business Bureaus handled some 3,000,000 inquiries and complaints from both businessmen and consumers. Besides this, they checked thousands of advertisements for posible deceptive and fraudulent presentations, and released and circulated reports, pamphlets and bulletins to alert the public.

Reproduced by permission of the Better Business Bureau of Metropolitan New York, Inc.

The following examples of alertness by Better Business Bureaus demonstrate how these organizations help to maintain a healthy climate in which legitimate business can flourish and the public is assisted at the same time.

A small retail toy store in a residential area of Brooklyn, its windows draped in its Christmas finest carried a large sign atop its storefront, which said, "Buy retail at wholesale prices." Once, it even offered $1,000 to any one who could disprove that claim.

One suspecting customer, however, called the store's claim to the attention of the Better Business Bureau of Metropolitan New York, and the organization looked into the situation.

The Bureau found that a doll, advertised in the store at the "wholesale" price of $3.98, could be purchased cheaper at any one of five different department stores. A toy gun, sold at $3.69, was priced anywhere between $2.22 and $2.27 in other stores.

In Milwaukee a local clothing store owner asked for a 30-day extension to his "Going Out of Business Sale" permit. Better Business Bureau representatives looked over the so-called "bargains" and found they were not from the store's regular stock. This testimony served to put an end to the fake sale and the city went to work to enact stiffer codes to cover such fraudulent operations.

Various Better Business Bureaus throughout the country have issued publications and alerts with regard to schemes and frauds which have the elderly as their prime target. The Senate hearings on health frauds and quackery have also emphasized the concentration on the elderly by gypsters and quacks. By publicizing fraudulent promotions, Better Business Bureaus are enabling the elderly to become alerted to these schemes and hopefully will enable them to resist the clever enticements which would take some of their limited funds and give them nothing in return. Of course, the introduction of Medicare should lessen the attractiveness of these phony schemes.

Old people had been duped by fly-by-night insurance companies that went out of business before people could collect on their polices. Others had signed for policies which, although within the letter of the law, contained vague and misleading stipulations in fine print.

In this instance senior citizens were at least warned against being misled by distortion of facts and "fast deals." This is an example of the valuable service rendered by Better Business Bureaus. It has been said that Better Business Bureaus' important aim of finding and eliminating conditions that eventually lead to complaints before the complaints are lodged is perhaps the least publicized aspect of their work.

Since the entire operation of every Better Business Bureau is based on the idea that honesty is the best policy and that business-men should conduct their businesses honestly and treat the consumer fairly, it is encouraging to be able to count them among the ever growing number of agencies dedicated to assisting consumers in one way or another.

Within the last thirty years a number of industries have formed associations of various types with the avowed purpose of standard-izing their products and making certain that acceptable merchandise quality is assured. Other purposes which these associations sought to emphasize were the establishment of public confidence in products and the creation of a favorable image in the eyes of consumers. We shall now briefly touch upon the work of some better known industrial groups.

Manufacturers of all kinds of machinery and appliances that use gas have the American Gas Association test their products for safety, durability and economy of operation. This association maintains testing laboratories in New York City and Cleveland for this purpose. Products that are found to meet the standards set up by the AGA are permitted to bear the association's seal of approval. It is interesting to note that over 95 percent of all gas-operated appliances in use at this time bear the AGA seal of approval.

A similar association designed to promote safety in electrical appliances is the Underwriters' Laboratories, Inc., which is supported by the National Board of Fire Underwriters. The UL stamp of approval bears great prestige. As a result, a consumer is assured of a product's safety when he purchases an item bearing the UL seal. Caution should be exercised when one buys electrical appliances to make certain that all parts of the product carry similar approval. This advice stems from the highly dishonest practice of clearly displaying the UL stamp on an electrical cord to imply that the appliance has been approved. In reality, the seal of approval was granted because the outlet cord met UL standards. As for the appliance, that is another matter.

Two other organizations that render valuable service to both their industries and many allied with them, as well as to the consuming public, are the National Institute of Dry Cleaning and the American Institute of Laundering. Both issue periodic bulletins containing information to their members with regard to the care and handling of different fabrics and materials. In these days, when new fabrics appear on the market almost daily, it is impossible for the individual businessman or consumer to determine the best method for caring for garments and products made from these fabrics.

The institutes operate training schools to prepare people for jobs in the laundering and dry cleaning fields. In addition, manufacturers of all products that can either be laundered or dry cleaned are most eager to acquire certification of their products by one or both of these industries. The "Certified Washable Seal" shows that manufacturers of garments and fabrics have met high standards in their products. Of course, availability of information provided by industrial organizations is of no value unless consumers make a conscious effort to use it. Very often a garment shrinks when laundered simply because it should have been dry cleaned. Failure on the part of the purchasers to read the important instructions for the proper care and cleaning of the garment may lead to unwarranted criticism of the product by the consumer. We should be on the alert to distinguish between unfounded accusations arising from situations like the one just described and the valid criticism of consumers who are victimized by sharp practices.

Several of our leading department stores, mail order houses and wholesale distributors have done much to encourage improvement of merchandise and control of quality, thereby aiding the consuming public. Macy's, for example, conducts its own Bureau of Standards which it proudly calls "the arbiter of the store's conscience." It is estimated that in a year over 7,500 products carrying Macy's own brand label are put through tests of fire, water, high pressure and simulated wear in order to see how they stand up.

The J. C. Penney Company, Inc., also conducts a research and testing laboratory for the purpose of testing merchandise quality before it is bought and offered for sale, and so do Sears, Roebuck and Company, Marshall Fields and Company and Gimbel's.

PROFESSIONAL ASSOCIATIONS

The welfare and interests of consumers have been served very effectively in many instances by the work of professional associations. These groups conduct activities in a number of areas: they issue information; they prepare educational literature; and they attempt to influence legislation where necessary. Three outstanding examples of professional associations that have given continued benefits to the nation's consumers are the following:

THE AMERICAN MEDICAL ASSOCIATION

As the name implies this is the national organization of the medical profession. It endeavors to promote improvement in patient care, better health for all citizens, and to raise and maintain the level of medical practice. Through its publications, meetings, councils and special committees, the AMA helps to raise national health standards. It publishes a popular monthly magazine, *Today's Health*, distributes pamphlets, and even sponsors educational radio and television programs for the purpose of permitting the public to receive authentic health information.

AMERICAN DENTAL ASSOCIATION

Like the AMA, this association is the national professional organization of dentists. About 90 percent of the country's dentists belong to the ADA. Its Council on Dental Therapeutics makes studies and issues authentic information concerning dental therapeutic agents which are available for use both by the dental profession and the consuming public. If a product is accepted by the Council it means that it has met the prescribed standards as to composition and the manner in which it is advertised. However, acceptance by the ADA does not mean that a product is recommended.

AMERICAN HOME ECONOMICS ASSOCIATION

The American Home Economics Association has for over half a century proved to be one of the leading national groups having as its chief interest the protection and assistance of the consumer. Its work is primarily educational and the association works through high school and college teachers of home economics. However, its effect should not be interpreted as being limited to young people. The nation's adult population has been assisted through the buying guides that the American Home Economics Association issues and which cover a broad range of interests. The concern of this association extends to the areas of food, housing, clothing, family care, and social welfare.

In general, the Association supports all movements and legislation devoted to serving consumer interests either by setting up standards of product quality and identification or by preventing fraudulent practices and the sale of harmful products.

Since an objective of consumer education is to stimulate the consumer to acquire as much information as possible about the products and services he purchases, he should studiously learn as much as he can about the private agencies discussed in this unit. In fact, he should do more than that—he should constantly be on the alert for other avenues of consumer information.

Even though some agencies are not directly motivated toward providing assistance and protection for consumers, they do manage to establish minimum standards of performance and hence ultimately benefit them. Producers have long recognized the value of subsidizing these private agencies so that they may be able to compete more successfully. Seals of acceptance and stamps of approval certainly aid manufacturers. At the same time the consuming public is assured that when purchase of tested products are made, the likelihood of acquiring merchandise of acceptable quality is greater.

CONSUMER UNDERSTANDING CHECK

1. Despite the existence of many sources of information, consumers as a whole do not avail themselves of these services to the degree that they should. How do you account for this apparent consumer indifference?

2. Explore all possible sources of assistance to the consumer in your community. Which ones would be of particular benefit to you?

3. In 1965 the American Medical Association actively engaged in a campaign to affect national legislation of great importance to the country's senior citizens. What different interests were represented in the campaign? What other associations or agencies became involved in this legislation?

4. Why has the growth of cooperatives in the United States been relatively slow compared to their development in western Europe and Scandinavia?

5. Why is the UL seal the most recognizable of all "seals of approval"?

6. Trace the production of a cotton dress from the planting of the cotton seed to the final point of sale. How many different organizations might be involved in assisting both producers and consumers along the way?

7. How do the following organizations add to the consumer's storehouse of knowledge?

    American Automobile Association
    American Bar Association
    American Retail Grocers Association
    National Retail Furniture Merchants Association
    AFL-CIO
    National Farm Federation

8. Consumers Union Magazine, **Consumer Reports,** is one of the most popular periodicals in the nation's libraries. It does not, however, enjoy similar popularity among purchasers of newsstand magazines. Why?

9. Why should businessmen establish Better Business Bureaus and Chambers of Commerce?

10. You are interested in buying an electric hair dryer. You have checked with an appliance store salesman concerning a particular brand and model; you have also consulted with a neighbor who owns that brand and model, and finally you check **Consumer Bulletin** and **Consumer Reports** for information about hair dryers. The information you receive appears to be conflicting. How do you then go about making your decision?

4. advertising—pros and cons

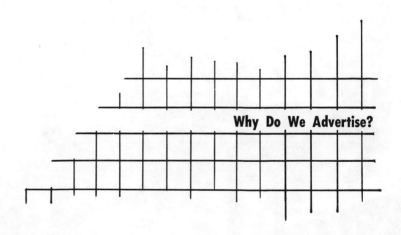

Why Do We Advertise?

Colonial Williamsburg photograph

THE BACKGROUND

From TV screens, billboards, radios and the printed page, we are bombarded every day with thousands of trick words, trademarks, brand names and symbols, all designed to sell, sell and sell some more. We are now living in an era of heavy competition, ever growing numbers of products, and mass communications. The almost 400,000 trademarks registered with the United States Patent Office represent much more than identification marks because identification alone is not enough to reach the American consumer. Marketing specialists contend that since the consuming public is now forming opinions faster than ever before, it becomes imperative that the corporations and manufacturers say who they are, what they do, and how they differ from competitors—and all this must be done quickly and efficiently.

Business spends in excess of $15 billion a year in advertising. Why? The answer is simple: to persuade people to believe that they require the products advertised. In other words, advertising's direct aim is to influence consumers. When our country was young and we had not yet experienced the full effects of industrial expansion, mass production, and the other pertinent characteristics associated with the business climate we recognize today, there was no need for a middle man. People satisfied their needs by direct buying. Manufacturing in advance of demand was unknown. If a farmer needed a set of horeshoes he went to a blacksmith and had them made, or he made them himself.

In Colonial times well over 90 percent of the new country's population was comprised of virtually self-sustaining farmers. They raised the food products they required, the fibers they needed for clothing, and they constructed their own homes from the natural resources that were available on the lands about them.

Industry as we understand the term today, did not exist because the colonists were required to depend upon England for manufactured goods. England carefully guarded her industrial rights since she was the mother country. Under the mercantile system colonies supplied raw materials for manufacture and later purchased the finished products. These products were primarily those of an essential nature: tools, implements, textiles, glass, etc. Luxury items had to be ordered directly and were not generally available for sale in shops. Moreover, the very limited market for manufactured goods did not encourage duplication in retailing or selling—there was only one shop of a kind in most communities.

An early American shop in the year 1800 advertised the nature of the articles or services that were available in it rather than brand names. For example, the barber of that era was a jack of all trades. He cut hair, he acted as physician, surgeon, and sometimes as dentist; and he also made wigs. In his capacity as surgeon, the barber would display a blood-soaked towel or cloth on his barber pole whenever his surgical efforts met with success. Very often the blood would drip down around the pole causing a circular design. That is how the tradition of alternating large red and white stripes on the barber poles developed. These have become the trademark of the profession.

The early bootmaker, in similar fashion, displayed a large boot in a conspicuous location to make people aware of the nature of his business. Every specialty shop made certain that the symbol of the trade or the product involved was used to advertise what could be obtained there.

But 1800 and 1966 represent eras as different as the horse and buggy on one hand and a Cadillac automobile on the other. Today few producers can effectively deal directly with consumers. Business is so complex that there has developed an entirely new and separate operation by which producers make their goods available. This is known as the marketing or distribution process. A very necessary component of this process is advertising whose major function, as stated before, is the creation and stimulation of demand for goods or services.

WHAT ADVERTISING SEEKS TO DO

Think of the problem in these terms: advertising is absolutely necessary in our complex mass-production society. A society that can boast of producing 9 million automobiles in one year must utilize advertising in order to stimulate the sale of that many automobiles. There are likewise many products which would remain unrecognized were it not for the success of advertising in promoting their sale. Let us use the illustration of the now popular ball point pen. The last decade has witnessed the end of the fountain pen as the popular writing instrument. In its day, the fountain pen was considered the best writing instrument and certainly modern, as well. Then came the much heralded ball-point pen that could write without being tied to a bottle of ink. Once the nation's advertisers got behind the product they succeeded in creating a demand for this entirely new writing instrument. It is probably safe to say that annual sales of ball-point pens far exceed the best year ever enjoyed by fountain pen manufacturers. Thus, advertising created demand for a newer and better product.

Another function of advertising is to promote more extensive use of an already existing product. Artificial sweeteners such as saccharine were at one time used primarily by those individuals who were required to restrict their intake of natural sugar. Through the medium of advertising, saccharine and other artificial sweeteners have now become "musts" for the food and beverage industries who find it necessary and profitable to cater to the needs of diet-conscious Americans.

There are very few people who are not familiar with the TV commercials concerning Kraft food products. These successful advertising programs have awakened in America's housewives an awareness of the many different uses of their products. Every week millions of viewers are exposed to tempting, new recipes. Cheese and mayonnaise have become romantic products.

Advertising's greatest success to date has been in the area of brand name identification. Consumers ask for Kleenex instead of facial tissues, Jello instead of gelatin and Frigidaires instead of refrigerators. Haven't you heard the name Levis used instead of the word dungarees? Users of chewing gum frequently refer to gum as Chicklets, Spearmint or Juicy Fruit, all brand names. Advertising has given identity and status to ever so many common products through their brands. Think of the power and magic of such brand names as Bayer, Ajax, Gillette, Band-Aid, Kellogg's, Listerine, and Nylon by DuPont.

ADVERTISING TECHNIQUES

Advertising is a complicated business, composed of the companies which make products and pay to advertise them, agencies which prepare and place the advertisements, and the newspapers, magazines and broadcasting stations which carry the message to the public. In the trade, the latter are called the media.

Regardless of what medium of advertising is selected to make the strongest appeal for a given product, the techniques employed by the advertising profession seem generally to be as follows:

(a) The ad must create an emotional appeal for the product involved. Such appeals are directed to the consumer's pride, vanity, desire for status, or his desire to keep up with his neighbors.

(b) Logical reasons must be given for preference of the advertised product over other brands of the same product. Emphasis is placed upon special ingredients, performance, and unique qualities which all blend to establish the picture of the best possible product available to consumers.

(c) Endorsements of a product by celebrities tend to cause consumers to identify themselves with the famous people who are shown using the advertised product and hence the consumers are very likely to buy the same product for their own use.

(d) A case is made for the superiority of a product on the basis of the claim that "everybody" uses a certain brand. The basic drive of human beings to "belong" is the psychological background for this approach.

(e) The advertisement plays up the consumer who wants to be treated as an individual or who fancies himself or herself to be creative.

The agencies who dominate the advertising scene at the present time have at their command specialists who use logical as well as irrational or irrelevant appeals. Sometimes it is virtually impossible to determine when logic begins and irrationality ends when viewing some of our "high powered ads." After all is said and done, the advertiser must get the consumer's attention—how effectively he does

THE FIVE APPEALS

EMOTIONAL

LOGICAL

CREATIVE

TESTIMONIAL

PSYCHOLOGICAL

this will determine whether he will prosper (some firms gross over 460 million a year), or lose out to more creative competitors.

STATUS OF ADVERTISING IN THE UNITED STATES

The December 1965 edition of *Newsletter,* the publication of the Council on Consumer Information, reports that the United States' advertising volume of over $14 billion in 1964 was ten times greater than the next country, Great Britain. Moreover, it was stated that this figure was greater than the total of the other 29 nations, all major industrialized nations (it reported volumes for thirty nations in all).

As industries are ranked, advertising is relatively small when compared to our industrial giants such as the steel, railroad, automobile, food and chemical industries. However, dollar totals and influence have little or no correlation in this instance. How can we slight the importance of an industry that directly or indirectly affects and guides consumer expenditures that exceed $400 billion a year?

Advertising also forms the backbone of financial support for newspapers, the radio, magazines and television. Without advertising these communication media could not continue to exist. Consider this fact: were it not for advertising the cost of the Sunday edition of the *New York Times* would have to be in the neighborhood of $6 or $7 instead of the current price of 30 cents (locally). Moreover, the advertising industry provides some 50,000 jobs for highly skilled and trained personnel.

Whereas the sole purpose of advertising in the early days of the industry was to sell and place advertising copy in a newspaper or magazine, the emergence of the so-called "omnibus" agencies in recent years emphasizes how different and complex the agency business is today. A modern advertising agency will handle every kind of study or research that a manufacturer may require. It engages in market research to study consumer demand and problems of product distribution, it studies which media are best suited to a client's advertising, and sometimes it does product research in order to test consumer acceptance of new products. Some agencies even act as public relations specialists for their clients.

Why has advertising grown? Simply because it pays for producers to advertise. Advertising has proved its worth because products have sold in increasing quantities when pressure has been placed upon the public through adroit advertising. Producers will continue to rely on advertising and generously subsidize the industry as long as consumers continue to demonstrate indecision and uncertainty in the marketplace. Whenever a shopper approaches the marketplace in the above fashion advertising moves in to direct his choice of goods or services.

THE PRODUCER'S VIEW OF ADVERTISING

Every producer's goal is to move his goods into the hands of as many consumers as possible. He is convinced that it pays to advertise because advertising has proved to be the best way to market goods and services. Businessmen aim to make a profit. Therefore, if profits did not materialize year after year, it is hardly likely that businessmen would continue to spend billions of dollars for services that failed to prove themselves in a very concrete way.

YEAR	'35	'40	'45	'50	'55	'60	'61	'62	'63	'64	'65
TOTAL IN BILLIONS	1.7	2.1	2.9	5.7	9.2	11.9	11.8	12.4	13.0	14.0	15.0

Advertising Expenditures in the U.S., 1935-1965

In the final analysis advertising is the best technique ever devised for mass selling. Our business firms are convinced of this and see specifically that when they place their wares in the care of top-flight advertising specialists they can look forward to these benefits:

1. A consumer preference will be created for a particular brand of a product. Every producer of the same kind of article has to make a decision as to how much to produce. But the selling capacity, or the market for the product will be the factor which will determine the manufacturer's growth potential. This means that the advertiser must distinguish his product, if not on basic points then on trivial ones, and he must forcefully emphasize this distinction by using a brand-name and by exposing this name to the consuming public. Only when a brand-name

is kept alive in a competitive, expanding market can a producer be assured of a place in the race.

Americans accepted Colgate Dental Cream as a direct result of the famous Ted Bates and Company advertisement which stated: "What's new in Colgate Dental Cream that's Missing—Missing—Missing in every other leading toothpaste?"

2. A new product will be accepted and used. About two or three years ago the General Electric Company introduced a new product—the electric knife. Its uses and advantages had to be forcefully demonstrated to the nation's shoppers to spark a demand for this new product. All advertising media were immediately called upon to saturate the market place. At the present time electric knives are among the fastest selling appliances and have become very popular gift items. The evidence of advertising's success in popularizing this relatively new product is that now there are forty manufacturers engaged in producing 110 models of electric knives to meet the new demand.

3. New uses will be publicized for products already in existence, thus increasing sales. Chocolate pudding and gelatins have long been recognized as popular American desserts. Recently, however, advertising has focused a new spotlight on these old products in order to achieve wider distribution and increased sales. Today they are widely used in the preparation of pies and cakes and even as trimmings for food platters.

Another interesting example of an increase in use of an already existing product is the heavy consumption of cigarettes by women today. At one time (until the early part of the 1920's) it was considered shameful and in very poor taste for a woman to smoke either in public or privately. However, when the advertising industry brought its big guns to play on the social barrier that was keeping down the consumption of cigarettes, the worm quickly turned. Such slogans as: "Blow a little my way," "Reach for a Lucky instead of a sweet," "Be nonchalant, reach for a Murad" and "Not a cough in a carload" went a long way toward making cigarette smoking by women fashionable and socially acceptable.

In 1931 almost 150 billion cigarettes were manufactured in this country, but in 1961 the figure had risen to 550 billion. How was this dramatic increase in the use of cigarettes "helped"? By advertising, of course. In only one year, 1961, to be exact, the tobacco industry spent over one billion dollars in advertising. The bulk of this sum naturally was used to promote the use of cigarettes, despite the warning issued by the Surgeon General that cigarettes are a cause of cancer and other diseases.

4. A continuous contact between seller and consumer will ensure a constant level of sales. Each seller wishes to maintain at least his share of the market. He realizes that any relaxation on his part in promoting his products will result in loss for him and possibly in gains for his competitors. Therefore, it is necessary to keep the most favorable image of a product before the public. Advertising has repeatedly proved to be the most effective method for establishing this required seller-buyer contact. In addition, it makes the buyer aware that the product is available for purchase. In other words, advertising very often becomes the insurance factor guaranteeing that the consumer cannot overlook a certain product when he is deciding which product to buy.

The illustration that appears very appropriate in conjunction with the above advertising benefit is that of Kellogg's Cornflakes. It can be safely stated that most American homes that use cornflakes are likely to prefer Kellogg's. This is so because Kellogg's was the first name associated with this famous American breakfast cereal. Effective advertising securely established this brand name as a household word and has succeeded in giving Kellogg's Cornflakes a commanding lead over competing brands.

5. Increased sales through successful advertising create the need for increased production. When a seller produces greater quantities of a product he can cut production costs through economical purchase of raw materials and supplies, labor saving devices and more effective use of plant facilities. Very often such economies can absorb the cost of advertising and even result in greater profits for the seller.

In 1947, 250,000 television sets were in use in this country. The price of a television receiver at that time was rarely below the $450 to $500 range. In fact, the largest screens sold for close to $1,000 during that period. However, by 1962 the television industry with the aid of advertising had succeeded in changing the status of that medium of communication. In fifteen years television had become a necessity instead of an expensive luxury. In 1962 there were 40 million TV sets in the nation's homes, and the price of a good set was approximately a quarter of what it was when television first appeared on the scene. Television manufacturers today are enjoying much greater profits as a result of increased production. It is interesting to point out that history is once again repeating itself in the case of color TV. Currently manufacturers of color TV sets find that they cannot meet the heavy demand for receivers. Production is at an all-time high, profits are soaring, yet the price of a large screen color TV set is lower than before. Increased competition among TV manufacturers has tended to reduce prices. This, in turn, has stimulated the demand for color sets. Television networks have seen in this new demand a market potential for commercial sponsors and have therefore converted a large number of their programs into color.

THE CONSUMER—TARGET OF ADVERTISING

The target of America's advertising specialists is the weekly paycheck of every wage earner, the allowance of every teenager, the social security or pension payment of every senior citizen and any other disposable income available to the nearly 200 million people who watch, listen and read.

Even though a good case can be built to support the contention that advertisers attempt to help consumers to purchase wisely and economically, it is a fact that the basic motive of advertising is to sell goods. Of course, there are several proven benefits that accrue to consumers as a result of the growth of large scale advertising as we know it today, and it is appropriate that consumers should be informed about them. Let us consider the following positive values of advertising from the consumer's point of view.

1. ADVERTISING IS EDUCATIONAL.

Through advertising, consumers learn of new products that appear on the market, products that may appreciably improve the level of living, contribute to better health and, in general, lead to increased satisfaction in our daily lives.

2. ADVERTISING IS COMMUNICATION.

Advertising is the brain child of our mechanized society; it is a recognized form of mass-produced communication. Without communciation we definitely would not have achieved the individual well-being of which our country can proudly boast.

3. ADVERTISING LEADS TO BETTER MERCHANDISE AT LOWER PRICES.

The consumer gains in this way. By making it possible to deliver goods at a lower cost, advertising permits consumers to have more purchasing dollars for other merchandise, thereby creating a demand for other advertised products.

4. ADVERTISING PAYS FOR MOST OF OUR MEANS OF COMMUNICATION.

It goes without saying that the real reason for advertising's generous support of such media as newspapers, magazines, radio, television, billboards, etc., is not a desire to appear as philanthropic agencies. Purely and simply advertisers are interested in their personal stake. Nevertheless, the public does benefit through such support. As we stated before in another section of this book, a newspaper's cost would be beyond the reach of all but the wealthy were it not for advertising. The press, a large part of the entertainment we see on television, radio and our magazines are to a very large degree supported by advertising.

5. ADVERTISING SERVES THE PUBLIC.

In many ways the public welfare has been aided by advertising. Many worthy causes such as the Red Cross, the March of Dimes, and the Crusade Against Cancer have received the assistance of business and advertising groups. All of us are familiar, we are confident, with advertisements that urge citizens to keep their communities free of litter, announce campaigns to prevent forest fires as well as those that urge us to vote in national and local elections. Such advertising benefits citizens everywhere.

6. ADVERTISING INFORMS CONSUMERS ABOUT WHERE TO SHOP.

There isn't a day of the week when consumers are not advised of special sales in department stores, supermarkets or specialty shops. Whether the community in which you live is a large city or a small town, the end results are the same—as a consumer you are directed to the places that sell products you desire by one or more of the avenues of advertising. Who hasn't had the experience of being helped by the advertising contained in the telephone directory's "yellow pages"?

7. ADVERTISING PROVIDES CONSUMER HELP.

Regardless of whether a consumer purchases one brand or another of the thousands of products that are advertised, much valuable information flows through advertising media. Homeowners receive valuable hints on gardening and lawn care, and tips on how to use and care for tools and appliances, as well as guidance in the matter of proper product selection for the many home tasks that every family has to undertake at one time or another.

8. ADVERTISING MAINTAINS HIGH STANDARDS.

High product standards are protected and maintained as a result of advertising. This represents another plus for the consumer. Since in the vast majority of cases products succeed in acquiring a reputation which leads to good public acceptance as a direct result of effective advertising, the sellers are forced to assume the responsibility for maintaining the original specifications of the products they seek to sell.

On March 15, 1962 the late President Kennedy in his message to Congress dealing with the need for consumer protection said, "If consumers are offered inferior products, if prices are exorbitant, if drugs are unsafe and worthless, if the consumer is unable to choose on an informed basis, then his dollar is wasted, his health and safety may be threatened, and the national interest suffers." Leaders in the government had been aware for some time of the dangers of advertising abuses, but steps taken to correct such abuses had always been too slow and too late.

Congress has begun several investigations in an effort to discourage deceptive advertising, but in most instances has met with strong opposition from powerful interests which hide behind so-called states' rights or local home rule arguments. Where large firms are involved in questionable advertising practices, it becomes almost impossible for local agencies to take effective steps to regulate their activities. And so where these conditions exist the consumer is as much exposed to the effects of shady advertising as a crow perched on a telegraph pole would be to a farmer's shotgun.

SOME NEGATIVE ASPECTS OF ADVERTISING

In the remaining portion of this section we shall attempt to acquaint the reader with some of the techniques used by certain advertisers to convince or persuade consumers, even though they suppress information when they do so.

Unscrupulous advertisers can present a cigarette in such a light that consumers can easily be persuaded that it contains very little nicotine. No matter what amount of nicotine is cited for the particular brand of cigarette, it often develops that the amount advertised is in fact greater than that of other cigarettes sold on the market and moreover, certainly not low enough to genuinely protect health. Can all brands be the best?

Every one of us is bombarded daily by misleading descriptions. Vendors advertise wearing apparel to be color fast or shrink-proof. When tested in a laboratory, many samples of the fabric used are found to be lacking in the advertised qualities.

According to findings of the Food and Drug Administration, advertisers of drugs, foods, cosmetic preparations and vitamins frequently misrepresent their products by label and advertising literature containing such words as "twice as much," "works faster than any other known product," "your money will be cheerfully refunded" or "because of its secret ingredient." How buyers are attracted by the magic of the words!

"The consumer has no quarrel with advertising as such. His basic quarrel is simply that this medium has been misused. As a whole, it has been designed to inform but has been powered for a lesser objective—the promotion of brands. And being so powered, it has less often led to consumer enlightenment than to consumer bewilderment."[8]

Another example: Two popular brands of toothpaste are advertised as containing special ingredients possessing almost miraculous cavity-preventing virtues. Both have won the endorsement of the American Dental Association. It is interesting to note that in each case the advertised special ingredient is in reality basically composed of a common chemical known as stannous fluoride. In each case the special ingredient is trademarked and proudly heralded by the advertisers as a means of presenting the products they are promoting as being distinctive. We see here a deliberate attempt by advertisers to give unique status to their products and to place them beyond the range of competition.

It would seem that a more honest approach is that employed by Bristol-Myers, the company that manufactures Fact toothpaste. The latter product is advertised as containing stannous fluoride without additional fanfare. Evidently the American Dental Association must have thought well of Fact toothpaste, otherwise it would not have permitted Bristol-Myers to use its endorsement.

Besides creating confusion and bewilderment in the minds of the

---

[8] Speech by Dr. Colston E. Warne, Professor of Economics, Amherst College, before the Boston Conference on Distribution, October 17, 1961.

unwary consumer, advertising very often wins even greater victories through the use of appeals to subsconscious needs, desires and ambitions. It has been estimated that billions of dollars have been spent for products and services simply because advertisements succeeded in penetrating the public's conscious guard. Modern advertising specialists have learned to successfully control feelings of guilt, fears, loneliness, doubts and insecurity. One might properly classify the advertisers in this category as vultures who feast on the secret miseries, misfortunes and weaknesses of human being. They work on man's mind and his soul.

"The Weiss and Geller advertising agency became suspicious of the conventional reasons people gave for buying home freezers. In many case it found that economically, the freezers didn't make sense when you added up the initial cost, the monthly cost added on the electric bill, and the amount of frozen leftovers in the box that eventually would be thrown out. When all factors were added, the food that was consumed from the freezer often became very costly indeed.

Its curiosity aroused, the agency made a psychiatric pilot study. The probers found significance in the fact that the home freezer first came into widespread popularity after World War II when many families were filled with inner anxieties because of uncertainties involving not only food but just about everything else in their lives. These people began thinking fondly of former periods of safety and security, which subconsciously took them back to childhood where there was the mother who never disappointed and love was closely related to the giving of food. The probers concluded: 'The freezer represents to many the assurance that there is always food in the house, and food in the home represents security, warmth, and safety.' People who feel insecure, they found, need more food around than they can eat. The agency decided that the merchandising of freezers should take this squirrel factor into account in shaping campaigns."[9]

The great emphasis recently has been on what advertising psychologists call the depth approach. Clever advertising copy is es-

[9] *The Hidden Persuaders,* Vance Packard, David McKay Company, Inc., New York, 1957, pp. 72-73.

pecially aimed to promote purchasing through nonrational and impulsive bases instead of rational and logical approaches. The advertising involved becomes professional persuasion to manipulate the consumers' buying attitudes. Consider the following:

"When the Mogen David wine people were seeking some way to add magic to their wine's sales appeal (while it was still an obscure brand), they turned to motivation research via their ad agency. Psychiatrists and other probers listening to people talk at random about wine found that many related it to old family-centered or festive occasions. Some talked in an almost homesick way about wine and good old days that went with it. A hard-hitting copy platform was erected based on these homey associations. The campaign tied home and mother into the selling themes. One line was: 'The good old days—the home sweet home wine—the wine that grandma used to make.' As a result of these carefully 'motivated' slogans, the sales of Mogen David doubled within a year and soon the company was budgeting $2,000,000 just for advertising—the biggest ad campaign in the history of the wine industry."[10]

We know that some advertising is misleading, deceptive or actually false. Consumers have every right to register indignation at any attempt to deprive them of the right to correct, honest information about a product which is placed on sale for their consideration. If the facts are clearly stated then the consumer alone will be responsible for making his decision. But when false advertising appears before the public the purchaser cannot make wise decisions.

In July of 1965 the Federal Trade Commission issued a consent order prohibiting the Home Delivery Food Service of Springfield, Massachusetts from misrepresenting its freezer-food plan. The company had falsely advertised that a trade-in allowance of $200 would be given with the purchase of a new freezer or refrigerator-freezer combination.

The Commission stated that the selling price was so inflated that any trade-in allowance would be absorbed so that no saving from the trade-in would be realized. Furthermore, the Commission proved that purchasers of the freezer-food plan could not receive

---

[10] *Ibid.*, pp. 80-81.

both the freezer and the foods at payments as low as $9.99 per week. It was shown too that a substantial portion of the meats provided under the plan were not "U. S. Choice" or "U. S. Prime" grade meats, inspected and graded by inspectors of the U. S. Department of Agriculture.

As a result of a recent Supreme Court decision, the Mary Carter Paint Company was prohibited from including a free paint offer in its advertising. The Federal Trade Commission had previously charged that the word "free' was misleading, on the ground that the company had been offering substantially two cans for the price of two cans. It is interesting to note here that in 1964 the Mary Carter Paint Company spent $2 million dollars for this advertising.

The two cases cited above illustrate flagrant violations of proper ethics in advertising. Unfortunately, it is impossible to determine how many consumers may have been victimized by such misleading advertising before the Federal Trade Commission was able to halt the misrepresentation. While the government does provide some safeguards for all of us against advertising abuses, its effectiveness is limited by legislation which has not kept pace with the rapid expansion of our nation's economy. In fact, one well-known author has stated in his criticism of the ineffectiveness of federal regulation that we have horse and buggy laws that try to cope with modern advertising abuses.

Advertisers reap rich dividends from the knowledge that consumers on the whole are gullible and that few people have mastered the art of reading advertising material with a critical eye. For these reasons it is indeed like looking for the proverbial needle in the haystack or a contact lens in a swimming pool to collect a good sampling of straight, honest advertisements.

OTHER COMPLAINTS ABOUT ADVERTISING

Intelligent consumers have long pointed to the tendency of advertisers to portray all phases of life in glowing terms. Every product is placed in a luxurious setting, where there is nothing but joy, elegance, well-being, gracious living and apparently a never-ending supply of money. The poor or middle income person rarely becomes the central figure in any advertisement. Psychologically, advertisers

No problems here! Everything's rosy.

are attempting to make us so dissatisfied with what we already own that we shall immediately discard those items. Naturally, it follows that we shall have to replace them with more modern products—more luxurious, more elegant, more expensive, etc. So we see that the more dissatisfied a consumer becomes, the more he will be likely to spend in the market.

Some of our most important industries (clothing, automobiles, and cosmetics) rely exclusively upon advertising's success in down-grading last year's model or design. Who is not aware of the race for status which begins every fall when the new automobile models appear in showrooms? The atmosphere becomes electrified: many consumers who have been convinced that their ego will suffer if they have to drive their old car (it might well be only one year old) for even another month or so, pant with excitement as their eyes feast upon ribbon-decorated new cars, or the beautiful streamlined models on the TV screen, or when they hear a radio commercial praising the performance of a new car.

When people cannot afford to purchase all the wonderful products advertising has assured them they must possess if they are to enjoy status in their community, and the high esteem of friends and business associates, they run the risk of suffering emotionally. Who knows how many cases of mental abnormality may have been triggered by emotional tension growing from such dissatisfaction?

Let us develop in more detail the concept of dissatisfaction resulting from advertising. When an individual is convinced that he is in need of a new expensive product he is likely to make the purchase whether he can afford the product or not. He will either borrow the money, buy the product on the installment plan or cut down sharply on his other expenditures in order to achieve his short-sighted goal. In other words, as Will Rogers once said, "Advertising makes us buy stuff we don't want with money we ain't got."

The advertising industry readily admits that, at least to some degree, it does cause people to spend money for unimportant or frivolous things when they should be purchasing important items. But then advertising has succeeded, since people have spent money —even if that money should have been employed elsewhere.

Another criticism that is often expressed relates to the manner in which advertising tends to discourage competition, thus limiting consumers' choices. Since advertising seeks to emphasize the uniqueness of products and to take them out of competition, then it logically follows that advertisers prefer to see monopolies of brand names established rather than continuing free competition within which buyers would continue to evaluate and compare products. Monopolies gain control of the market and make it difficult or even impossible for the small seller to survive. It is no concidence that the nation's largest corporations are also the nation's largest advertisers.

Advertising, considered objectively, is both good and bad. It is good when it gives us the information we need, but bad when it withholds or distorts information we should have in order to make up our minds about a product or a service.

Advertising has provided an effective means for distribution of goods and services. At the same time, it is questionable whether these goods and services are as good as they are advertised to be.

Advertising successfully stimulates consumption, which is beneficial to the nation's economic health. But advertising bewilders and staggers the consumer who finds it increasingly difficult to make choices. To repeat what was stated earlier, it is not possible for all products to be the best in their class.

Advertising frequently becomes the buyer's helper, but it should not become the directive force dictating the course of action that the buyer must follow. It was picturesquely stated once that advertising was in reality a numbers game with agency men playing the public like a piano.

Advertising has helped America to achieve the highest level of living ever known to man. The American consumer is better housed, paid, dressed, fed and treated than anybody living in any other country. We are a nation of abundance and affluence. At the same time, the enormous expansion of our market system had led not only to considerable waste, but to sharp variations in product quality as well. Advertising causes the market to be flooded with all types of products—good, bad and in between. Advertising is a business seeking its share of profits. Its only criterion for success is the degree to which it can mount a profitable sales campaign.

Advertising acts like a lubricant and keeps the wheels of mass production moving easily by causing many new products to be accepted by consumers. Yet as advertising accomplishes this it also promotes the concept of obsolescence. How can sellers ever get buyers for so many new products without seeing to it that new products replace others before their time? Obsolescence can be purposely built into a product or it may result accidentally from changes in design, fashion or function. When we hear the common complaint "they don't make things like they used to" there is more than a little foundation involved. It is not just a hunch. Consider, for example, the illustration of an appliance used in every home—the refrigerator. When the electric refrigerator replaced the old-fashioned ice chest it immediately assumed a dual role in the average household. Not only did it serve to preserve foods but what appeared to be of equal importance, it became decorative.

The first refrigerators lasted years and years and few people saw any need for replacing them if they functioned satisfactorily. But when the advertising industry along with manufacturers succeeded in promoting "new and improved" models which contained features that changed every year (to entice buyers, of course), demand for new refrigerators rose sharply. At the present time the average family prefers to change its refrigerator long before it wears out because it wants to be in style. This drive to keep up with what's new makes it easy for consumers to justify purchases of replacement products.

It should be borne in mind that in this world there are all kinds of people. There are honest people and there are some who are dishonest. We know also that greed is a characteristic of a certain percentage of human beings. Some of these people are consumers, not just producers. In fact, proportionately more consumers than producers fall into this category. It follows therefore that greedy consumers who are always on the alert for "the bargain of the year" are partially responsible for the direction that advertising takes. Advertising reflects the attitudes and the wants of consumers.

All the agencies that exist to protect consumers, whether they are private or governmental by nature, cannot protect the naive, gullible consumer who sees in advertising what he chooses to think the inducement really implies. The consumer should shoulder the greatest amount of responsibility for raising advertising standards. He alone can start the chain reaction leading to healthy changes in advertising, when needed, by accepting and using advertising that honestly supplies the information he seeks. He should reject misleading, deceptive and false claims as well as advertising that demonstrates poor taste and lack of maturity.

An alert, well-informed consumer is the best safeguard against abuses in advertising.

CONSUMER UNDERSTANDING CHECK

1. Describe your local supermarket as it might appear if there were no advertising of any kind in evidence.
2. What points of information do you think should be included in a good advertisement?
3. How would people shop if there were no advertising?
4. Go to your neighborhood or school library and get information on the characteristics of these advertising specialties:
   (a) institutional
   (b) public service
   (c) display
   (d) retail
5. How would buying habits among consumers change if all advertising had only logical appeals?
6. Compare the need for advertising in the Soviet Union with the advertising requirements of American industry.
7. Select from your local newspaper an example of what you consider to be bad advertising and also an illustration of honest, effective advertising. Compare both advertisements and analyze their composition.
8. The back page of a weekly magazine with a wide circulation sells for $54,000 to any advertiser who seeks effective display for his wares. How do you think the magazine justifies this price?
9. Until a few years ago **The Reader's Digest** stubbornly held to a policy of not permitting a single word of advertising in its pages. Can you think of possible reasons for the change of policy which led to inclusion of advertising material?
10. How do you react to the following advertising claims:
    "Actually makes your hair feel stronger—right away."
    "If you have a passion for the elegant casual, satisfy it with . . . . (a shoe)."
    "This iron tells you when to add water."
    "Because this man and his skilled research chemists devoted 25 years to the study of woman's skin chemistry . . . . today your skin can have that vibrant young glow you thought you'd never see again!"
    "When the occasion calls for moving . . . . . we dress your furnishings to travel."
    "The school lunches that get eaten are the lunches bagged in . . . ."

5. spending dollars with sense

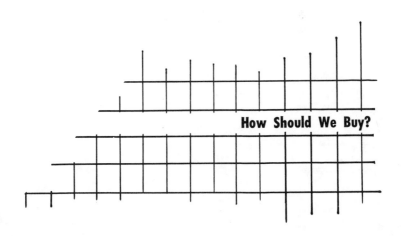

How Should We Buy?

WHERE DO WE GET OUR MONEY?

Consumers obtain the dollars required to meet living expenses when they sell their services to producers. When the individual's skills and talents are such that they are in great demand, producers will have to pay more for his services. Thus, the well-known law of supply and demand is an important factor in determining production costs. The greater an individual's rewards in his role as a producer, the greater will be his income and his ability to buy goods and services. It should be borne in mind, however, that such an individual will not necessarily receive more for his dollars than someone else with less purchasing power. Much will depend upon how well informed and trained he is to solve consumer problems.

Our largest corporations have for many years followed the practice of sending personnel specialists to the campuses of the nation's leading colleges in order to recruit talented young people for their organizations. In recent years the supply of engineering students has been much below the heavy demand resulting from the dawn of the "Sputnik Era" and the rapid growth in electronics, chemicals, oils, metals, and defense industries. We must also include here consideration of the tremendous effect of automation on the demand for engineers.

It is not unusual for a beginning engineer who has just completed his professional training to receive from $7,000 to $9,000 a year. Compare the average compensation paid to messengers, delivery boys, clerks, and other unskilled workers. The latter are in great supply. For this reason, producers do not have to compete for their services. Low pay rates become the inevitable fate of the nation's unskilled workers.

The foolish skeptics who doubt the value of education would do well to consider these eye-opening statistics:

Of all people whose incomes equal or exceed $15,000 a year, 40 percent have at least a college education. On the other hand, of the people earning less than $3,000 a year, which is now considered the poverty level in our economy, approximately 36 percent have less than eight years of schooling.

Let us now project the lifetime income expectancy in terms of educational achievement. A man with less than an elementary school education can expect to earn $125,000 during his lifetime. A man who has graduated from college (4 year), however, can look forward to earnings of at least $360,000 in his lifetime. *Education is the best investment you can make as a young person.*

All young Americans hope for a good life, a fair measure of success and a share of happiness. This is as it should be. Our democratic way of life has been the insurance which has guaranteed to all the right to aspire and achieve. Translated into dollars and cents the traditional "American dream" is basically this: we want to achieve so that we may gain a respected place in society for ourselves. With such achievement we can also acquire the material satisfactions of life. To reach this goal we naturally have to develop the capacity to earn more.

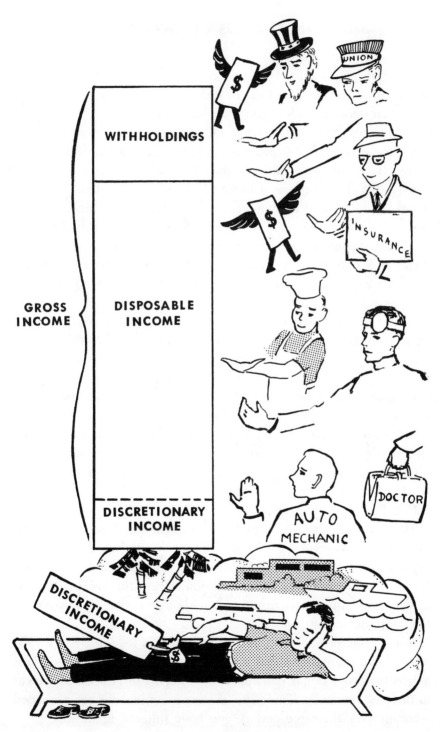

GROSS INCOME

WITHHOLDINGS

DISPOSABLE INCOME

DISCRETIONARY INCOME

DISCRETIONARY INCOME

There's always too little left.

AN ANALYSIS OF INCOME

The salary or wage a person contracts to receive is in reality a theoretical amount—he never receives all of that money. We'll explain why this is so. The total in dollars that a salary or wage contract represents is called gross income. But before any of this income becomes available to us certain deductions are made: income taxes, social security, unemployment insurance, pension fund, health and welfare insurance, and in some cases union dues.

After the deductions are subtracted from gross income, what remains is the amount of money that we receive. Technically this is known as disposable or net income. You will probably be more familiar with the term "take-home pay." This is the amount the individual or family has available to meet the usual needs and wants, all of which are basic and related to the requirements of everyday living.

After the necessities have been purchased, the remaining portion (if any) of one's disposable income then becomes discretionary income. As the term implies, there is wide discretion or opportunity for choice in the utilization of this remaining amount of income. Consumers' preferences and wants will determine the manner in which these dollars are spent, saved or invested.

Mr. Ernest Colville earns $700 a month. He is married and has one child. His payroll deductions from gross income amount to $108.50 a month, leaving him with a disposable income of $591.50. His total household expenses amount to $517 a month, leaving him with a discretionary income of $74.50.

Mr. Colville's financial situation is typical for Americans in the same income bracket. If, of course, a family increases its household expenses, the discretionary income will correspondingly decrease. Consumers learn this in painful fashion during the holiday seasons as they make greater commitments without a serious realization of the economic consequences.

A major factor affecting purchasing power is inflation. Since 1955 prices have increased about 1.6 percent each year. In effect, this means that your dollar has lost about 15 cents in purchasing power in the past ten years. Therefore, if your gross income has remained constant over the same period, you have suffered financially.

The sage advice out of the Orient which points to the superiority of one picture over a thousand words applies here. Look at the following chart. It tells the story emphatically.

A SAMPLING OF WHAT'S HAPPENED TO PRICES[11]

Average changes across the U. S.

	10 years ago	Latest	Change
Loaf of bread	$ 0.18	$ 0.21	Up 17%
Round steak, lb.	$ 0.90	$ 1.10	Up 22%
Bacon, lb.	$ 0.66	$ 1.06	Up 61%
Chicken, lb.	$ 0.53	$ 0.39	Down 26%
Milk, qt.	$ 0.22	$ 0.25	Up 14%
Man's suit, wool	$ 65.00	$ 80.00	Up 23%
Woman's cotton house dress	$ 10.00	$ 11.00	Up 10%
Nylon stockings	$ 0.95	$ 0.95	Down 7%
Rug, wool	$265.00	$300.00	Up 13%
Refrigerator	$225.00	$150.00	Down 33%
Laundry, 10 lb., finished	$ 1.75	$ 2.50	Up 43%
Doctor's fee, house visit	$ 6.50	$ 9.00	Up 38%
Hospital room, semiprivate	$ 15.00	$ 27.00	Up 80%
TV-set repair	$ 12.00	$ 14.00	Up 17%

Economists continue to concern themselves with the threat that the inflationary spiral poses for consumers, business and even the government. At the present time steps are being taken to contain inflation. While it is recognized that once inflation gets under way there is no way to halt it completely, there are ways to prevent it from galloping. If it creeps, we can apply the brakes and still continue to enjoy an expanding economy. Galloping inflation, if unchecked, can lead to a recession or even a depression. We must avoid this at all cost.

It is estimated that by 1975 the dollar will have lost an additional 15 cents in purchasing power assuming that price rises conform to the same pattern as in past years. From evidence available it appears that prices will rise even more in the decade ahead. Therefore, the American consumer can expect a greater pinch in his pocketbook.

While the ravages of inflation have an involuntary effect on income, there are other factors which also exert pressure on the amount of money we have for spending. Fortunately, in the case of

---

[11] U.S. News and World Report, January 24, 1966, p. 80.

these factors, the individual has some degree of control. That is to say, the consumer can make a decision provided he is alert to elements which, if uncontrolled, will reduce his purchasing power. Controllable factors include the following: changes in styles, fashions, tastes, income itself, social status, advertising and conspicuous consumption, otherwise known as "keeping up with the Joneses."

We shall refer once again to our hypothetical Mr. Colville to illustrate this point. When Mrs. Colville informs her husband that all the other ladies who belong to her Thursday afternoon bridge club own a mink stole and that therefore she feels out of place without one, Mr. Colville's discretionary income goes out the window for a period of time (until the mink stole is paid for). The desire to keep pace, to conform to the social level in which we find ourselves often ignores the cold, hard realities of wise financial planning.

WHERE DOES YOUR MONEY GO?

In every consumer's life there are four basic expenses: food, clothing, shelter and transportation. These are necessities which must be placed in a priority above all other spending categories, regardless of income level. Next in order of importance are expenditures for medical care, recreation, travel, insurance, and personal advancement.

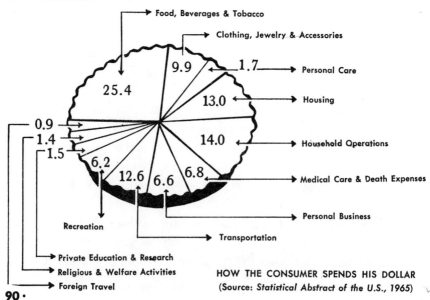

HOW THE CONSUMER SPENDS HIS DOLLAR
(Source: *Statistical Abstract of the U.S., 1965*)

In recent years consumer spending has risen for the second group of categories more than for the four essential ones. Whereas in 1950 consumers spent about 33 percent of their money for services such as medical care, education, travel and recreation, by 1965 they were spending almost 42 percent of their income for the same services. It is apparent that as disposable income increases in the years ahead even further gains will be the pattern in spending for services.

In 1950 the nation's consumers spent $195 billion for all goods and services not including purchases of homes. In other words, with a population that year of 150,698,000 the per capita expenditure amounted to $1,293. Fifteen years later the nation's consumers (population 195,826,000) spent $432 billion for goods and services. The 1965 per capita expenditure figure was $2,206. Let us examine what has taken place in the last fifteen years as far as the dollar's value is concerned. It has already been established that the dollars we earn now are worth less than dollars in 1950 and are worth much less than dollars of the depression year 1939. The purchasing power of the dollar has certainly been cut in dramatic fashion. But it must be emphasized also that we earn more now than in 1950 or 1939. The increase in dollars earned has been more than enough to compensate for the decrease in purchasing power. Here's the proof: the per capita expenditure in 1950 was $1,293. By 1965 it had risen to $2,206. Applying the 1.6 percent a year inflationary increase to the latter figure it is apparent that along with the decrease in the dollar's purchasing power there has appeared an actual increase in the number of dollars available for spending. The $2,206, when expressed in terms of the constant dollars of 1950, amount to $1,720, almost $500 more than the per capita expenditure of 1950. In simple terms, what we are saying is that despite inflation, people had more money to spend in 1965 than in 1950.

The average consumer has been fortunate—he has been regularly receiving additional dollars as the country's economy has expanded in healthy fashion. He has been enjoying a higher degree of flexibility in spending patterns than has ever been experienced in our nation's history. But in this period of plentiful dollars, consumers have tended to become careless and indifferent in the management of their money. Too many subscribe too readily to the "there's-more-where-this-came-from" school of thought. We have no crystal ball to assure us that we shall always have an ever-increasing supply of dollars. Prudent buying habits are a necessity for every consumer so that he may further increase his dollar's purchasing power.

THE FIRST QUESTION: SHOULD WE BUY?

So many purchases are the result of decisions arrived at on the spur of the moment that if the average consumer were asked this question he would probably consider it silly. Advertising has succeeded in creating an environment in which we respond to stimuli almost without thinking. We can be certain that modern young people in their teens, who spend approximately $15 billion annually for cosmetics, records, clothing, hobbies, magazines, books, cameras, and a host of other products too numerous to list here, rarely consider seriously whether they should buy or not. They want these products and they buy them.

We recognize that we must take care of our needs. We must buy food and clothing, and we must pay for our shelter and transportation. These are necessities in our life and most people appear to be able to meet these expenses in satisfactory fashion. The picture assumes different proportions when we turn to our wants.

Is there a teen-ager who doesn't dream of owning a "set of wheels"? Watch a used car lot on any Saturday afternoon. You will be sure to see groups of eager teen-agers experiencing great joy as they feast their eyes on the arrays of recently "doctored" and brightly polished "almost new" cars. In a good many instances boys (and girls, too) work during the summer, and hold part-time jobs after school just to be able to save enough money to buy a car. They may even consciously do without items that properly belong in the category of needs (clothing, medical care, etc.) in order to be able to afford a car.

When a young man in such circumstances pays $300 down for a used car and contracts to pay the remaining $600 over a period of two years, he is satisfying a want. However, at the same time he unwittingly forgoes the satisfaction of other needs and wants. The fact that he is in need of dental work, that he may need a new overcoat or that he should be setting aside money for further education, rarely interrupts his thinking when he aims to satisfy his desire for a car. In effect, the purchase of the car involves not only the dollar cost of the car, but the loss of the use or services of the other possible choices for which he could spend his money. Every individual has limited resources with unlimited wants. For this reason, it is vital that he make the best possible use of the revenues he has in order to achieve the highest standard of living. Higher standards of living can become a reality for all of us by managing your resources according to the guide lines that we shall now develop for you.

THE SECOND QUESTION: HOW SHOULD WE BUY?

The wise shopper is a person who decides what he wants before he shops. By entering the market place with your mind made up you automatically arm yourself with the resistance that results from rational thinking. You are not as likely to fall victim to the usual selling techniques. When you seek to make a purchase of an item you need, it represents a decision you have made. It follows that you will then search for maximum value for the price you expect to pay. In other words, like a soldier preparing for battle, you get ready to match your skill as a consumer with that of the seller. Some writers in the field of consumer education have referred to this contest as one of buymanship versus salesmanship.

If we were in a position to evaluate the skills of consumers and sellers it is a certain prediction that salesmen would have more "A" grades on their report cards than would consumers, as a whole. The salesman is a professional in his field of salesmanship, while the consumer is an amateur in the area of buymanship. This disparity in position is one of the primary reasons why consumer education's role is becoming increasingly important in the United States. Informed consumers will elevate the tone of our lives and will present the strongest defense against commercial mediocrity.

Private business and government on all levels, insist upon expert guidance by informed purchasing specialists before making a commitment to buy. These purchasing experts set up standards, find out where to buy at the best price, learn about the product in detailed fashion, ascertain the financial terms of the transaction and assure themselves of the reliability of the producer or seller. How many consumers do the same? Do you proceed as above when you get ready to spend your hard-earned dollars? You can't afford to make costly mistakes, but it is more than likely that you make a lot of them.

Follow this typical buying pattern. Does it sound familiar? The Colville's vintage washing machine has finally "given up the ghost." After hearing from the neighborhood repair man that the transmission needed replacement (cost was $76), the decision to buy a new washer was immediately made. Mr. Colville reasoned that $76 was too much to spend for repairs to a machine that had seen a decade of hard use. That evening, the Colvilles set out upon their shopping expedition. Do you know where they went? They went to the new giant discount center with a mammoth electric sign which flashed in red and green lights CHEAP-A-GO-GO. The parking lot was convenient and the advertisements in the daily newspapers had promised fantastic savings.

America's favorite sport—bargain hunting.

On the upper level, where appliances were on display, the Colvilles were greeted by the sales manager who lost little time in assuring them that they were about to get the "best buy of the season" in a washing machine. It just happened that CHEAP-A-GO-GO was featuring a well-known brand of washing machine at a ridiculously low price because the owner had managed to buy a carload of washers directly from the manufacturer. The manager went on to say that this machine, if purchased under normal circumstances, would cost $289.95. However, due to this fortunate "deal," the Colvilles could buy the washer for the embarrassingly low price of $199.61. Needless to say, the Colvilles swallowed the hook whole. They signed the sales contract on the spot. As they left the store and happily walked toward their car they congratulated each other for having been so quick to sense a true bargain. It was their lucky night!

It was a lucky night to be sure—but for the sales manager, not for the Colvilles. The purchase may very well have been "the bargain of the season" but neither the Colvilles nor you, the reader, could possibly evaluate the "deal" on the basis of the salesman's expert pitch. He neglected to present many facts. He had such factual information at his disposal, but the Colvilles did not require him to reveal it.

They should not have signed the sales contract before a thorough consideration of the following:

1. *What washers sell for.* The Colvilles should have determined in advance the range of washing machine prices and they should have decided exactly how much they could afford to spend for a new washer.

2. *What kinds of machines are on the market.* Which type should they have selected? Purchasers can choose from three general types of power washers—the nonautomatic washer, the automatic washer and the combination washer-dryer. Each type appears on the market under a number of brand names.

3. *Features to be carefully considered.* The Colvilles were totally unaware of the following:

(a) Some washing machines employ a common type of tumbling mechanism. Agitators tend to be harder on clothing than tumblers.

(b) Washers load in two ways—from the top or from the front. Do you know that front-opening washers use less water per fill than top-opening washers? But consider a compensating factor. If you load from the top you don't have to stoop or bend as you do when you load through the front.

(c) Washers vary greatly in capacity. Small washing machaines have a capacity of about 8 pounds, while larger ones can launder up to 14 pounds in one washing. The Colvilles never gave a thought to what size washer was most appropriate for their family.

(d) Good washers afford flexibility of use. This means that the appliance permits a variety of fabrics with different laundering requirements to be washed safely and effectively. For example, the best washers are designed to combine the appropriate wash water temperature, level of water, washing time, and speed of washing and spinning in response to the operator's selection of one or two key controls.

(e) Washers must be safe to operate. Every washer should have a safety switch to stop movement when the lid is opened during the cycle. Moreover, every machine must be grounded to prevent shock to the operator.

(f) All washers should have porcelain-enameled or stainless metal tubs.

The Colvilles were guilty of further negligence or defective buymanship because they did not:

◆ Determine whether the model they purchased was a new one or a discontinued number.

◆ Find out about the terms of the guarantee or warranty.

◆ Inquire about installation requirements. They found out, much to their dismay, that they required the services of a plumber to connect the hoses (cost, $19.50).

◆ Get information about service arrangements. Would they have to pay for service calls during the first year?

◆ Measure the washer to see whether it would fit into the space occupied by the old washer. Happily, for them, the new washer did fit.

The Colvilles' most serious blunder, however, was in accepting with blind faith the salesman's statement of the original price—$289.95. The discount center, in this case, had followed the familiar tack of advertising a deceptive price in order to give the impression that a great saving would automatically result for all who paid their "special sale" price. It should be noted here that the Federal Trade Commission has uncovered many instances where sellers have made use of what is known as in-store comparative pricing. In these cases the vendors placed tags or signs on the merchandise showing the lower, sale price as well as a higher figure with such terms as "Comparable Value," "Was," "Regularly," "Value" and "Mfg. List." The higher price, of course, was only a device for the purpose of deceiving the purchaser. The products were never sold for those prices.

We have presented the illustration of a relatively simple decision to go out and purchase a washer in order to forcefully emphasize that there are a number of very important factors applicable in virtually every transaction where the consumer buys goods or services. Isn't it just as important to shop wisely whether you spend $2.98 for a frying pan or $3,500 for an automobile?

Don't consider the question to be silly. It is far from it. It is unfortunate that there are so many poorly trained shoppers, persons who are not in a position to afford mistakes. They would be the first to say, "Sure it's important to shop wisely!" Yet, because of lack of training, experience and understanding of what's involved in buying, they spend from a dollar to hundreds and even thousands of dollars without reference to any guidelines or criteria. They are the ones who are victimized by the sharp practitioners of the art of salesmanship.

A PRESCRIPTION FOR INTELLIGENT SHOPPING

As we have repeatedly indicated, the intelligent use of your income is the basis of your consumer power. This power, stated in other terms, is your capacity to make the most of your real income.

Study the suggestions that follow and strive to utilize them every time you prepare to make a buying decision.

KNOW YOUR REQUIREMENTS. If you wish to become an intelligent shopper it is important to decide what you want and why you want it *before* you go shopping. Planning ahead of time will make it easier for you to obtain the item that best suits your needs.

BECOME A COMPARATIVE SHOPPER. Once you have decided that you wish to purchase a specific item, make a survey of a number of locations where the item may be obtained. In general, the more expensive the item, the more extensive should be the survey. Obviously, it is not necessary to visit five or six stores to purchase a toothbrush. But if one were going to purchase an automobile it would be entirely in order to evaluate the reliability, service record, as well as prices of perhaps six or seven dealers.

MAKE USE OF BUYING GUIDES. You can become an informed shopper by reading articles that appear in magazines and newspapers, consumer information publications, product rating services, and advertisements. Government agencies supply a wealth of information about products and services.

READ THE LABEL. Look for important facts about the product. A good label should provide you with information about contents, quantity, quality, trade name, price, how to use the product, grading, and special instructions for care of the product.

CHECK FOR ECONOMY AND VALUE. Don't be misled by the myth that the large jar or package is always the most economical size to buy. To prove our point: can you quickly decide which of these represents economy buying?

6¾ ounces for 35 cents
9¼ ounces for 59 cents

Another factor that you should consider, is the possibility that a large amount of a food product or any product that deteriorates with the passage of time (certain drugs, paints, etc.) can turn out to be wasteful purchasing even though the initial price might compare very favorably with that charged for a smaller quantity.

CHECK YOUR BILL OR CONTRACT. We all make mistakes. Sales personnel, clerks, executives as well as consumers are subject to human error. To protect your own interests you should take time to carefully examine the figures that represent the dollars that you are spending. Arithmetic is only one of the things you must check. Of equal importance, is the written portion of a bill of sale or sales contract. The salesman in his enthusiasm and eagerness to make his sale, can and often does represent a product in very glowing terms. In addition, he may orally promise little extras or may advance claims certain to lower anybody's sales resistance. If all that is promised is set down in writing in the contract or on the bill, you are protected. Therefore, check to see that what you have agreed to orally is written into your contract before you sign it.

PAY CASH, IF POSSIBLE. What a pleasant feeling one has when he buys something he desires and he knows that it is completely paid for. A feeling of independence is only possible when you are free from obligations—when you do not owe money to anyone. Pay cash whenever possible, and avoid being swayed by salesmen who advocate the use of credit. Remember, credit adds to the cost of your purchases.

THE THIRD QUESTION: WHEN AND WHERE SHOULD WE BUY?

The best time for shopping varies with the kind of product or service you are seeking. But whenever you shop, time will prove to be an important factor in stretching your shopping dollar. To decide when to shop consider the following:

◆ Purchases made during the "off season" generally will prove to be better buys. For example, the home owner who buys his storm windows and storm doors in April or May will be in the "driver's seat." He undoubtedly will be able to get his merchandise at a lower price than the home owner who goes shopping for the same items after the first frost has arrived.

◆ Sale time is bargain time. If a sale is legitimate, it will afford you an opportunity to buy what you require at lower prices without sacrificing quality. Retail stores run sales for the purpose of stimulating demand. Regardless of the adjectives that may be used with the word SALE (going out-of-business, clearance, off-season, inventory, end-of-season, anniversary, etc.)

sales are a good time to buy. Be on the alert for sales in your neighborhood stores or at least in shops that can be reached relatively easily.

◆ Timing is important in shopping. The day of the week and the time of the day should enter into one's shopping plans. Timing may not have any bearing on prices, but it does relate to comfort, the quantity of merchandise available, service, and the treatment you are apt to receive from sales people. In general, you will find it advantageous to shop during those hours when traffic is light. During those periods salesmen can give you the best attention and service and you can make your selections from a wide variety of merchandise. Avoid the lunch hour and the late afternoon hours. Also, if at all possible, beware of Saturdays.

You, the consumer, should realize that it is difficult to prescribe specific recommendations concerning where to shop. Selection of stores and locations for *your* shopping ventures must be guided by your individual preferences.

Some people do not mind crowds, the inconvenience of traveling great distances, lack of service, the possibility of receiving lower quality merchandise or limited varieties of goods in order to obtain savings. Other shoppers prefer to patronize stores that provide a pleasant, comfortable shopping atmosphere as well as superior service and a wide variety of merchandise. Prices in such stores tend to be higher because of the many services they offer, but their customers appear to be willing to assume the additional cost.

If the shopper fully realizes that he is paying a higher price for superior services and he derives satisfaction from shopping in such an environment he is then making an informed decision. The intelligent consumer who arrives at such a conclusion should have no regrets. He is acting in his own best interest and makes purchases where he can have his personal shopping tastes satisfied.

Let it be understood very clearly that we get what we pay for. It is foolhardy to expect top quality merchandise at bargain basement prices in every discount house. To be sure, bargains can be obtained in outlet stores, discount centers, bargain basements and on plain pipe racks. The practiced, alert shopper may spot such opportunities often sandwiched between merchandise of less value. However, to assume that everything for sale in such environments will prove to be a genuine bargain is unwise. The dollars "saved" by indiscriminately shopping in such places will surely prove to be an economic illusion.

The ultimate responsibility for intelligent buymanship rests squarely on your shoulders. Only you can find the right answers for the questions that confront you.

To summarize what has been presented in this section it is appropriate to emphasize that while it is very simple to dispose of your dollars, it takes time and effort to spend with common sense.

THE SEVEN-WAY TEST OF BUYMANSHIP

1. Should I buy?

2. How should I buy—cash or credit?

3. What exactly (specifications) do I seek to buy?

4. Which product (brand) should I buy?

5. When should I buy?

6. Where should I buy?

7. Am I getting what I want?

CONSUMER UNDERSTANDING CHECK

1. Apply the SEVEN-WAY TEST to the following buying situation: you wish to purchase a tape recorder. What problems will you encounter in finding answers to each of the seven basic questions?

2. It is a known fact that movie stars earn much more money than surgeons, nuclear scientists, professors and members of other learned professions. Can you justify such high earnings on the basis of their worth as producers?

3. Legitimate business men prefer to deal with informed customers. Why?

4. Formulate a label for any product with which you are familiar. Include all the information which you feel a good label should reveal.

5. A large discount house advertises a 23 inch well-known brand television set at a "drastic reduction"—$179.95; your neighborhood TV sales and repair center displays the same model at $205. How would you arrive at your decision where to buy, assuming that you wished to purchase that particular make and model?

6. Price and brand name are indicators of value and performance. Discuss the validity of this statement.

7. How can you determine whether an advertised sale is genuine or merely a device designed to dispose of substandard or old merchandise?

8. On the chart entitled "A Sampling of What's Happened to Prices" prices of chickens, nylon stockings and refrigerators have decreased over a ten-year period. Why do you think those items decreased in price while all the others listed increased?

9. Whenever you are involved in a financial transaction involving a large purchase your signature can very well prove to be your most valuable possession. Explain what is meant by this statement.

10. Advertising makes us buy. What other factors motivate us to go out and spend our money?

6. buying food and clothing

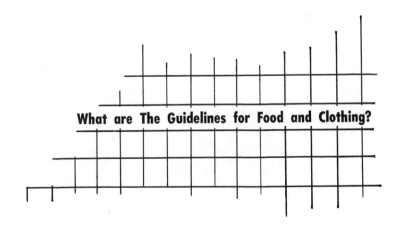

What are The Guidelines for Food and Clothing?

BUYING FOOD AND CLOTHING

HOW SHOULD YOU BUY FOOD AND CLOTHING?

BALANCING YOUR DIET AND YOUR BUDGET

Your family food purchases are highly important—they are investments in health. It is the duty of every family to learn how to buy food wisely to provide for good nutrition within the limitations of its budget.

A balanced diet is essential for health. We require a variety of foods to supply the needs for building and repairing our bodies, for energy and for keeping the body working normally. The problem that the average family faces is that of obtaining this healthy food balance despite income limitations. The task is challenging enough to tax the ingenuity and skill of the nation's homemakers.

The purpose of this section is to stress the need for sound buying practices so that you may obtain the best nutrition and the most palatable food at the lowest prices. Remember, when you economize on food it does not mean that you have to skimp or sacrifice quantity or quality. It is definitely within the power of every family to eat better for less money. This in turn, makes it possible to have more money to spend on the other items that tend to make life more enjoyable.

Not all families with good diets have large incomes, and not all families with poor diets have low incomes. This points to the fact that learning how to select a balanced diet is more important than a large budget for food.

HOW TO MANAGE YOUR FOOD DOLLARS

PLAN YOUR MEALS AROUND DAILY FOOD NEEDS

Your family is one of some 50 million attempting to obtain good food to keep healthy and be productive. Of course that is not an easy task. It requires careful planning, selecting, buying, preparing and serving so that all members of the family will receive the basic food nutrients—proteins, minerals and vitamins.

You would do well to give serious consideration to the recommendations of the U. S. Department of Agriculture's nutrition experts who have developed the following daily food guide for physical fitness.

The guide[12] presents four food groups: the milk group, the meat group, the vegetable and fruit group and the bread and cereal group. Their recommendations in each group are the following:

I. The Milk Group

Foods Included:

Milk—fluid whole, evaporated, skim, dry, buttermilk.

Cheese—cottage; cream; cheddar-type—natural or processed.

Ice cream.

Contribution to Diet:

Milk is our leading source of calcium, which is needed for bones and teeth. It also provides high-quality protein, riboflavin, vitamin A, and many other nutrients.

Amounts Recommended:

Some milk every day for everyone.

Recommended amounts are given below in terms of whole fluid milk:

	8-ounce cups
Children under 9	2 to 3
Children 9 to 12	3 or more
Teenagers	4 or more
Adults	2 or more
Pregnant women	3 or more
Nursing mothers	4 or more

Part or all of the milk may be fluid skim milk, buttermilk, evaporated milk, or dry milk.

Cheese and ice cream may replace part of the milk. The amount of either it will take to replace a given amount of milk is figured on the basis of calcium content. Common portions of various kinds of cheese and of ice cream and their milk equivalents in calcium are:

---

[12] *Food for Fitness—A Daily Food Guide.* Leaflet No. 424, U.S. Department of Agriculture.

1-inch cube cheddar-type cheese	=	½ cup milk
½ cup cottage cheese	=	⅓ cup milk
2 tablespoons cream cheese	=	1 tablespoon milk
½ cup ice cream	=	¼ cup milk

II. The Meat Group

2 or more servings.
Beef, veal, pork, lamb, poultry, fish, eggs.
As alternates—dry beans, dry peas, nuts.

Foods Included:

Beef; veal; lamb; pork; variety meats, such as liver, heart, kidney.
Poultry and eggs.
Fish and shellfish.
As alternates—dry beans, dry peas, lentils, nuts, peanuts, peanut butter.

Contribution to Diet:

Foods in this group are valued for their protein, which is needed for growth and repair of body tissues—muscle, organs, blood, skin, and hair. These foods also provide iron, thiamine, riboflavin, and niacin.

Amounts Recommended:

Choose 2 or more servings every day.
Count as a serving: 2 to 3 ounces of lean cooked meat, poultry, or fish—all without bone; 2 eggs; 1 cup cooked dry beans, dry peas, or lentils; 4 tablespoons peanut butter.

III. The Vegetable and Fruit Group

4 or more servings.

Include:

A citrus fruit or other fruit or vegetable important for vitamin C.
A dark-green or deep-yellow vegetable for vitamin A— at least every other day.
Other vegetables and fruits, including potatoes.

Foods Included:

All vegetables and fruit. This guide emphasizes those that are valuable as sources of vitamin C and vitamin A.

SOURCES OF VITAMIN C

Good sources.—Grapefruit or grapefruit juice; orange or orange juice; cantaloup; guava; mango, papaya; raw strawberries; broccoli; brussels sprouts; green pepper; sweet red pepper.

Fair sources.—Honeydew melon; lemon; tangerine or tangerine juice; watermelon; asparagus tips; raw cabbage; collards; garden cress; kale; kohlrabi; mustard greens; potatoes and sweet-potatoes cooked in the jacket; spinach; tomatoes or tomato juice; turnip greens.

SOURCES OF VITAMIN A

Dark-green and deep-yellow vegetables and a few fruits, namely: Apricots; broccoli; cantaloupe; carrots; chard; collards; cress; kale; mango; persimmon; pumpkin; spinach; sweet-potatoes; turnip greens and other dark-green leaves; winter squash.

Contribution to Diet:

Fruits and vegetables are valuable chiefly because of the vitamins and minerals they contain. In this plan, this group is counted on to supply nearly all the vitamin C needed and over half of the vitamin A.

Vitamin C is needed for healthy gums and body tissues. Vitamin A is needed for growth, normal vision, and healthy condition of skin and other body surfaces.

Amounts Recommended:

Choose 4 or more servings every day, including:

1 serving of a good source of vitamin C or 2 servings of a fair source.

1 serving, at least every other day, of a good source of vitamin A.

If the food chosen for vitamin C is also a good source of vitamin A, the additional serving of a vitamin A food may be omitted.

The remaining 1 to 3 or more servings may be of any vegetable or fruit, including those that are valuable for vitamin C and vitamin A.

Count as 1 serving: ½ cup of vegetable or fruit; or a portion as ordinarily served, such as 1 medium apple, banana, orange, or potato, half a medium grapefruit or cantaloup, or the juice of 1 lemon.

IV. The Bread and Cereal Group

4 or more servings.
Whole grain, enriched, or restored.

Foods Included:

All breads and cereals that are whole grain, enriched, or restored; check labels to be sure.

Specifically, this group includes: Breads; cooked cereals; ready-to-eat cereals; cornmeal; crackers; flour; grits, macaroni and spaghetti; noodles; rice; rolled oats; and quick breads and other baked goods if made with whole-grain or enriched flour. Parboiled rice and wheat also may be included in this group.

Contribution to Diet:

Foods in this group furnish worthwhile amounts of protein, iron, several of the B-vitamins, and food energy.

Amounts Recommended:

Choose 4 servings or more daily. Or, if no cereals are chosen, have an extra serving of breads or baked goods, which will make at least 5 servings from this group daily.

Count as 1 serving: 1 slice of bread; 1 ounce ready-to-eat cereal; ½ to ¾ cup cooked cereal, cornmeal, grits, macaroni, noodles, rice, or spaghetti.

The above four food groups should be supplemented by such foods as butter, margarine, oils and sugar. You will find these ingredients in baked goods and mixed dishes. They are foods that supply the body with calories and add those little extras to meals.

You will find that your food shopping list is your guide and handiest aid in selecting the kind and amount of food to buy. An up-to-date list will prove to be a time saver and will, in the long run, save you energy as well as money.

Always shop from a carefully prepared list. Make your list *before* you go to the store. Don't be an impulse shopper! Buy only those items you have on your shopping list and try to plan your week's menus in advance.

To construct an adequate shopping list:

◆ Keep a note pad handy for jotting down items you need as your food supplies run low. Organize your list by grouping together the same kinds of foods and supplies since you will find them in that arrangement in any store.

◆ Note all foods you wish to buy. Be sure to check menus and recipes for amounts and foods needed. Inspect your refrigerator, freezer and shelves to determine what you have on hand and what you need.

◆ Check current market prices, especially weekend specials in the newspapers or in other advertisements. Also, take advantage of foods that are in season. Each month the Department of Agriculture lists in newspapers those foods that are in plentiful supply. Such foods are at the peak of quality and tend to be offered at reasonable prices.

◆ List perishable and frozen foods last to minimize delay in proper storage. These items should be purchased just before you leave the store.

◆ When your shopping list is completed, reexamine it with a critical eye. Make certain that it contains those items which are among the foods needed each day for your good health. Spend your money first for those items, then include the other foods that you can afford within your budget. Acquire the habit of roughly estimating the cost of the food items you have listed.

SHOPPING FOR YOUR FOOD

After having prepared your shopping list you are ready to make your purchases. Since you have already determined what you wish to buy, one might say that you have won a third of the battle. Now you must make two other important decisions—*WHERE* you should shop and *HOW* you should shop. Both factors will affect the value you will get for your food dollars since shopping techniques can either result in profit or loss for you. Remember also that prices vary from store to store.

As a general rule, shopping in person will result in the greatest value for the money you spend. There is no good substitute for this practice. You have the opportunity to select foods, you pay cash and you carry your purchases home. By so doing you are participating in the most economical transaction there is. Some individuals who are forced by circumstances beyond their control (sickness, residence far from stores, weather) to shop by telephone, to have food delivered to their homes and to charge food purchases will find that their shopping costs are greater. They pay extra for these conveniences.

The big decision that you now face is WHERE to do your marketing. Naturally the handiest location would be the neighborhood food store closest to your home. However, prices, selection of foods, quality and service may not be to your liking. Therefore, it is important that you determine which store will offer the best values, the variety of items from which you can make your selections and last but not least, the quality of service that gives you satisfaction. You have a choice ranging from the gourmet specialty shops that offer tempting food products of the highest quality, to supermarkets, discount stores and self-service drive-in centers. The decision as to WHERE to do your shopping is YOURS ALONE and you should arrive at it on the basis of your family's requirements and budgetary limitations. It may develop from comparisons you make that you will do better by shopping in a number of stores rather than in one store exclusively. Shopping around for the foods you want at the lowest available prices is still the best practice.

Now to the HOW of shopping—perhaps the most important aspect of buymanship! It is strongly recommended that you follow these suggestions. In fact, they are so valuable that we prefer to call them "The Shoppers Commandments."

◆ Shopping trips should be planned to save time, energy and money.

◆ Use advertising to your advantage: don't let it be your sole guide to buying.

◆ Don't compromise. Insist upon obtaining the quality you want at the best possible price.

◆ Use grades in making your food purchases. Government grades will enable you to be sure of the quality of the food you buy and will permit you to make more accurate price comparisons.

◆ Look for government inspection stamps on such products as meat, poultry, fish, and their by-products to be assured that you are buying food that is wholesome.

◆ While brand names in most instances represent high quality, you should not overlook the possibility that a store's own brand may be of comparable or even higher quality. Experimentation is the key to selecting the best brand for you to buy.

◆ Read all food labels thoroughly. Make sure that the ingredients listed are satisfactory for you.

◆ Compare costs of foods in their various forms—fresh, frozen, or canned. Select the form that best meets your requirements.

◆ Check the net weight of the container to figure the cost per ounce or fluid measure. The number of servings suggested by packers in their literature is another guide for estimating cost.

◆ Buy reasonable quantities of food in accordance with size of family, its preferences and the amount of storage space available.

HINTS FOR FOOD SHOPPERS

1. When buying frozen foods check containers. Never buy an item which is covered with frost. Also, make sure that you select food which is stored below the freezer line at 0° or below.

2. Permit the season of the year to guide you in determining which form of foods to buy. For example, if you crave watermelon in February or March, settle for frozen melon packages. They are not only less expensive, but handy and easy to use.

3. Be on guard against shady advertising. Don't be taken by surprise when you see such words as: "jumbo half-gallon," "giant quart" or the "new and improved large pint." The container will hold at capacity just so much and no more. The adjectives are just "come-ons" to "take" the customer who is very hungry for bargains.

4. When buying fruits and vegetables consider color, shape, weight, size, maturity and freedom from defects.

5. When buying meat, consider the amount of lean meat, not the cost per pound. The number of servings you obtain from your selection will then determine actual cost.

6. When purchasing poultry look for clean skin, relatively few pin feathers and absence of bruises or discolorations. Poultry is less expensive than other cuts of meat.

7. Fish is high in nutritive value, but low in cost. Peanut butter and dry beans are also good, inexpensive substitutes for meat.

8. Eggs are a less expensive source of protein than most meats. They should be purchased by comparing grades as well as sizes.

9. Buy packaged foods by weight, not by size of package.

10. You'll save money by cooking your own cereal. Ready-to-serve cereals in individual containers may cost up to three times more than the same cereal in a large box.

11. Baked goods that are homemade are less expensive than those prepared commercially.

12. Select bread for its weight and food value. Don't consider size of loaf.

13. Choose the type of pack or grade in a canned product that is appropriate to your cooking method. When preparing stew or sauces, use a lower grade of canned tomatoes for economy. However, for use as a vegetable you will want a top grade of tomato.

14. Think twice before deciding to purchase the so-called "ready-to-eat meals" that require nothing more than heating. While it is true that you save time and energy, these savings are more than counter-balanced by the excessive cost of the packaged food. A well-known frozen food called gravy with sliced beef sells for 25 cents for a five ounce package. The actual cost of the beef, which constitutes only thirty percent of the contents, comes to approximately $3 a pound.

15. Check the dates on all dairy products and baked goods. Select only dairy items that bear the latest date mark. Give consideration to the possible savings you may make by purchasing baked goods that are a day or two old. This slight aging in no way reduces the food value of the products.

16. Watch the scale and the cash register to prevent mistakes that could be costly to you. The scale should register at zero before your items are weighed and it should bear a stamp certifying that it has been inspected for accuracy. Make sure, also, that the clerk or attendant clears the cash register before beginning to total your purchases. Make certain that only one figure is registered for an item. Don't hesitate to demand a "recount" if you suspect an error. Timidity is no virtue before a cash register.

The food shopper should have no difficulty finding a variety of wholesome, nourishing foods at a wide range of prices. These foods come in all forms—fresh and processed—packed or packaged for convenient storage and use. Tasty, nutritious meals at costs within one's budget are more possible today than ever before. But you alone can decide which food buys are best for you. Through the acquisition of good shopping habits you will not only get more for your money but you will be doing your part to encourage the continued production and efficient marketing of good food products. As a consumer-shopper you should read, ask questions, observe, compare, and try out different foods. Education plus imagination can prove to be two excellent ingredients which go to make up the recipe for successful management of your food dollars.

MEETING YOUR CLOTHING NEEDS

CLOTHES MAKE THE MAN

An old Arabian proverb states the following: *Eat whatever thou likest, but dress as others do.* From what we know about human nature it is apparent that most people follow this advice even though they do not know of the proverb. Without a doubt clothing is one of the most important status symbols. It certainly does much more than keeping us warm. Clothing gives us pleasure, serves as a means of display, and advertises our tastes, styles and social position.

In today's competitive society clothing and grooming play important roles. Appearance is extremely important socially and vocationally. How one dresses will definitely be included among factors having a bearing on employment. Moreover, there exists a feeling among employers, school administrators, teachers and law enforcement agencies that nonconformists in the area of dress will be very likely to perform in erratic fashion. A top-flight employment agency would frown upon a client who appeared without a tie, wearing scuffed shoes, and a dirty shirt. A "Beatle" hair style and a shaggy sheep dog beard do not blend with a white collar job either.

Yes, clothing can make or break the man! These days designers and manufacturers of clothing are producing attractive and functional clothes on all price levels. One does not have to be rich to dress well. In fact, many people whose appearances invite praise spend relatively little on their wardrobes. On the other hand, some people spend large sums of money for their clothes, yet they fail to appear well dressed. Plan carefully before you spend and take good care of what you buy. If you do these things you'll find that your clothing dollar can be stretched.

YOUR WARDROBE

A good wardrobe does not have to be large. It should, however, provide suitable wearing apparel for the variety of activities that are part of your living pattern. Since people's needs differ, it is not a wise procedure to attempt to plan your wardrobe along the line of someone else's.

Each individual should evaluate his existing wardrobe on the basis of how it meets his requirements. Perhaps the existing wardrobe is large enough in its present state, though few will ever admit this. Consider the following: What kind of clothing do I need for my job? What kind of clothing do I need for use during my leisure time? What social activities do I have that require special clothing?

A good plan to follow as you think through your wardrobe problems is to make a list of the apparel you have on hand, a list of the clothing you think you will need in order to participate in your everyday activities, and last, a list of items you would like to buy in order to complete your wardrobe. The latter, of course, must be viewed in terms of two specific factors: (1) whether the items constitute needs or wants, and (2) your own finances—that is, what you can afford to buy.

Since your work income enables you to live, it is vital that you consider first the clothing requirements of your particular job. It may well be that your work clothing is also suitable for leisure time use. For example, if you work in a department store as a sales clerk you are required to wear appropriate attire—a business suit or a simple, conservative dress. The same items of apparel are entirely adequate for after-work activities. Therefore, when you select your clothing keep this fact in mind. Bear in mind also that by planning everything to go with one or two basic colors, the need for duplicating accessories is lessened and you then have more clothing money for other purchases.

You naturally will be limited as you plan your wardrobe by the amount of money you can afford to spend for clothing. Even though most people spend about ten percent of their yearly income for clothing, it must be realized that clothing expenses are among the more flexible expenditures. How much you spend will depend upon your income, what your other expenses are and just how much importance you give to clothing in your pattern of living.

How to Manage Your Clothing Dollars

After you have completed your list or plan for your wardrobe, as well as a plan for spending, you are then ready to go shopping. Attention to valuable hints and to the time-tested rules for clothing shopping will go a long way toward helping you to become a skillful shopper. Learn your lessons well—you'll save money by doing so. By all means KEEP YOUR CLOTHING PURCHASES WITHIN THE AMOUNT YOU HAD PLANNED. Don't permit yourself to be tempted or to be carried away by a sensational deal. Keep within your budget.

1. Buy exactly what you set out to buy. Don't go home with a cashmere coat when you intended to buy a raincoat.

2. Compare values on the basis of quality, style and price.

3. Evaluate a garment's quality in terms of the purpose for which the clothing will be used.

4. Remember that medium-priced clothing usually wears the longest.

5. Avoid extremes in style—high-fashion styling becomes dated very quickly.

6. Buy only items that go well with apparel you already own. Don't be swayed by "bargains." A red and white striped sport shirt (horizontal bands) on sale at $1.95 instead of the regular $5.50 price will prove to be an unwise purchase for a very short man. The first time he looks at himself in the mirror he'll be displeased with his judgment.

7. Compare values at several stores. Very often clothing is on sale in competing stores at prices that differ considerably.

8. Make sure that your clothes fit properly. Proper fit is absolutely essential for good appearance and comfort. Moreover, it adds to the life of a garment.

9. Select uncluttered styles. Avoid many trimmings and drapings. A solid blue wool dress can be suitable for any number of occasions—a dance, a party, or the office.

10. Insist on top quality of fabric and workmanship in all garments that you plan to use for many seasons.

11. Read the label to learn about fabric, finish and maintenance instructions.

12. Take advantage of clothing sales conducted at reputable stores.

13. Buy on a cash basis. Remember that credit adds to cost.

CLOTHING CARE

It is of no value to spend much time and a great deal of energy shopping for best value in clothing unless we are willing to go one step further—to give clothing the proper care it deserves. A little extra attention in this area will permit garments to continue to look their best and to last longer. Good care of clothing is highly recommended and includes proper storage, cleaning, laundering, pressing and repairing. The manufacturer's instructions should be followed in every case and the labels that purchasers are so prone to discard as soon as the garment is unwrapped should be retained for reference. Very often vital information for the user is provided on the label.

Here are some suggestions which, if followed, will add long life to your clothing (that's a saving also):

◆ Like human beings, clothes need air. Don't crowd clothing in a closet.

◆ Brush your garments after every wearing.

◆ Put clothes on hangers immediately after you wear them. Keep shoulders in place and fasteners closed. Be sure to store knitted garments and loosely woven items like sweaters on a flat surface.

◆ Mend garments as soon as repairs are indicated.

◆ Never store stained garments. Delay in removing spots or strains may result in permanent damage to the fabric.

◆ Follow manufacturer's instructions in the matter of cleaning a garment. Some garments may not be dry cleaned, others may not be laundered. On the other hand, there are some garments that can be either laundered or dry cleaned.

◆ Store all garments between seasons of use only after they have been thoroughly cleaned and protected against moths and other fabric-damaging insects.

◆ If possible, place clean clothes in boxes or garment bags and store them in a cool, dry place. This prevents mold and mildew formation.

It should be more than apparent now, that to a certain degree, the selection of clothing requires much more serious thought and advance planning than does the selection of food. One doesn't "consume" a suit of clothes like a box of cookies or a box of cornflakes. A suit is a long-term investment from which it is reasonable to expect considerable satisfaction. Careful thought before purchasing it and proper maintenance afterwards will immeasurably increase the value of this investment. The same pattern of reasoning applies to one's entire wardrobe. Good wardrobes don't just develop overnight. They require time, thought and regular care so that clothing is always fresh, clean and ready to wear on the various occasions when all of us are called upon at one time or another to appear at our best. There's no substitute for being well dressed. A good appearance and the right selection of clothes can increase your confidence and can spell the difference between success and failure. Oh yes, all this can be done within your budget.

CONSUMER UNDERSTANDING CHECK

1. What information should you look for on the label of a can or package?
2. Why is it preferable to judge the cost of meats on the basis of servings rather than pounds?
3. Why is it considered poor taste for a short, stocky person to wear clothing with large, horizontal stripes or designs?
4. From the Food Guide contained in this section prepare a three-meal menu for one day that you would consider acceptable.
5. Check the products on your storage shelves at home against similar products on the shelves in your supermarket. Do you think your purchases represent best buys. If not, on what basis were the items purchased?
6. If you go to your local supermarket you will find two or more sizes of grade A eggs for sale side by side. Study these comparisons and then decide which size grade A egg gives you the best value for your money. Use these USDA standards for comparing large, medium and small sizes of eggs: Large — 24 ounces per dozen, minimum weight; Medium — 21 ounces per dozen, minimum weight; Small — 18 ounces per dozen, minimum weight.

    At the EAT-MORE EMPORIUM eggs are priced as follows:

    Large grade A eggs — 69 cents a dozen
    Medium grade A eggs — 63 cents a dozen
    Small grade A eggs   — 49 cents a dozen

7. Make a list of all the advertising blurbs which add no information to the consumer's storehouse of knowledge. Every supermarket abounds with them (i.e., "super-quart," "jumbo-pint," etc.).
8. Why do so many people say, "I have nothing to wear" even though they have closets filled with clothes?
9. Why is it easier to be well-dressed today than it was 50 to 75 years ago?
10. Why are food and clothing budgets different for every family? List at least six factors that have a bearing on budgetary differences.

7. buying automobiles, appliances and furniture

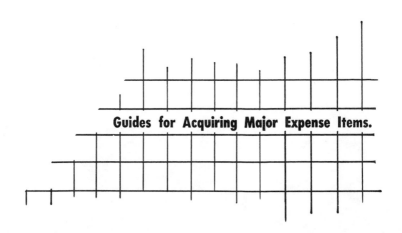

Guides for Acquiring Major Expense Items.

HOW SHOULD YOU SELECT AN AUTOMOBILE?

Why do you wish to buy a car? Do you need a car to earn a living or to get to and from school? Does your family *require* a car for transportation? Will you use the car strictly for pleasure? Do you feel that your prestige will suffer if you don't have a car? These questions should be considered and honest answers provided before you go out to purchase an automobile.

If you can honestly conclude that an automobile represents a real necessity, and that either you or your family would suffer serious inconvenience as a result of being without one, then you should proceed to the first step in a careful plan for buying your car. If you find that even though a car is not a life or death proposition in your particular case but that you would derive pleasure and satisfaction from owning one, by all means buy one provided you can afford to do so. Don't strap yourself financially, however.

The automobile has broadened our horizons and social habits, has changed our pattern of recreation, has improved our standard of living, and has brought us new services and conveniences. Owning a car has become a necessity for many, a convenience for others, and a pleasure for all. The initial price, the added costs of special equipment and accessories, and the expenses for maintenance and operation make it well worth anyone's time and effort to buy a car thoughtfully, and to maintain it efficiently and economically.[13]

Consider the fact that in the course of a lifetime the average car owner will spend more money for automobiles than he will for any single consumption product, including a home. If a young man purchases his first automobile at the age of 23 and he invests $2,800, if he follows the normal pattern and replaces his old car every four years he will probably buy about eleven cars during his lifetime, at a minimum. Since he would have to pay at least $2,100 plus his car in trade every time a new car is bought, his total expenditure would equal at least $23,000. This figure would be significantly increased if he were to do as most Americans who continually "trade up." If your young friend were to become a car buff and were to

---

[13] *Money Management, Your Automobile Dollar,* Household Finance Corporation, 1965, Preface.

react as do many persons who feel they must have a new model as soon as it comes off the assembly line, he then would probably spend in excess of $40,000 to satisfy his whim ($1,000 a year).

For many, the decisions involved in purchasing a car make the venture an ordeal. They become so confused and bewildered that they go about the job of selecting their car haphazardly. In the end they may complain of having been "stung." It should not be this way at all. In fact, buying a new or a used car can be a pleasant and interesting experience.

Whether you should buy a brand new car or look for a good buy in a used model is a matter for you to decide primarily on the basis of capacity to pay the required cash or to obtain sufficient credit. First, you should have a definite idea of how much you can afford to spend for a car. Then decide, if your available cash or credit must be limited in amount, whether it will be more advantageous to buy a low-priced new car or a good used car which originally sold for a higher price. Let's assume that you decide to buy a new car. You have many decisions confronting you because there are so many makes, models, sizes and extra equipment available. A wise bit of advice worth taking is to make your decision concerning the size, price range and style of car to buy *before* you enter any show-room. *By all means, avoid settling on any one make of car in advance.*

WHAT SIZE SHOULD YOU BUY?

Size is the first thing for you to decide. Preference will dictate the size you ultimately choose. Remember, however, that the larger the car, the more it will cost to operate and the greater the initial cost. Compact cars are produced to meet the needs of economy-minded consumers. The intermediate or full-sized car, on the other hand, will offer a quieter, smoother ride than a compact model and will provide more interior room and comfort. Large cars do consume more gas, are more difficult to park and generally cost more to repair.

WHICH TYPE ENGINE SHOULD YOU SELECT?

In choosing your engine type you must consider whether full

economy or power is what you want. Then too, one must take into account the initial cost. If you decide to buy a foreign car or an American compact, then the size of the engine is not necessarily a matter of choice since those small cars generally come equipped with a four or a six cylinder engine.

However, a recent trend initiated by American car manufacturers is that of offering optional engine sizes to prospective purchasers of any size automobile. If you are in the market for a car you should be guided in your thinking by the following:

◆ In general, the larger the number of cylinders, the higher the horsepower. However, horsepower varies in engines having the same number of cylinders. One make of car might have a six cylinder engine that can deliver 140 horsepower, while another make of car with an engine of the same number of cylinders might have much less horsepower. Late model Chevrolets come equipped with eight cylinder engines that may have from 160 to 300 or more horsepower.

◆ A lightweight car with a low to medium horsepower engine may be as peppy as a heavy car with a larger engine.

◆ If you are accustomed to carrying much heavy luggage or drive long distances, it is advisable to consider higher horsepower than if you drive most of the time within city limits.

◆ High horsepower engines generally require premium fuel—that means higher operating costs.

◆ The larger the engine, the lower the economy.

◆ Larger engines have higher original costs, but are worth more when trading or selling a car.

WHAT TYPE OR MODEL SHOULD YOU BUY?

Whether you buy a new or a used car you will have a choice of many styles and types. And within each type you will be able to select from a host of special items of equipment, colors and engines. For example, people who entertain the notion that a car should be sporty will probably select a convertible. As one ad states, the convertible means "fun in the sun." For a small family or for business use, the two-door sedan will probably be ideal. As a good

STATION WAGON

CONVERTIBLE

2-DOOR SEDAN

4-DOOR SEDAN

2-DOOR HARDTOP

all-round family car the four-door sedan is best. If one has a large family or does a great deal of camping or vacation traveling, station wagons are the best bet. It is interesting to note that nowadays the two-door hardtop is the most widely sold body type. It is considered by young and old alike a prestige car. Moreover, the extra price you pay for this model will come back to you when trade time rolls around.

WHAT ABOUT THOSE EXTRAS?

Bear in mind that the price tag or label of every car includes different items. What is standard equipment on one model may be optional or extra on another. You should inquire just what equipment and accessories are standard on the model in which you are interested. Determine also whether the price the salesman quotes includes any extras and what the cost is for every piece of equipment or accessory you would like to consider.

Some extra-cost items may well be worth the additional expense because of the safey features they provide or the increase in comfort or attractiveness. This is especially true if you can get more for your car when you trade it in because the car is equipped with such optional equipment or accessories. For example, power steering always adds $50 to $100 to the value of a car when it is being traded in or sold. However, if extras represent mere frills which will add little or no value at resale time, then one should not consider them. Fancy seat covers, special color combinations, rear radio speakers and special audio equipment belong in the category of frills which retain little value as the years pass.

A word of caution—the larger the number of accessories you add to your car, the higher will be the maintenance cost. A lot can go wrong with accessories as they get old.

Don't let yourself be trapped into accepting a model equipped with extra equipment which you honestly feel you don't need. Salesmen have a convincing way of pushing "loaded" models. If you desire a certain model with specified extras, insist upon obtaining that model. Pay no attention to the explanation that the dealer doesn't have it in stock. He can order it from the factory or get it from some other dealer. A short wait can save you money.

FACTORY-INSTALLED EXTRA-COST EQUIPMENT

Mfr's Suggested Retail Prices		A	B	C
Air Conditioner(1)	$375.05	Extra	—	Extra
Dual Air Conditioner (Wagons Only)(1)	573.09	Extra		
Air Foam Front Seat	11.72	Extra(3)	Std.	Std.
Bumper Guards, Front	13.95	Extra	Extra	Extra
Bumper Guards, Rear (N.A. Wagons)	13.95	Extra	Extra	Extra
w/Step Pad (2-Seat Wagons) (Std. on 3-Seat Wagons)	16.68	Extra		
Cleaner Air Pkg. (California Only) (Mandatory)	24.82	Extra	Extra	Extra
Defogger, Rear Window (N.A. Wagons & Conv.)	20.06	Extra	Extra	Extra
Differential, Sure-Grip	48.35	Extra	Extra	Extra
Disc Brakes (Req. Power Brakes)(9)	108.91	Extra	Extra	Extra
Electric Clock	15.20	Extra	Extra	Std.
Emergency Flasher (Mandatory N.Y. State)	12.51	Extra	Extra	Extra
Glass, Tinted All Windows	41.45	Extra	Extra	Extra
Windshield Only	27.80	Extra	Extra	Extra
Heater Delete (N.A. w/Air Cond.)	85.99	Cr.	Cr.	Cr.
Mirrors Left Outside—Remote-Control	5.42	Extra	Extra	Std.
Inside Glareproof	4.13	Std.	Std.	Std.
Moldings (Door Upper Frame) (4-Dr. Sedan)	21.05	Extra		
Moldings, Sill (Wagons)	25.92	Extra	N.A.	N.A.
Molding, Two-Tone (N.A. Monaco Wagons & All Convertibles)	27.36	Extra	N.A.	N.A.
Paint, Buffed	20.80	Extra	Extra	Extra
Engines: 383 V-8 2-Bbl.	N.C.	Std.(5)	N.C.
383 V-8 4-Bbl.(10)	34.24	Extra(5)		Std.
440 V-8 4-Bbl. Sgl. Ex. (N.A. Wagon) (Available w/TorqueFlite Only)	118.15(6)	Extra(5)		
440 V-8 4-Bbl. Dual Exhaust(10)	162.76(6)	Extra(5)		
Power Assists Auto-Pilot (Available w/Torque Flite & Power Brakes Only)	82.75	Extra	Extra	Extra
Brakes	41.45	Extra	Extra	Extra
Bench Seat (6-Way)	93.08	Extra(3)	Extra	N.A.
Bucket Seat—Left (6-Way)	89.65	Extra(2)	Extra	N.A.
Deck Lid Release (N.A. Wagons)	10.73	Extra	Std.	Std.
Door Locks (2-Dr. Models)	35.99	Extra	Extra	Extra
Door Locks (4-Dr. Models)	53.86	Extra		
Steering	93.08	Extra	Extra	Extra
Windows	103.45	Extra	Extra	Extra

Mfr's Suggested Retail Prices		A	B	C
Radios Music Master	$ 60.71	Extra	Extra	Extra
Astrophonic	86.43	Extra	Extra	Extra
Rear-Seat Speaker (N.A. Wagons)	13.95	Extra	Std.	Extra
Seat Belts, Retractable (2 Front & 2 Rear)	9.59	Extra	Extra	Extra
Steering Wheel, Tilt & Telescope (Available w/Power Steering Only) (N.A. w/3-Spd. Man. Trans.)	86.18	Extra	Extra	Extra
Steering Wheel, 3-Spoke	15.00	Extra	Std.	Std.
Sun Visors, Padded	6.31	Extra	N.A.	Extra
Suspension, Rallye	15.79	Extra	Extra	N.A.
Tachometer	48.35	Extra(2)	Extra	Extra
Tires, Set of 5 (See Chart Below)				
Transmissions 4-Speed Manual, Console-Mounted(7)	215.21	Extra(2)	N.A.	N.C.
TorqueFlite (Column-mounted; Console On Polara 500 & Monaco 500)	215.21	Extra	Std.	Std.
Undercoating w/Hood Insulator Pad	15.29	Extra	Extra	Extra
Vinyl Roof (2- and 4-Door Hardtops)	90.20	Extra(4)	N.A.	Extra
Vinyl Trim (Sedans and Hardtops)	24.92	Extra(4)	N.A.	Extra
Wheel Covers (15")	18.07	Extra(3)	Std.	N.A.
Wheel Covers, Deluxe (14") w/Disc brakes only	27.70	Extra(4)	Std.	Std.
Wheel Covers, Wire (14")	47.61(8)	Extra(4)	Std.	Std.
Wheelhouse Opening, Rear Skirt (N.A. Wagons) (N.A. w/Del. covers)	24.53	Extra		N.A.
Station Wagon Items Roof Luggage Rack	95.16	Extra	—	
Rear Compartment Lock	10.43	Extra	—	
Assist Handles	15.94	Extra	—	
Power Tail-Gate Window (Std. on 3-seat wag.)	31.82	Std.	—	

Tires—Set of Five	Except Wagons	Wagons
(15" available only w/Disc Brakes; 14" N.A. w/Disc Brakes)		
8.25 x 14" WSW 4PR	$40.66	N.A.
8.55 x 14" BSW 4PR	17.73	Std.
8.55 x 14" WSW 4PR	62.15	$44.48
8.55 x 14" BSW 8PR. Nylon	63.89	46.22
8.55 x 14" WSW 8PR. Nylon	108.22	90.55
8.45 x 15" WSW 4PR	44.48	N.A.
8.45 x 15" BSW 8PR. Nylon	46.22	Std.
8.45 x 15" WSW 8PR. Nylon	90.55	44.48

STANDARD EQUIPMENT

	A	B	C
Alternator, 35-amp	Std.	Std.	Std.
Armrests, Front and Rear	Std.	Std.	Std.
Ashtray, Lighted	Std.	Std.	Std.
Automatic Choke	Std.	Std.	Std.
Backup Lights	Std.	Std.	Std.
Battery, Self-Adjusting	Std.	Std.	Std.
Cigar Lighter—Front	Std.	Std.	Std.
Cigar Lighter—Rear (in Console)	Extra	—	Std.
Clock, Electric	Std.(2)	N.A.	N.C.
Closed Crankcase Ventilation	Std.	Std.	Std.
Directional Signals	Std.	Std.	Std.
Engines 318 Cu. In. 2-barrel	Std.(2)	N.A.	N.A.
383 Cu. In. 2-barrel	Std.	Std.	Std.
383 Cu. In. 4-barrel	Extra	Std.	Std.
Floor Covering Formed Color-Keyed Carpeting	Std.	Std.	Std.
Heater & Defroster	Std.	Std.	Std.
Mirrors Inside Glareproof	Std.	Std.	Std.
Left Outside—Remote-Control	Extra	Extra	Std.
Oil Filter	Std.	Std.	Std.
Parking Brake Warning Light	Std.	Std.	Std.
Padded Instrument Panel	Std.	Std.	Std.
Safety Seat Belts (2 front and 2 rear)	Std.	Std.	Std.
Seats, Front Bucket	Extra	N.A.	Std.
Bench (Std. in Monaco 4-Dr. Sedan)	N.A.(1)	N.A.	N.A.
Bench w/Folding Center Armrest & Bright Seat Side Shield (All except 4-Dr. Sedan)	N.A.	Std.	N.A.
Foam Cushion, 1¼", Plus Cotton Pad	Std.	Std.	Std.
Foam Cushion, 2¼" Full-Volume Foam	Extra	N.A.(1)	Std.
Steering 6-way Manual	Std.	Std.	Std.
2-spoke w/Partial Horn Ring	N.A.	Std.	N.A.
3-spoke w/Full Horn Ring	Std.	N.A.	Std.
Tires 8.25 x 14" Black Sidewall (Except Wagons)	Std.	Std.	N.A.
8.55 x 14" Black Sidewall (Wagons)	N.A.	N.A.	Std.
Transmissions 3-speed Manual (Col. Mounted)	Std.	Std.	N.A.
TorqueFlite	Extra	Extra	Std.
Wheel Covers	Std.	Std.	Std.
Wheel Covers, Deluxe	Extra	Std.	Std.
Windshield Washers	Std.	Std.	Std.
Windshield Wipers, Variable-speed Elec.	Std.	Std.	Std.
Power Tail-Gate Window (Std. on 3-seat Wagons)	Extra		—

Who says these are little extras? They amount to a lot of money— $1900.

No reliable guides have yet been found to prove conclusively that it is best to trade in a car at a specific time. One person may find it to be convenient and satisfying to trade in a car every year. Other people keep their cars two, three, four, five, or more years. They apparently are equally satisfied. When to buy a new car will involve consideration of a number of factors:

1. How much driving you do in a year.
2. The condition of the car you own at present.
3. Your temperament—is prestige a very important thing?
4. Your financial position.

Most automobiles are relatively trouble free during the first 15,000 miles they are driven. After that, there is a strong possibility of greater maintenance cost. Brakes wear out, shock absorbers need replacement, tires must be replaced, and many other defects begin to appear. After 50,000 or 60,000 miles repairs can become very costly.

Since timing can become a factor in your favor when you set out to purchase a car, give serious thought to those special buying opportunities that develop at various times throughout the year—summer sales, winter "white sales," etc. Many people prefer to buy their new car just before the next year's models appear in the showroom. Generous price reductions have been the pattern in the past few years. Do take into account, however, that cars purchased late in the season depreciate about 30 percent the moment the new models appear.

Savings realized through purchasing a new car a month or before the new models appear disappear when the car is traded in. Buying the new car as soon as it appears in the showroom will result in a greater initial expenditure, but in the long run, the additional cost will be balanced by a higher trade in value.

FROM WHOM SHOULD YOU BUY YOUR CAR?

A DEALER'S REPUTATION IN HIS COMMUNITY SHOULD BE YOUR TOP CONSIDERATION. Do not permit tricky auto ads to lure you to showrooms with promises of "no money down," "atomic trade-ins," "block buster bargains," etc. Don't believe signs that tell of pricing below dealer's cost, or anguished cries that over 100 cars must be sold before the end of the month in order to meet a quota. Be equally skeptical of free gift offers, bonuses and the host of "come-ons," all concocted to entice hungry buyers. Price is not everything when you buy a car.

Who hasn't experienced personally, or at least heard of instances where a car that in the beginning looked to be the world's best deal turned out in the end to be one of the most expensive and least satisfying? You will derive satisfaction only when you succeed in dealing with a reputable automobile dealer who provides good quality service and who stands behind the warranty that goes with the car.

A quick glance at a dealer's service shop is highly recommended. It can be very revealing. A small, cramped shop might mean that the dealer cannot afford to give you too much attention. On the other hand, a large, spacious service area with cars of all makes generally speaks well of the reputation of the mechanics. Finally, it is always desirable to compare car costs by going to several dealers.

HOW DO YOU RECOGNIZE A "GOOD DEAL"?

The first requisite when you go shopping for a car is the ability to protect yourself against aggressive salesmen. Remember that you're in the driver's seat until you sign your name to the sales contract. YOU should dictate the terms. You will be spending your own money.

Consider the list price posted on the car as a starting point. The dealer will lower it if he has to. Whether he actually does so or not will depend on how good a shopper you are.

If you do not have a car to trade in then you have a right to expect a discount from the quoted list price. Here are some suggested guides: a 12 percent discount on compact models, a 15 percent discount on full-sized models and an 18 percent discount on luxury type automobiles. If you will be turning in a car as a trade, you should expect to receive the same discount in the form of additional allowance on the car you are turning in. Consider also the possibility of selling your car privately.

The best method for ascertaining the prevailing market value of the used car you expect to turn in is to indulge in judicious comparison shopping. The time spent in visiting two, three or four dealers' showrooms will prove to be profitably spent. Prices do vary from one dealer to another. Careful shopping among reputable dealers can be profitable for any car buyer.

WHY NOT A USED CAR?

If you can afford to purchase a new automobile it will be to your advantage to decide in favor of it and against settling for a used model. The tested axiom holds true in this case: "When you buy a used car you buy someone else's headaches."

Nevertheless, a one or two-year-old car which has not been abused can prove to be a very satisfactory investment since the heaviest depreciation has already taken place. As a rule, a two-year-old car can be purchased for about half the original price when new. Thus, if one's finances are limited, he would do well to consider the alternative of buying a used car.

Since it is imperative that you investigate most thoroughly and carefully before investing in a used car, you should follow accepted guide lines in making your selections. It will be to your advantage to heed the advice that follows. It will help you to make a good choice for your particular needs and your pocketbook.

ON-THE-LOT-TESTS[14]

"1. Study highlights and reflections along body sides (omitting fenders) and top. Do this in a good light. Repainted or ripply areas on the sheet metal indicate possible damage to the car's basic structure; consider the car for rejection (but see Test No. 20, below).

"2. Probe by thumb or finger pressure along the lower edges of body, doors and trunk area for signs of weakened or rusted metal. Pimples or flaking of paint, as well as actual rust spots, are indications of internal rusting, which is difficult and expensive—and may in the end be impractical—to repair structurally.

"3. Run windows up and down; if they don't work, repair is fairly

---

[14] From *Consumer Reports*, Sept., 1962, pp. 426-427.

expensive. Open the doors and close them without slamming; if they don't seem to fit, or if they sag, drop down on opening, or must be slammed to close, they will usually be hard to fix and, worse, may indicate a bent frame.

"4. Look at a car's interior for signs of hard usage or abuse (broken cushion springs, worn pedal pads, paint off steering wheel, etc.), and at all five tires. If the tires are badly worn—or new-looking—any late model has probably run up at least 20,000 miles. Unevenly worn treads on any wheel indicate that the front end has been, or is, out of line. Realignment costs up to $15; rebushing, up to $90.

"5. Press your foot steadily on the brake pedal for a minute or so. If it sinks slowly under pressure, there is hydraulic leakage. Consider making Test No. 19. Failure to repair is hazardous, and repair cost runs from $10 to $50.

"6. Start the engine. Check all instruments, or flashing lights and gauges, to make sure they are functioning. A warning light or ammeter can show that the generator is not charging. Cost to repair or replace, $20 to $50.

"7. Stoop facing a front wheel, grasping it at the top with both hands. Shake it to and from you with vigor. Clunking sounds, or a lot of free play, is a sign of loose or worn wheel bearings or of worn suspension joints. Repair of the latter, $20 to $90.

"8. Push down rhythmically at one corner of the car at a time, so as to set it bouncing. The car should, when you release it, move up or down, then stop at an equilibrium position. Freer motion—as up and down—signals worn shock absorbers, which should be replaced for safety as well as comfort (at $15 to $20 per pair).

Driving Tests

"If a car looks good to you after running through the tests above, take it out on the road. A road test is essential before you buy. While you have the car on the road, keep listening for serious-sounding rattles, knocks, or squeaks. Too many should lead you to give up the car.

No fast, expert, or strenuous driving is necessary for the following tests.

"9. Start off from rest several times. Once you are used to the clutch, if any, it should give you smooth engagement, forward or backward—no jerk, grab, or chatter. If these symptoms persist, adjustment or replacement of parts is needed. Replacement will cost $40 to $80.

"10. Check the transmission at the same time. A manual transmission should not give out intermittent groaning noises, offer difficulty in shifting gears, or howl under slow speed acceleration with floored accelerator. A full overhaul costs $100 to $250. An automatic transmission also should give smooth starts in either direction, shift at well-spaced intervals, not allow the engine to race, or break away, on light-accelerator shifts. Other irregularities, each possibly a symptom of trouble, can come to light in an hour's driving. Overhaul of an automatic transmission can run very high—$100 to $300.

"11. Accelerate briskly several times from 10 or 15 mph to 40 or 45 in high gear or in Drive range with an automatic. The engine should pick up smoothly, without hesitation or bucking. If it does not, engine tuning or other work may be needed; don't buy without making Test No. 18.

"12. Pick a straight, quiet street or road, stand or kneel behind the center of the car, and have it driven slowly away from you. A car that travels a little crabwise, with front and rear wheels not in line with each other, may have suffered accident damage and should be rejected. Bent or wobbly wheels, however, can be replaced, if no further damage is discernible; see Test No. 20.

"13. Drive the car around some sharp left and right corners. There shouldn't be a lot of looseness in the steering, and it must not bind; only if these troubles are adjusted, should you accept it. Power steering shouldn't be lumpy in feel, nor lose its power to assist if turned rapidly. Overhaul of power steering costs $20 to $100.

"14. Find a wide, straight road or street, and, with no following traffic, make several stops from 40 to 45 mph, braking harder each time. The brake pedal should remain well above the floor and feel solid, not spongy; the stops shouldn't cause swerving, or grabbing or chattering of the brakes. Misbehavior may require major adjustment, new linings, drum refacing, etc., costing from $20 to $40 (see Test No. 19).

"15. If practicable, descend a grade of some length with your foot off the accelerator. (In a flat area, decelerate from 50 mph to about 15, without using the brake.) Then step hard on the accelerator, watching for a puff or cloud of blue exhaust smoke. Heavy smoke is a reliable warning that new piston rings soon will be needed or that the engine may have to be overhauled. Costs are listed in Test No. 18, following.

"16. A short ride over a really rough road will show up rattles and squeaks that need attention and allow you to check for jerky, "kicking," or uncertain steering, looseness of the whole front end, and lack of shock absorber restraint.

"17. If you can arrange it, drive the car long enough to find out if it is going to overheat. A long, slow pull uphill or driving in slow-moving traffic will help to demonstrate the fault. If overheating can be traced to the radiator, bear in mind the cost of repair or replacement: $15 to $110.

Shop Tests

"Even though a car you are considering has passed on-the-lot and driving tests, much more can be found out about it by having an unbiased mechanic make the tests that follow. He should make them in his own shop, at a cost of $5 to $15. He may suggest others. He shouldn't, of course, be connected with the dealer you plan to buy from.

"18. The condition of the engine's valves—and, to some extent, of its piston rings—can be learned by taking the compression pressure of each cylinder with a compression gauge. Engine overhaul costs: $10 to $35 for major tune-up; $40 to $70 for a valve job; $150 to $200 for minor overhaul; $200 to $400 for major overhaul.

"19. Have the mechanic remove a front wheel and brake drum. He can then note easily whether the drum is scored and needs reconditioning, what shape the brake lining is in, whether the hydraulic-brake cylinders are leaking, and the condition of the front wheel bearings. Repair costs: drum grinding, $2 to $3 per drum; brake overhaul, including hydraulic system (4 wheels), $20 to $90; front wheel bearing replacement, $15 to $35.

"20. With the car raised on a lift, the mechanic can examine it for grease leakage, from worn or broken bearing seals, on to wheels, tires, rear axle housing, etc. (cost of seal replacement varies, according to where the seal is; parts cost is usually minor). He can observe signs of exhaust gas leakage from damaged or rusted-out mufflers (repair, $10 to $60). He should also study the frame, suspension, and steering parts for indications of collision repairs: welds, heated areas, bent or straightened parts, etc. If he finds them, reject the car—and consider the mechanic's fee a good investment in safety.

"If CU's three sets of tests have been intelligently performed, the resulting picture of a potential used-car buy will be as complete as a moderate expenditure of time and money can make it."

HOW DO YOU CLOSE THE DEAL?

Study these statistics: In New York State legal interest charges for new car financing may vary from 4½ percent to 7 percent. On a used car up to two years old, the rate is higher—from 7 to 10 percent. On cars older than that, the rate may be as high as 13 percent. Bear in mind that your state's rates will probably be higher since rates in New York State are among the lowest in the country. The meaning should be very clear. Whether the car buyer realizes it or not, such finance charges are as much a part of the cost of the car as would be the addition of some costly extra equipment.

Even if you do some careful comparison shopping for a good credit deal, you'll probably wind up paying about $400 over a three-year period if you need $2,500 to buy your car—that is, provided the interest rate is only 5 percent. If your state allows higher rates, the chances are that you will pay up to $600 or even more to borrow the same amount. Therefore, the $3,000 car, if purchased on credit with a down payment of $500, will cost the purchaser from $3,400 to $3,600 or even more.

Using cash to pay for a car is without a doubt the very best policy for YOU—NOT FOR THE DEALER. He profits from selling you the car and also from his share of the charges on any credit transaction that he arranges.

If you have the money, pay cash. But if you do not have sufficient ready cash available then it is your responsibility to obtain the best possible credit terms that will suit your particular requirements. Once you have definitely decided on how to finance the purchase you should proceed to examine the contract. Every sales contract should be checked carefully to make certain that the terms are clearly stated and understood.

If you're paying cash, the contract should show the amount of the down payment, including the value of your trade-in, if you have one, the total price of the new car, an itemization of every extra accessory or piece of equipment with prices. You should insist upon a statement of all standard equipment, as well. A reputable dealer will have no hesitation in providing this for you. In addition, a contract involving financing should reveal the following:

(a) The agency to whom you will pay the balance due, since your dealer most likely will turn the contract over to a bank or a finance company.

(b) Special terms covering refunds if full payment can be made before the end of the contract.

(c) Exact specifications concerning the rights of the contract holder in the event that you cannot meet your obligations.

Insist that every condition is included in the contract. Do not be satisfied with a salesman's promise. Again we remind you that consumers are educated amateurs, at best. The dealer is a professional.

An important investment should be protected by the proper type of insurance. In another section (11) specific recommendations will be given concerning the protection that every car owner should have.

HOW SHOULD YOU BUY FURNITURE AND APPLIANCES FOR YOUR HOME?

Consumers who are in the market for furniture should first develop a basic overall plan to achieve the effect desired. Furniture is something you live with for a long time. Therefore, it should be selected with preference for quality materials and construction rather than for extreme and fancy design.

Furniture should be functional, should have simplicity of design, colors that harmonize with the room, and must be in proportion to the dimensions of the area in which it will be used. Avoid gaudy, massive units and showy fabrics. Another point to consider—the furniture you select should be appropriate and tasteful in any setting. People do move.

Very few consumers possess adequate knowledge of woods, fabrics, finishes, design, or hardware. For that reason, furniture hunting can become a risky venture for the average consumer. Even for the "expert," the experience will be costly from the standpoint of time. He will recognize that high prices do not indicate superior value in furniture and will spend much time examining construction, fabric, finish, etc.

In the bibliography the reader will find listed excellent publications that provide authoritative information about many aspects of decorating your home, including the wise selection of its furnishings. This treatment in no way attempts to condense them. The main purpose is to highlight broad guides which will serve to focus attention on mistakes to be avoided.

SELECTING A STYLE OF FURNITURE

As with everything else in life, a good style is one that you personally like. However, you will get your money's worth if you buy relatively simple modern furniture which tends to be durable and easy to care for. A variation known as Danish-modern is also very functional. The design is attractive, construction simple and prices moderate. Moreover, because the finish is of an oil type, it does not scratch as easily as does a high-gloss finish.

Contemporary designed furniture makes use of strong material, robust construction and avoids upholsteries and coil springs. Instead of bulky, heavy wood, contemporary furniture manufacturers often use metal rods, plywood and foam rubber. The result is a clean, durable product. Such pieces go well in compact dwellings.

Other popular styles of furniture include pieces of early American design, found very frequently in bedroom furniture, and the more elaborate type known as provincial. If you are attracted to curved legs and chair backs and somewhat larger pieces, then you may wish to consider French or Italian Provincial styles.

WHAT SHOULD YOU LOOK FOR IN CONSTRUCTION?

If a piece of furniture is well constructed it will stand firmly. Do not purchase wood furniture that has its parts nailed together. Joints should be made in such a way that the frame is held securely. For durability, which is so very important, a piece of furniture should be constructed with dowel or mortise and tenon joining technique (see illustration below). Good design, fine wood or even the most exquisite finish are of no value if the construction is poor—good furniture is made to last. Of what good to you is a chair that soon wobbles or cracks?

The following construction guides, which appear in the publication *Money Management, Your Home Furnishing Dollar* (Household Finance Corporation, 1964), offer valuable pointers to all who seek to purchase furniture.

"Backs of chests, desks or buffets made of 3-ply veneer. In high and medium priced furniture, they are inset and screwed into the frame. In high quality pieces, backs and undersides are sanded and color stained. In budget furniture, backs may be flush with the sides and tacked or nailed in position.

"Drawers constructed with dovetail joints for a secure fit . . . with center or side guides for easy operation . . . with smoothly sanded surfaces . . . with stops to prevent accidentally pulling out. An exact fit is essential for drawers that are flush with the surface of furniture. Overlapping drawers need not fit as snugly. Joints should be firm and sturdy. Dust panels between drawers help keep stored items clean and add to rigidity.

"Knobs, pulls, handles attached firmly, placed evenly, easy to grasp and harmonious with furniture.

"Sides made of wood in the color and grain to match the front and top. Back surfaces should also match if furniture is to stand away from the wall.

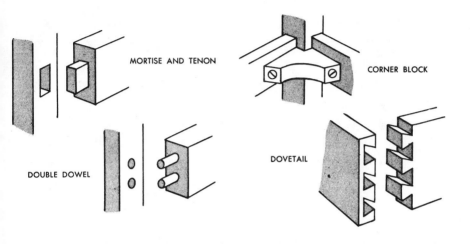

Examples of good joint construction

"Joinings made to hold frame firmly. (See illustration.) For durability, mortise and tenon or double dowel joinings should hold outer frame together . . . corner blocks, notched and screwed into place, should be used for reinforcement at points of strain such as chair and table leg joinings . . . dovetail joints should be used to join corners of drawers. When additional rigidity is desirable look for reinforcement of joinings with corner blocks, glue and screws. If metal is used for structural parts, joints should be securely bolted, riveted, welded or screwed.

"Interior surfaces sanded smooth in all pieces. They may be lacquered or waxed in high priced furiture. Any metal used should be rust resistant . . . if painted, it should be chip resistant."

◆ Suites of furniture are obsolete. Avoid sets consisting of many pieces. More often than not dealers make up such sets from cheap items that have little value.

◆ Buy few pieces, but good, durable ones.

◆ Buy only from the most reputable dealers who will stand behind their merchandise.

◆ Select wood finishes that are hard, scratch-resistant and less likely to show dirt. Lacquer finishes are superior to varnish finishes.

◆ Ask for a written guarantee when salesmen assure you that a piece of furniture is made of solid maple, solid walnut, or solid mahogany. Very often furniture is made from cheap wood and then a thin veneer of good wood is placed on top.

◆ When buying sofas and upholstered chairs examine the bottom portions. Look for heavy muslin coverings and strong coils. They assure rugged construction. Also, make sure that the frame is of hardwood.

◆ Be on the lookout for sales in department stores. February and August are usually excellent months for good furniture buys.

APPLIANCES FOR YOUR HOME

Whether you reside in a large city like Chicago or Los Angeles or in a suburb or a rural area, your private home, rented apartment or cooperative will require certain basic appliances. These will include a refrigerator, a gas or electric range, and at least one piece of communication equipment—TV or radio receiver. Beyond these basic items what other appliances are desired will depend upon how much money you have at your disposal, your particular needs and the general standard of living that you set as your goal. It would be rare these days to find a residential community whose homes did not have all or most of the following appliances: air conditioners, freezers, dish washers, washing machines, clothes and hair dryers, electric toasters, mixers, grills and broilers, vacuum cleaners, sewing machines, garbage disposal units, floor waxers and polishers, irons, and a wide assortment of electric appliances used for cooking.

Your actual requirements as well as a careful analysis of your future needs should be the basis for determining exactly which appliances to buy. Moreover, in selecting appliances you should likewise give thought to the specific needs such appliances satisfy. For example, if you are anxious to cut down on food costs it might prove to be economical if you were to purchase a food freezer. This would hold true especially in a large family situation. On the other hand, if washing clothes by hand becomes an arduous task, obviously you will wish to purchase a washing machine to conserve energy and to make washing more convenient, more effective and less time consuming.

Whatever your appliance needs may be, avoid purchasing them by impulse. Do not allow an attractive sign in a window to persuade you to buy the first item you see.

AN APPLIANCE CHECK LIST

1. Do you know exactly which appliances you want?
2. How will you pay for them?
3. Have you determined in advance the special requirements that apply in your situation? Which is better for you, gas or electric operated items? How much space do you have? Should the appliance, if it has a door, open to the left, the right, or on top?
4. What will be your installation requirements and costs?
5. Have you checked with others who own such appliances? Have they encountered special problems? Are they satisfied?
6. Have you checked *Consumer Reports* or *Consumer Bulletin* for product ratings?
7. Have you checked prices and the availability of various makes and models with a number of dealers?
8. Have you paid attention to advertisements?
9. What warranties or guarantees are available?

10. Are you satisfied with the appliance's safety rating as evidenced by a UL seal of approval or some other well-known certification of approval?
11. Does your dealer stand behind the products he sells? What is his reputation regarding service and replacement of parts?
12. Can delivery be made within a reasonable period of time?

The same general advice that is appropriate for purchasing furniture and automobiles applies when you are in the market for appliances. The consumer must look at himself in the mirror and should make a firm determination to play the game fairly and above board. He must be willing to pay a fair price for goods and services. Too often, consumers hope to get something for nothing. In life, this doesn't happen. No dealer can remain in business without making a profit. If the consumer attempts to squeeze the dealer's profit margin, he must be prepared to sacrifice some value in terms of product or attendant services. This is the way business operates.

The natural urge to want a lot for a little has fostered the mushroom-like growth of discount operations in this country. Discount houses thrive on consumers' greed. Hungry-for-bargain shoppers are always those who are "taken" most quickly and thoroughly. You only get what you pay for. The consumer who becomes dazzled and confused in a tempting market never knows what value he's getting for his money. Price must be considered along with all the other factors that have already received mention in connection with automobiles, furniture, appliances, food and clothing. Certainly the consumer should always be on the alert for good buys—only fools will knowingly pay more for items than they should. However, somewhere along the line every fair-minded consumer strikes a balance because he recognizes that square dealing is like a two-way street. There must be give and take on the part of the buyer and the seller.

CONSUMER UNDERSTANDING CHECK

1. The ownership of your first automobile brings with it a number of responsibilities that did not exist before. What are they, and what decisions result from them?
2. A brand new compact car can be bought for about $1,800, whereas a two-year old car of the "luxury" model type can be bought for $2,200. Assuming that you had enough money to buy either one, which car would you buy? Why?
3. It has been said that "the best time to buy a new car is during a blizzard." What is the reasoning behind this statement?
4. As our economy has boomed so have the sales of luxury cars. The **Wall Street Journal** told of a young man in the mid-west who paid $6,000 for a Cadillac Coupe de Ville convertible. His yearly income was $15,000. Do you think that status is a sufficiently strong reason for investing 40 percent of one's income in an automobile?
5. In the May 1965 issue of **Consumer Reports** there appeared an article entitled "Why Auto Dealers Don't Like Cash Buyers." How has consumer greed led to this condition?
6. What reasoning would spur the buyer of a convertible to accept an air conditioner as one of the extras on his car?
7. Shopping for furniture will pose a number of problems that are far more complex than those facing the buyer of a car. How should one go about shopping intelligently for furniture?
8. Examine your furniture at home and check its construction against the guides provided in this section. Without considering price, do you think your furniture meets the described standards?
9. For many years home washers and dryers were always sold as separate appliances. Recently, combination washer-dryers have appeared on the market. What advantages or disadvantages do you see in such a combination unit?
10. Make a survey of all your home appliances, room by room. Estimate the approximate cost of these appliances. Do you still feel that "two can live as cheaply as one"?

8. budgeting

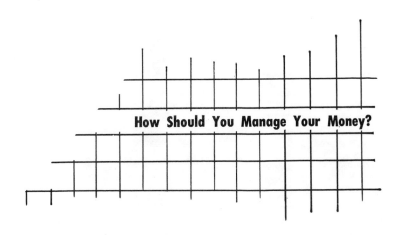

How Should You Manage Your Money?

HOW SHOULD YOU MANAGE YOUR MONEY?
WHAT IS A BUDGET?

A simple yet basic definition of the term budget must include the concept that it is a logical plan for managing your income. Virtually everyone has income or is dependent upon someone who has income. To utilize income wisely one must develop a plan.

Government decides first how much money it will need to function and then proceeds to obtain the necessary income to do so. The individual, on the other hand, begins with a predetermined amount of income from which he must meet his obligations. As his income changes, he must revise his spending habits. Do you remember our consumer-friend Ernest Colville? His monthly income was $700. As was emphasized in section 5, a variety of payroll deductions makes it impossible for him to receive his gross income (the amount for which he is hired). His take-home pay, or disposable income is that amount of money that is available to him. Of course, this does not imply that Ernest Colville can do what he likes with it. Before he can decide to save or spend at will, he must allot a sufficient amount of money to pay for the basic expenses of living. After all obligations have been taken care of he has free choice in the use of what is left—if there is any.

Mr. Colville, like the rest of us, will never be able to adjust to living within income until he learns how to effectively plan his spending and to wisely manage his dollars for maximum satisfaction in his daily living. Since income has limits, only by adhering to a personalized budget plan will it be possible for him and all of us to derive the full benefit from earnings.

HOW DOES A BUDGET WORK FOR YOU?

Poets and writers have frequently alluded to the fact that dollars seem to grow wings and disappear from the scene in a hurry. Perhaps that is the reason man devised the budget—he recognized the need for anchoring money in some way. And that is exactly what a budget can do. A sound budget can assist you to obtain the things you want—all of the necessities, as well as the extras to which you are entitled—within the framework of the income at your disposal.

To put it in other words, when you have a plan for spending your dollars are utilized more fully for greater satisfaction. A certain orderliness or discipline is injected into an individual's spending pattern.

It is not difficult to list reasons for having a budget. Here are the most important ones, in our opinion:

1. A plan for spending enables a person to satisfy his short and long-term objectives.
2. A budget helps you to manage your money efficiently.
3. A budget forces the individual to place each single expenditure in proper focus.
4. A budget leads to better understanding of the power inherent in money.
5. A budget provides valuable economic education for the entire family.
6. A definite plan for handling your income gives you a feeling of well-being and security.

One could list many more advantages or reasons for having spending plans, guides or budgets, but to do so here would be like carrying coal to Newcastle. A brief discussion of the six benefits listed above should serve to convince the reader that one has to put effort, time and thought into living in such a manner that hard-earned dollars will not vanish into thin air. You owe it to yourself to know where *your* money goes.

1. Through a budget you can learn to see how your living pattern should meet the day-by-day or short-term goals as well as the plans or goals that take a long time to achieve. For example, if your electric range needs repairs you cannot wait a month or two before calling a repair man. The necessary repairs represent an immediate expense—you will have to spend money to have the range fixed NOW. However, if the range has been giving continued aggravation by virtue of requiring very frequent repairs over a period of time, it might be wise to start putting aside a fixed amount of money for the time when you decide to replace the range. Since your goal will then involve action in the future, it properly must be considered

a long-term aim. In other words, by planning early for the future purchase of a new electric range, you are doing the following:

(a) You are lessening the shock. It is always hard to take when you are suddenly faced with the need to spend large amounts of money that you don't have.

(b) You have the right to determine the conditions under which you will replace the range. In other words, you can decide exactly when to trade it in. You will not have to wait until it breaks down once and for all. Moreover, you are better able to take advantage of special sales to get what you want.

(c) You save money by being prepared for the purchase of your new range. You will be using money you will have saved rather than credit. Remember, loans cost money. They add to the original cost of whatever you buy.

It should be emphasized that long-term goals must never be permitted to interfere with basic daily needs. It is not recommended that you put off going to the dentist because you're saving to buy a new car.

2. A budget is one of the best deterrents of impulse buying. A predetermined plan does help you to avoid wasteful spending of your dollars. So many people become heavy spenders on pay day. As soon as they receive their wages they embark on spending sprees. A spending plan will point out how much all those "little" things cost, and will force you to realistically balance how much goes out against how much you have coming in. Of course, the plan or budget can only help if the person who makes it out has the courage and steadfastness to stay with it.

3. Bear in mind that when you prepare a budget you are really preparing a priority list of your needs and wants. You are determining the comparative importance of them in your life pattern. By so doing you apportion the money that you are willing to spend for each item. What we are saying is that a budget forces the individual to place each expenditure in proper focus. Doesn't this family scene seem familiar? The mother would like to have a new refrigerator, the father expresses a desire to buy a more powerful outboard motor

for the coming summer's boating season up at the lake, the sixteen-year-old daughter wants a new hi-fi set on which to play her Rock and Roll records, and her fourteen-year-old brother never misses a chance to appeal for a four-speed English racing bicycle. The budget cannot be stretched to make all these desires possible. Therefore, the family must have a conference to decide whether all the items the individual members have requested are justified. Even if agreement is reached that the items are justifiable, a priority plan must be formulated in order to separate immediate needs from long-term wants. Limited funds make this necessary.

Let's examine the basis for the family's decision. It was agreed that the boy should have his bicycle because next month he would be going to junior high school—and the school is a mile from home. Moreover, he would need the bike for his recently acquired newspaper route. Johnny agreed to pay for part of the cost of the bicycle from his earnings as a newsboy. Mother's refrigerator came next. There was no doubt about the need for a new one since the one they had was fifteen years old and groaned continually. In addition, the appliance refused to manufacture ice cubes during the summer months. As for the outboard motor—well, it was decided that $15 a month would be set aside for it. When next summer came it would be possible to have enough money on hand to purchase it. It was decided that since Mary's record player was in working condition, the hi-fi purchase would be made the following year. The family thus set a priority for spending based on decisions that reflected their needs and wants. All such decisions are individual acts and do not necessarily meet the requirements of others.

4. Money possesses the power to obtain for you the things you desire. However, random purchasing patterns without planning can seriously decrease your money's power. One need only point to the large number of persons who succumb to the temptation to spend beyond their means as the Christmas season approaches. Is it not foolhardy to spend $85 for assorted toys and decorations when one's rent is due and the refrigerator is almost empty? Wise financial planning in advance might very well be the preventive in these cases. The consumer should be the master of his money and should always be in control of its power. Money should not be man's master. A budget is the only known effective control of expenditures.

5. Money is the medium of exchange whereby we use the money we receive as producers to obtain the goods and services we require as consumers. In effect, we acquire through budgeting an understanding of economic principles as they apply to our everyday living. For example, life in every family unit provides concrete experience relating to the law of supply and demand. After all, the family's *supply* of money is limited, while its *demands* are usually unlimited. The budget acts as a tool permitting us to adjust both elements. Inherent also is the concept of scarcity, which in this application, refers to the limitation of dollars that are available to either an individual or a family. Thus, everyone must assume responsibility for a choice. In all cases this means that one must forego the use or benefits of the item or items not chosen.

Let's consider the problem faced by George Brown, a high school senior who has earned six dollars mowing lawns on a Saturday afternoon. He must decide whether to go to the shopping center near his home to buy some records he's been anxious to own, or to buy a pair of skates. George is also tempted to take his girl friend Mary to the movies. Another remote possibility that crosses his mind is that of depositing the six dollars in his small savings account. The big question is—what should he do? Regardless of which course of action George selects, the economic concept of *opportunity cost* will enter into the picture. His expenditure for the movies, if that is his choice, is actually increased by the realization that he is denying himself the benefits of the other three alternatives. Through the awareness that one acquires in proper money management, it is hoped that effective choices are made possible more easily. If George's family utilizes a budget he will have had the experience of participating in decision making with regard to use of income.

6. The knowledge that your income is properly apportioned to meet all possible expenses, with some left over to spend or save as you please, provides real satisfaction and a feeling that "things are looking up." It is a known fact that the greatest cause of domestic friction and broken homes is the family's inability to cope with money problems. In most cases a large amount of emotional tension and anxiety could have been avoided by proper money management beginning with a budget geared to the particular family

situation. Security is something all of us should enjoy and a budget can put us on the road leading to the realization of our dreams and aspirations. Like a compass, a budget gives us direction in life. Remember, drifting leads nowhere.

A budget can give you a feeling of satisfaction.

THE BUDGET AS A PERSONALITY

With many families, the budget occupies a place of real importance. In fact, one might say that the big "B" is regarded as another person, and they shower this personality with both praise and blame. The budget assumes the role of a watch dog. "I'd like to go away with you folks for the weekend, but the budget won't permit it." "My budget saved me so much money that I can now afford to buy a new tape recorder." We're all familiar with similar remarks make by those who think of the budget as a discipline, a deterrent, a savior, a guiding spirit, to mention but a few of the terms that apply.

BUDGET FORM		
Expenses	Weekly	Monthly
Rent		
Food		
Car		
Insurance		
Clothing		
Medical		
Personal		
Savings		
Entertainment		
Education		
Miscellaneous		

The budget is your conscience.

Perhaps you should consider the budget as your conscience since it is a reflection of you. If there is moral value in letting your conscience be your guide, there is equal merit in permitting your budget to guide your financial decisions. Remember, however, that a budget cannot pull rabbits from a hat. It cannot increase your income, nor can it save your money for you. It can, however, assist you to establish a healthy balance between those things that you need for everyday living and others that are not exactly essential.

Do not permit your budget to dictate every move you make. To guide is one thing, to confine and restrict is another. It certainly would be foolish to become emotionally upset attempting to track down a $1.57 which you can't account for. Your budget should never be like the tail that wagged the dog.

You should decide how you wish to spend your money. You will shape the personality of your own budget by your action. When you say "my budget" you are in effect saying that you are going or not going to do this or that. Therefore, there is little value to be gained from making the big "B" a villain when you are dissatisfied with your financial management. Analyze the problem honestly.

WHAT DO YOU BUDGET?

A budget may be prepared for any desired planning period—a week, a month, a year, or even a longer period. Figure out how much disposable income you will have for the desired budget period. Be sure to include all wages, or salaries for you and any other family member whose income is to be included, as well as any other income such as rents, interest, dividends, profits from business transactions, etc.

The next step is to set down all of your expenses that must be met during the same period, as well as savings that you consider appropriate. Every budget should contain the following expense items:

FOOD—this should include not only all foods purchased for the home but the cost of all meals that have to be eaten away from home.

HOUSING—this includes (a) rent or mortgage payment; (b) utilities; (c) heating; (d) property taxes; (e) repairs and maintenance; (f) all household insurance—fire, theft, liability and mortgage.

CLOTHING—new clothing, repairs, cleaning and laundry charges.

TRANSPORTATION—cost of public transportation and/or your automobile. This includes gas and oil, insurance, license fees, tolls, repairs and maintenance.

HOUSE FURNISHINGS—appliances, furniture, draperies, linens, credit payments on these items, rugs, repairs and maintenance.

MEDICAL—medicine and drugs, medical and dental expenses, hospitalization and health insurance.

INSURANCE—life, and any other special form of insurance you may carry.

RECREATION—entertainment, vacations, sports, clubs and costs associated with them (i.e., babysitting).

CONTRIBUTIONS—charitable and religious; other donations.

PERSONAL—allowances to cover all incidentals.

SAVINGS—banks, stocks, bonds, mutual funds and credit union shares.

MISCELLANEOUS—gifts, books, magazines, hobbies, newspapers, dues and fees.

Rarely does the initial budget attempt succeed, simply because you don't really know with accuracy where your money goes. After several realistic adjustments made to suit your individual pattern of living, you will, if you are determined, succeed in making the plan which you have improved work for your benefit.

Your budget is as individual as your finger prints. No two families can function in the same way. Only you can draw up a plan that will meet your requirements and desires. Don't try to model your budget after someone else's—it won't work.

SOME IMPORTANT CONSIDERATIONS ABOUT BUDGETING

◆ A budget does not have to include every penny to succeed. It should not be a maze of trivia, nor should it become a noose around your neck. If it assumes the shape of a strait jacket, you'll soon find ways to avoid using it.

◆ One does not "look cheap" or lose status by following a budget. Bear in mind that government and business wouldn't think of operating for five minutes without a budget. Why should you?

◆ How much money you make is not necessarily most important—it's how you use what you have.

◆ Don't limit yourself to functioning within the narrow range of the often cited percentage guidelines. For example, 25 percent of one's income is considered the average expenditure for food. However, it must be realized that none of us is average. This average is a composite of what all people spend for food. Your tastes are individual—you may properly expect to spend more or less for food. Your only restriction should be the amount of money you have to spend.

Make every attempt to involve all members of the family in the preparation of the budget. By doing so, they will all become acquainted with and appreciate the goals you set for yourself and the family. This will insure their cooperation through establishment of incentive.

HOW DO YOU BUDGET?

The budget or financial plan that is best suited to your needs cannot be prepared quickly. Budget planning is not like writing a letter —it cannot be completed within a specified amount of time. On the contrary, you will find it necessary to record actual expenses for several weeks, months, or longer if the period for which you are attempting to plan is a long one (a year, for example). How revealing those records will be! Such records will then form the basis for the financial plan you have in mind.

It will soon become apparent upon studying the records that your spending and saving will have a pattern—not always the same perhaps, but they will nevertheless reveal certain similarities. You may even be pleasantly surprised to learn that you've been budgeting all along since your expenditures and savings have been within your income. Should that be so, you merit congratulations. Too often, however, congratulations cannot be offered—expenditures exceed income and not a dollar is available for saving. To a degree, a person in the first category has his problem—though not as serious a one as does a person in the latter case. Neither one has given any thought to the long term objectives that are so very important. A day by day existence, even though it may be within income limits, has many weaknesses. No provision is made for the future and no direction in life is nourished.

We must be realistic in the case of the individual or family that has to live on a very small income. We recognize that only the smallest savings are possible, if at all. Therefore, it would be unrealistic to expect that any budget plan could make a difference as far as more discretionary income is concerned. But it might serve to alert the individual or family to the fact that something must be done to improve the financial position. Perhaps some part-time work might prove to be the answer, or even re-training to increase earning potential. The "shock value" of a budget can conceivably become the motivating force for self improvement.

In the case of persons who make ends meet with something left over for savings, a budget can really make a difference. It can make them redirect their actions so that increased discretionary income becomes a reality. Obviously, the more one saves the greater are his chances for realization of long-term goals at a later date.

Budgets, believe it or not, are likely to be of greater benefit to those persons in the upper income brackets. We'll explain why. The greater one's income, the greater will be the temptation to spend in large amounts. Persons who earn $50,000, $100,000 or more per year tend to lose perspective. Money comes to them easily and leaves them even more easily. It flies away. It is a known fact that many people who enjoy incomes of the size mentioned above discover to their horror that when April 15th approaches they are "behind the eight ball," financially speaking. They often find it necessary to borrow to pay their income taxes. Proof of this is the fact that celebrities such as movie and TV stars, professional athletes and entertainers almost always engage the services of a business manager, who usually is an accountant. His main job is to keep them solvent and to guard the health of their husky incomes. It is axiomatic that you have to spend money in order to make money and celebrities do spend. Many corporation executives fall into the same category. Their large incomes also require careful management. It is not unusual for their financial advisers to assume complete control of their clients' income. They place their clients on strict allowances, they pay all their bills and make a concerted effort to establish for them a firm financial foundation.

Now let us examine a specific case—the Colville family. Mr. Colville's gross income is $700, which amounts to a disposable income of approximately $600 after deductions. The $600 is budgeted as shown on the next page. On the surface this would appear to be a budget possessing very little flexibility. However, even this plan can be adjusted so that the family can increase spending in any desired areas or decrease spending in order to permit greater savings. Now we shall perform some surgery.

$120

$130 HOME SWEET HOME

$40

$50

$50

$40

$25 POLICY

$30 MOVIES TONITE

$20

$50 SALE RECORDS

$25 BANK BOOK

$20 PAPERS

All of us would be able to increase spending in any one of the categories. That is very simple. Reducing expenses is another matter. Here's how to save in each category.

FOOD

Economies which would really make a difference in terms of dollars and cents are the following:

1. Substitution of store brands for nationally advertised brands.
2. Hamburger meat in place of steak.
3. Margarine in place of butter.
4. Purchase of foods in their least expensive form (fresh beans rather than frozen).
5. Purchases of foods that are in abundance (in season, when costs are low).
6. Planning meals around items on sale.
7. Quantity buying when the price is right.

HOUSING

One should not spend for rent an excessively large percentage of his income. If you feel that your rent is drawing too heavily upon your income, look for less expensive housing.

CLOTHING

You can save by:

1. Repairing instead of buying new clothes.
2. Shopping at discount houses.
3. Buying clothing for multi-purpose use.
4. Avoiding high-fashion clothes that will go out of style within a short period of time.
5. Economizing on clothes maintenance (home or self-service laundering, ironing, and self-service dry cleaning).

TRANSPORTATION

The most valid approach to a sound evaluation of your transportation requirements involves a determination of need, cost, convenience, alternatives, time and status. A person who resides in a large city but works in a suburb twenty miles away would probably do well to concentrate upon automobile transportation unless bus or railroad lines exist and offer efficient, convenient service between the two areas. Where one has alternative means of transportation from which to choose, cost, convenience and service should be the criteria upon which to make the decision. Status or prestige should occupy last place among all considerations.

One can effect economies by:

1. Using public transportation rather than buying and maintaining an automobile.
2. Buying commutation or monthly tickets, wherever available, in order to effect economies.
3. Purchasing a car for performance rather than style.
4. Selecting a new car without extras; the "standard package" deal. Avoid optional equipment.
5. Locating a good used car that sells for less than the lowest price new car.
6. Joining a car pool to reduce the cost of going to and coming from work.
7. Giving your car the attention it deserves in order to prevent expensive repairs.

HOUSE FURNISHINGS

Worthwhile savings will be realized if you:

1. Buy merchandise rated high by *Consumer Reports* and *Consumer Bulletin.*
2. Buy only furniture and appliances that are essential. Don't fall for every gadget you see in a store window.
3. Compare prices, performance, style, service and dealers before making your decision to buy.
4. Pay cash. Avoid additional charges for credit.
5. Check the written warranty.
6. Buy products whose specifications meet the family's requirements, not those of the salesman.
7. Build your savings to purchase better quality furniture which will be more durable. This will reduce long-term

furniture costs. This procedure should be followed with all purchases, if possible.

MEDICAL

By maintaining adequate medical protection through a Health and Accident Policy, your out-of-pocket expenses will be minimized. When you accumulate adequate reserves over a period of time you will not be hurt by an emergency.

INSURANCE

For a comprehensive treatment of the many aspects of insurance and how to cut its cost to you, see Section 11.

RECREATION AND CONTRIBUTIONS

In these areas simple common sense should apply. You donate or spend *what you can afford*. Don't follow the leader. Conspicuous consumption (keeping up with the Joneses) can cause very serious financial difficulties. Set aside a definite amount for recreation and stick to it. Don't borrow from the food money to spend an evening on the town.

PERSONAL ALLOWANCES AND MISCELLANEOUS

It is foolhardy to pinch nickles and dimes from this category. You'll never become a tycoon by depriving yourself of your favorite morning newspaper. Remember what we have said: "A budget is not a strait jacket."

Everyone needs some spending money. You do too. Why spoil your fun by attempting to account for every penny? The only sensible advice appropriate here is this—don't go overboard in the matter of allowances. Whatever amount you set for personal spending in your financial plan should be large enough to meet your needs, yet modest in terms of the total picture.

SAVINGS

Everyone should save some money from his or her disposable income. The amount you save each pay period need not always be exactly the same since expenses do fluctuate. Nevertheless, it is a good procedure to deposit a fixed amount in your savings account as soon as you are paid. Should you find later that your expenses are larger than expected, you can withdraw the required amount from your account to "balance your budget." A detailed treatment of savings will be found in section 12.

WHERE DID MY MONEY GO?

Have you ever stopped to take stock of where your money went from the time you left your house in the morning to three o'clock on a Saturday afternoon? If you are like most of us you probably will find it most difficult to account for every penny unless you keep a written account of every expenditure.

A plan or record of spending will serve not only as a valuable record of money spent but even more important, it will provide guidelines for future spending. You will be able to tell where your money goes and you will be able to examine your spending habits. With the knowledge acquired you will be able to make adjustments in order to achieve maximum effectiveness.

A good budget represents a record to be taken seriously but not to be considered as a drudge and a tiring experience. You and you alone will be its master and your budget will work to the degree that you will want it to work. Paper work will not perform miracles for you. Your determination and will power, however, will guarantee that your budget will work for you. Your record keeping can be made interesting with a little imagination—it need not be a chore. Whatever system you decide works well for you should reflect sound business methods that can be applied to individual or family income. Such a plan will pay rich dividends.

CONSUMER UNDERSTANDING CHECK

1. What kinds of income other than wages and salary can an individual receive? How do they qualify as income?
2. The Colville family wants a color TV set, the daughter wants a new gown for her junior prom, Mrs. Colville would like an electric knife, and the father would like a new putter. The family budget cannot handle all four wants. If you were a member of that family, how would you rank these wants in relative order of importance assuming that it would be possible to set aside $25 a week for their purchase?
3. Keep a record of every expenditure you make during the period of one week. Then analyze how you have spent your money to see if you can improve your spending habits.
4. A budget can be an effective weapon in dealing with the forces of inflation. Why is this statement made?
5. "I have so little money, it wouldn't do me any good to have a budget." Do you agree or disagree with this statement often offered by persons who are reluctant to adhere to a plan for money management? Why?
6. How does budgeting lead to the acquisition of improved understanding of economic principles?
7. What is meant by the term "opportunity cost"? Give a concrete illustration of the term's application in a situation with which you are personally identified.
8. How would you counter the argument "I make ends meet without a budget"?
9. Assume that you are the head of a family having a weekly disposable income of $200. How would you budget this amount of money in order to achieve maximum utilization and provision for savings?
10. How much money do you have at the present time? When will you be receiving more money? What will be your expenses between now and that time? If your expenses will exceed the amount of money that will be at your disposal, what surgery will you perform on those expenses?

9. credit and lending institutions

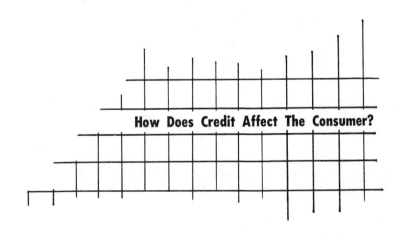

How Does Credit Affect The Consumer?

HISTORICAL DEVELOPMENT OF CONSUMER CREDIT

In our early days only the most reputable business firms or well-to-do people could obtain credit. In fact, the very mention of the word "debt" was enough to create the reputation that a family or individual was financially incompetent. The people whose incomes were small had to save money in tiny amounts for years before they could make a major purchase. However, as our economy expanded production of all kinds of goods increased rapidly. Merchants soon realized that if they wanted to stay in business they would have to let the poor and those with modest incomes have the goods they needed and permit them to pay in small amounts, by the week or month, rather than waiting until they saved enough cash to make purchases. This plan of credit we recognize, of course, as *installment credit*.

Toward the beginning of the nineteenth century installment credit became well entrenched in the American way of life as families began to buy such items as sewing machines, books, furniture and pianos on an increasingly large scale. Within the century many department stores and retail establishments began to extend credit to their customers. This marked the beginning of the pattern with which we are thoroughly familiar—the *charge account*. For the first time, wage earners and people of moderate means found a feast of new merchandise available from which they could select at will even if they lacked cash at the time to make purchases.

Though installment buying became increasingly popular and was accepted by members of the business community, there continued to exist, nevertheless, social prejudice against it. The whole area of installment selling and borrowing money to be able to buy was the target of condemnation. It was not considered to be the pattern of life of gentile, refined, successful people. Only the lower classes—the irresponsible, borrowed to pay for goods and services. The jails were filled with delinquent debtors, and money lenders were regarded as persons of low character.

Producer credit, however, enjoyed a respectable status during the same period. The government and business firms borrowed money then just as they do today. The distinction, of course, lay in the fact that borrowing for consumption was synonymous with being improvident, a faulty manager of money. Borrowing to expand a business, thus leading to increased profits, was another matter. That was respectable.

But people's attitudes change. Outright condemnation gave way to a grudging acknowledgment that installment credit did hold some advantages. But many continued to emphasize the disadvantages and to maintain that consumers ought to save their money and pay cash for almost everything they bought. Now, however, installment credit has even acquired respectability in this country. There is wide acceptance of installment plans as very useful techniques that can be used advantageously, provided they are not abused.

CONSUMER CREDIT AND THE POST-WAR YEARS

Experts in the field of credit frequently refer to consumer credit as a phenomenon of the post-World War II era. During the war years America's civilian and military population had accumulated tremendous amounts of cash which, the moment the war was over, made its way into the market place as eager consumers bought cars, houses, appliances, and furniture and house furnishings of all types. War-starved appetites had to be satisfied. Demand was so great and supplies so limited that an inflationary spiral resulted. Elimination of the price controls that had been in effect during the war years in order to keep a ceiling on price levels proved to be one of the basic reasons for the sudden spurt both in the demand for products and the prices they commanded in the market.

By 1948 American industry had increased its production levels of consumer goods to the point where prices began to decline. Supply had succeeded in equaling demand and, in many cases, had exceeded it. The savings that had been accumulated during the war were now depleted. The nation's giant two-year spending spree had taken its toll. The desire for consumer goods—from houses to refrigerators—was not exhausted, however. At this point, the use of credit became widespread and began to acquire a new brand of respectability. Its advantages came to be appreciated as the nation changed from a war to peace economy.

All sectors of the nation's economy were quick to see in consumer credit advantages and merits ideally suited to their varied needs. An examination of the statistics that follow will reveal how tremendous has been the growth of consumer credit since 1945.

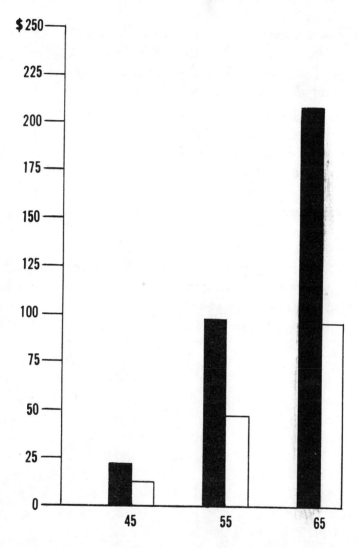

Dramatic Growth of Consumer Credit in post-war years.

In 1945 the mortgage debt for urban homes of one to four families was approximately $18 and a half billion, and outstanding short and intermediate term consumer credit amounted to slightly over $5 and a half billion. Ten years later, mortgage debt amounted to $88 billion. In other words, housing credit had increased about 500 percent in a ten-year period. Short and intermediate term consumer credit reached $39 billion—a jump of almost 800 percent. By 1965, our national mortgage debt was $213 billion and short and intermediate term credit reached the $86 billion mark. Mortgage debt in twenty years increased 1,200 percent and short and intermediate term consumer credit increased 1,700 percent.[15]

People are buying things today which are far more costly and durable than ever before. The prices of such durable items as TV sets, washing machines, automobiles, motor boats and trailers do not permit the average citizen to buy them from his discretionary income. But people want the satisfaction of owning one or more of such items even though they may not have ready cash. Credit becomes the answer. Credit is a word derived from the Latin verb *credere,* which means *to trust,* and is the term used to mean that payment will be expected at some future time for some item of intrinsic value given on trust. It can be said that we are actually living in the age of credit. One can obtain almost any item or service on credit these days. We hear over the radio and TV so many commercials inviting us to "fly now and pay later," eat on credit, charge everything from flowers, books and gasoline to funerals, and the ever increasing pleas to avail ourselves of the many credit card plans, revolving charge accounts or budget accounts in order to enjoy a host of services as well as goods of every conceivable description. You can even make telephone calls on credit. Believe it or not, cash seems to be going out of style. Persons who pay cash are considered "square"; but if your wallet is filled with credit cards you automatically step up a notch and join the ranks of the "in" people. It looks like credit is here to stay—a useful tool to be sure. But so is a razor blade. You must know how to use it.

---

[15] Statistics from *Economic Report of the President,* January 1966, U.S. Government Printing Office.

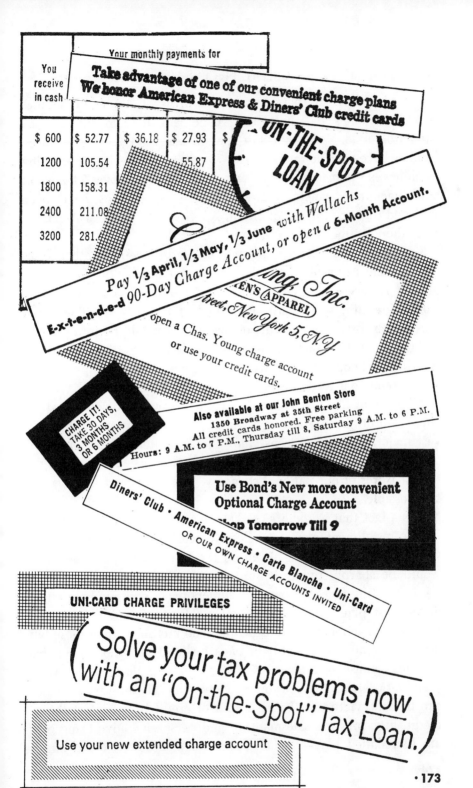

IS CREDIT NECESSARY?

Consider the fact that almost three-fifths of American families own their homes and that about 70 percent of them own at least one automobile. Virtually every home has a radio, 98 percent of all families have electric refrigerators, 75 percent have electric washing machines, 93 percent have at least one TV set and over 74 percent have vacuum cleaners. Many of these acquisitions have been achieved through the use of credit. Approximately half of America's 55 million families have some oustanding debt.

Since most of our homes, automobiles and the various other forms of consumer's durable goods have been bought on the installment plan, it is very clear that without credit, ownership of such goods would not enjoy wide distribution. Only the relatively affluent persons with substantial amounts of ready cash would be in a position to buy them. Certainly the use of installment credit has made it possible for people in the lower and middle income groups to enjoy costly items that could never be purchased otherwise.

Whereas in many parts of the world homes, automobiles, appliances and other durables are owned only by the wealthy, here the vast majority of our citizens enjoy the same items. Lack of wealth does not prevent persons of modest circumstances from sharing in the pleasures of our national economy. Installment credit has made this possible.

It is a fact that in today's marketplace sellers of durables will sell on the installment plan as well as for cash. They realize only too well that if they refused to sell on the installment plan their sales would be sharply reduced. Students of sales psychology point to the interesting fact that once consumers make one purchase on the installment plan they become better sales prospects. The records point to consumers in debt as people who buy more than those who do not owe anything. Let it be clearly stated that though this pattern may cause merchants to smile, it is one that merits critical examination from the consumer's viewpoint. The unwary consumer can become victim to the easy kind of credit because installment-credit, high-pressure salesmanship and persuasive advertising operate like skilled players who are members of the same team. By strategic manipulation the stage is set so that the consumer buys things he doesn't need with money he doesn't have.

Now that easy credit is available almost for the asking, it is easier to sell goods to consumers. The temptations to buy were never greater. As a result, there are many who owe their souls to loan sharks, credit companies and banks. Like drug addicts, they cannot resist temptation. They fall prey to the salesman's cunning—"no down payment needed in this case and we'll give you up to 150 weeks in which to pay." Thus another item is acquired and the weight of debt is increased accordingly.

Credit availability has certainly led to financial irresponsibility. Note that despite the unprecedented prosperity of our economy, the number of bankruptcy cases filed in 1965 (163,000) shows an increase of almost 150 percent over the 1935 figure of 69,153—a time when America was suffering from a very serious depression. Even though we recognize that the population increase has been one of approximately 50 percent since 1935, the increase in bankruptcies has been about 3 times that amount. As the saying goes, "we must be doing something wrong." Our view of this potentially dangerous condition is that people are not exercising caution in the use of credit. There are too many customers who attempt to expand their purchasing power through credit without full realization of the responsibilities that go together with substitution of credit for cash purchases. There's always the day of reckoning ahead no matter how easy the terms may look when the sale is made.

While credit does increase consumers' appetites for merchandise of all kinds, the relative ease with which the average consumer can obtain credit leads him to misuse this potentially beneficial tool. Just because credit is abundant in supply is no reason for consumers to use it indiscriminately. The decision concerning the advisability of "buying on time" must always be based on the ability of the consumer to meet the credit obligation. Sadness and want become the end products of foolish buying on credit in too many instances. Consider the young man whose sad plight is unfolded in this case history:

Young Joseph Scarletti, father of two infants, is "desperate" because of the bills his 19-year-old wife continues to pile up. "But, he cannot control her," reports an attorney who just handled a bankruptcy action for Mr. Scarletti. Even though the couple ended their first years of marriage with some $3,000 in debts, Mrs. Janet Scarletti doesn't seem concerned. Nor does it worry her that her husband felt he was fighting a losing battle and could see no way out except to declare bankruptcy.

Married three years, Joseph and Janet are both of "lower middle class immigrant stock," the lawyer notes. Urban Massachusetts residents, they both completed ninth grade. This is nine years more education than their own parents had, however. Although he didn't complete high school, Joseph is a semi-skilled worker, the lawyer reports. He works full-time and grosses about $90 a week. Last year, his total income was about $4,680.

Mr. Scarletti is an "earnest and hard working young man," the counselor emphasizes. Although he entered marriage with no more conception of money management than his wife, he is "much more responsible," particularly when it comes to feeling obliged to repay debts.

Janet, on the other hand, seems to have a "general attitude of sour resentment. She feels that she is saddled with two children at age 19 and that she is missing all the fun that her unmarried friends are having. She pays only cursory attention to the children or the housekeeping chores." Mostly, it seems, she lolls around the house listening to records that she hasn't paid for.

Her marriage has given her one thing, though—the "power to spend money." She never handled money of her own before and this has "simply overwhelmed her," the attorney suggests. Evidently, "she never learned that it is not honest to buy something that she has no intention of paying for," the lawyer says. She'll order anything that can be ordered by simply signing a coupon and sending away for the merchandise. She's piled up debts for record clubs, book clubs, and so on. She makes the necessary down payment, gets the merchandise, and never makes another payment. She simply can't seem to "cope with the idea of going into a store, buying merchandise, and charging it," the attorney says. Her credit buying has repeatedly sent the family into a tailspin. When bills become too pressing, Joseph goes to a local small loan company or credit union and borrows. When he recently filed bankruptcy, he owed $1,100 to three finance companies and one credit union . . . just for money borrowed to pay off bills accumulated here and there.

Eventually, about two years after their marriage, the Scarlettis let all their bills fall behind—utilities, rent, and so on. They couldn't even afford to pay the hospital or doctor for services involved in Janet's second pregnancy. When all the bills really began to pile up, Mr. Scarletti often made matters just that much worse, the lawyer notes, by going to the dog or horse track "hoping to make a hit. This never happened, though, and the few dollars that the family might have had left at the end of the week were lost."

Finally, when the situation became completely unbearable, Joseph turned to bankruptcy. At that time the Scarlettis had $3,160 in debts, all of which were discharged in bankruptcy. These debts included:

$907 owed to three different loan companies;
$ 42 owed to two mail order record clubs;
$150 to four different mail order book clubs;
$108 to four different department stores, a jewelry store, hardware store, and curtain store;
$100 in past due rent;
$ 82 to the telephone company;
$174 to three utility companies—gas, electricity, and heating fuel;
$300 to a doctor;
$111 to a hospital;
$196 to a credit union;
$ 90 to a dairy; and
$100 to a toy company that sells through home parties.

After the Scarlettis were absolved of responsibilities for all these debts, the fact was stressed to them that they couldn't file bankruptcy again for another six years. Whether their first years of married life indicate a future of credit buying, juggling funds, and trying to evade creditors remains to be seen. It all depends on "whether Mr. Scarletti will be able to curb his wife's irresponsibility," the lawyer says. Or, "perhaps with a little more age and maturity she will learn on her own to curb her desire to buy anything that she can get and then let her husband worry later about paying."[16]

Is credit necessary? We feel the question should be answered affirmatively. There can be no doubt about the fact that the generous use of credit in the United States has been a solid force behind the achievement of the highest level of living in the world. The debt incurred by the nation's army of consumers has resulted in great material comforts for our people, more jobs, greater profits in industry and an overall expansion of our national economy. By itself, debt is not evil. But when so many of the nation's consumers who buy on credit blindly permit themselves to think that credit is a substitute for cash, unpleasant consequences are bound to follow. The wise use of credit requires understanding of the power of money and the limitations of income.

WHAT KINDS OF CREDIT ARE AVAILABLE TO THE CONSUMER?

Since one can buy almost anything imaginable on credit—from a Cadillac car to a college education—there obviously exist many types of credit plans designed to make it easier for consumers to buy. The one word, credit, includes a variety of possibilities when applied to consumers.

LONG-TERM CREDIT

This is a form of credit for which repayment is extended over a period of time in excess of three years. This form of credit is usually restricted to use by persons seeking mortgages on real estate.

INTERMEDIATE-TERM CREDIT

Usually such credit must be repaid within 5 to 7 years. It is commonly used to finance major home repairs, improvements and modernization.

---

[16] *The Spender Syndrome,* Center for Consumer Affairs, The University of Wisconsin, University Extension, 1965, pp. 115-116.

SHORT-TERM CREDIT

This form of credit is used to acquire both durable and nondurable goods. It is also used very frequently to obtain money. In the latter case, we call it *cash credit*, whereas in the former it is called *sales credit*. But both categories represent either *installment* or *noninstallment* credit. All goods and services that involve a substantial amount of money generally may be acquired through credit that is repaid over a period of time with a specified number of payments (two or more).

Though many of us use installment credit sometime during our lives, all of us make use of noninstallment credit. This involves credit which is repaid within a short period of time with one payment (usually 30 days). Every housewife who pays an electric bill, a telephone bill, a doctor's bill or a charge-account bill is making use of noninstallment credit.

Since space does not permit a detailed treatment of all the credit plans that one may encounter, we shall concentrate upon certain common plans that all will recognize as being basic in today's business world.

CHARGE ACCOUNTS

Everybody is familiar with this basic form of consumer credit. Regardless of whether it is a *revolving*, a *budget* or a *divided* charge account—whether it is a formal charge-plate system or the old-fashioned write-it-in-the-book plan, the end purpose is the same. The consumer obtains goods or services immediately without cash. Whereas retail stores were among the first to offer charge accounts to increase availability of goods to consumers, lately there has been an explosion of interest in charge accounts by such businesses as hotels, motels, restaurants, airlines, car-rental agencies, service stations, florists and theaters.

CREDIT CARDS

Credit cards are an outgrowth of the charge account. By having a credit card in his possession, the consumer finds it possible to buy on credit from a variety of businesses with a single charge account. Such plans offer nation-wide and even world-wide purchasing opportunities to holders of their credit cards. The American Express Company and Diner's Club are two well-known examples of credit cards that are recognized all over the world.

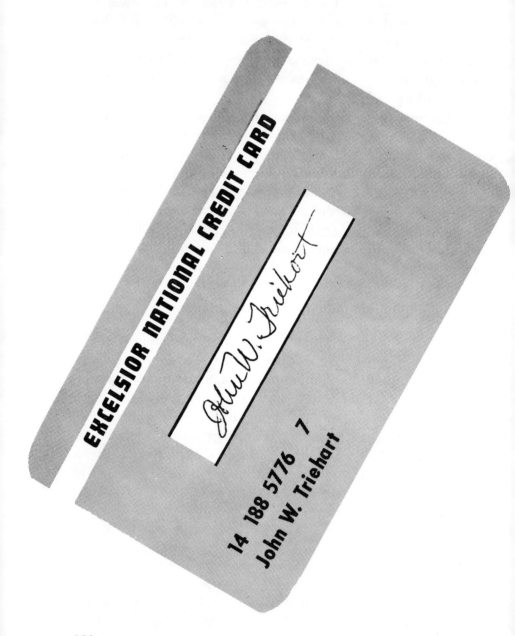

INSTALLMENT SALES CREDIT

This is probably the most common form of consumer credit in use today. Most readers will recognize it as "buying on time." Unlike the charge account, this credit plan extends payments over a period of time so that the purchaser may enjoy the benefits of goods or services while he is paying for them. Most merchants require that the buyers give some evidence of good faith by making a cash *down payment*. This partial payment serves a double purpose: (1) it gives the buyer equity which he naturally seeks to increase until full ownership is achieved, and (2) by obtaining the down payment the risk is minimized for the lender. In the event of the need for repossession, the lender can always get his share. The value of his loan will always be less than the market value of the merchandise. The lender tends to be well protected.

The six types of credit we have just described represent a direct transaction between a buyer and a seller. Another major type of credit, however, involves the transaction between a borrower and a money-lending institution. Credit which is obtained in this way is equivalent to the rental of money for a specific purpose or need. We shall now explore how a consumer can get money or cash credit.

WHERE CAN YOU BORROW MONEY?

There are all types of lending institutions from one end of the country to the other, eager and willing to rent money for a fee. That's why they are in business. As proof of the enormity of the loan industry we cite the fact that nearly half of all consumer credit in the United States is in the nature of cash loans.

Whereas in installment buying the goods or merchandise being purchased serve as security against the loan of credit, the institutions that extend cash or money credit must depend on the integrity of the individual. We can subdivide this concept of integrity into the three Cs of credit.

The three Cs of credit are: character, capacity and capital. In other words, they stand for the dependability and reliability of the potential borrower, and his ability to pay for what he has obtained on trust.

Regardless of type, all lending institutions demand satisfactory answers to such questions as the following:

(a) How long have you, the prospective borrower, lived at your present address?

(b) How long have you been steadily employed?

(c) Do you owe any money at the present time?

(d) Have you bought other merchandise on credit before?

(e) Do you own a car?

(f) Where do you do your banking?

(g) How much money do you earn?

(h) Do you have additional sources of income?

(i) If you own your home, is it mortgaged? If so, what is the the amount of the mortgage?

(j) Can you furnish three names of persons who will vouch for your integrity?

One would expect to be asked these searching questions since the lender has to be reasonably sure that the customer represents a sound credit risk. He obviously must be assured that you can pay for the credit you are seeking.

The wise consumer who goes shopping for a loan should examine every type of lending institution to determine which one will best meet his requirements. This is in addition to comparing the cost of the loan desired.

TYPES OF LENDING INSTITUTIONS

BANKS

Banks permit people to deposit savings and to operate checking accounts (commercial banks, only). In addition to these important services to consumers, banks perform another service which has reached mammoth proportions since 1900—offering consumer loans. In fact, commercial banks are the largest single source of consumer credit.

There are three types of banks to which one may go to in order to obtain a loan—a commercial bank, a savings bank and a savings and loan association. The person seeking a loan should examine the various types of regulations and restrictions since they are governed by different regulatory agencies. For example, a savings and loan association is permitted by law to offer larger home mortgages than either a savings or a commercial bank. Unsecured installment loans are offered only by commercial banks. The interest rates are competitive among all banks and will vary with the kind of loan desired. Where an automobile, a life insurance policy or stocks and bonds are offered as security when applying for a loan the interest rate will naturally be lower.

CREDIT UNIONS

Credit unions are "self-help" associations of people who have a common bond. They may be part of a cooperative, a housing development, a business organization, a public school system, a religious or fraternal organization or a union. They are chartered by the state or Federal government and make loans only to their members. The members pool their savings in order to make money available to those of their group who require loans.

The rate of interest on their loans is low—1 percent a month on the unpaid balance, as a maximum. Most credit unions charge lower rates (¼ to ¾ of one percent per month). Those who belong to credit unions are in a unique position because they usually may borrow money at highly favorable rates of interest. Credit unions show great personal interest in the financial needs of their members and as a general rule impose fewer special charges than any other type of lending institution.

SMALL-LOAN OR CONSUMER FINANCE COMPANIES

Small-loan companies also called consumer or personal finance companies operate under state regulation. They originally came into existence as a result of states' efforts to curb the operations of illegal money lenders or "loan sharks." People had been forced to borrow from the latter simply because they could not meet the requirements of commercial banks. In desperation, they had to pay fantastically high interest rates to the money lenders.

The small-loan company charges the highest rate of interest of any of the legal lending institutions. This is somewhat justified by the high risk these companies often assume in granting most loans and also because they are limited by law in determining the maximum amount that they may grant. At the present time no small-loan company may grant a loan over $2,000, although most loans are well under $1,000.

LIFE INSURANCE COMPANIES

Very frequently a prospective borrower will find that it is less expensive to borrow on the loan value of his life insurance policy and pay cash than to finance a purchase on the installment plan. Life insurance companies in many instances provide such loans. On the other hand, the policy may be used as security for a bank loan. One feature of this type of loan which is favorable or unfavorable, depending upon your personal viewpoint, is the fact that you don't have to pay back the loan as long as the insurance policy remains in force. The interest must be paid at regular intervals, of course. It must be emphasized that the amount of the policy is automatically reduced by the amount of the outstanding loan.

Life insurance companies also offer home mortgages at interest rates comparable to rates charged by banks.

ILLEGAL MONEY LENDERS

Though the loan shark can hardly qualify as an institution, mention of this fixture is certainly in order in this section. Every community has one or more of these vulture-like individuals who grow fat on the misfortunes of others. These money lenders operate outside the law and charge whatever the traffic will bear. Their victims are the unfortunates who have exhausted all legitimate means of obtaining credit. Loan sharks sell their cash in the form of loans at very high rates. They represent the shady fringe of the loan industry and should be avoided at all cost.

HOW MUCH DOES CREDIT COST?

Since consumer credit is usually offered in small amounts the cost is substantially higher than the cost that business has to bear when it enters the credit market as a shopper. It is cheaper for a lender to handle one large transaction than to engage in many small ones.

Most people appear to believe that 6 percent is the average or prevailing rate to pay for borrowed money. While it is true that many lenders and sellers of installment plans charge an apparent 6 percent rate, the figure of 6 percent is a myth. By using the technique of charging interest on the original amount that is borrowed throughout the period of the loan, instead of on the reduced balance, the real rate of interest is shown to be 10, 11 or 12 percent. A handy guide for estimating the true or effective rate is to double the apparent rate.

For consumers who are intelligent and properly concerned with determining the exact cost of the credit they are seeking, the formula used by the Federal Reserve System for converting charges into true annual interest will provide accurate information. The formula shown below may be used to determine true interest rates for credit which extends over periods up to 36 months.

$$I = \frac{2MD}{P(N+1)}$$

The symbols used refer to the various aspects of the credit agreement:

I   refers to the date of interest
M refers to the number of payments in one year
D refers to the total charges in dollars
P   refers to the total credit obligation
N refers to the total number of payments

Let us see how the formula works. Mr. Colville goes back to his favorite discount house CHEAP-A-GO-GO and falls in love with a handsome color TV set marked down to $400 from its "original" price of $499.50. The salesman informs him that he can have the set that very evening in time to watch the championship boxing match if he pays a mere $50 as down payment. He further adds that the balance can be conveniently spread over a two-year period with very small monthly payments—$18 a month. Mr. Colville immediately feels that he has walked into a really good deal because $18 a month will not torpedo his budget. For only 60 cents a day why shouldn t he enjoy color TV? Doesn't he deserve a little recreation after working so hard at the office? Of course he does.

Now let's see how good his deal really was. We'll apply the formula, $I = \dfrac{2MD}{P(N+1)}$

$$I = \frac{2 \times 12 \times 82}{350\,(24 + 1)}$$ (24 payments × $18 = 432. Subtract $350 to give you $82, the finance charges.)

$$I = \frac{1968}{8750}$$

$I = 22.5\%$ (the true annual rate of interest.)

Some deal! Mr. Colville's TV set will cost him $482. But he will be able to enjoy his set. The point we wish to stress is that you should know what you are spending and how costs are figured. The tragedy lies in the fact that buyers are rarely aware of the cost of credit. In the vast majority of cases credit costs are concealed in such a way that buyers cannot make valid comparisons.

Consumers can effectively reduce the cost of credit by obtaining a separate loan from a bank or a credit union and use the loan to pay the retailer the cash price. Even when this method is decided upon, however, it will pay to shop around for your loan. Rates do vary.

Here are some additional guide lines to help you understand credit costs:

HOW TO FIGURE DOLLAR COST OF CREDIT

Multiply amount of monthly payment by number of monthly payments to be made.

Subtract from that total the amount financed.
   (Cash price minus down payment)

DIFFERENCE will be dollar cost of credit.

EXAMPLE: A refrigerator costs $300 and can be paid by making a
   $12 down payment and 12 monthly payments of $25.92 each.

MULTIPLY payments × months to
   be made ($25.92× 12) $311.04

SUBTRACT the amount financed
   (Cash price minus down payment) $288.00

DOLLAR COST OF CREDIT $ 23.04*

Total cost on credit ($300 cash price
   plus $23.04 credit cost) $323.04

*Cost of credit equals $8 per $100 per year on unpaid balance of
$288. This is equivalent to a simple annual rate of 14.8%. See
chart below.

TYPICAL CREDIT CHARGES

If charges are based on the beginning amount owed and are included in the 12 equal monthly installments:

If Charged:		Simple Annual Rate is:
$ 4 per $100	or	4% per year 7.4%
$ 6 per $100	or	6% per year 11.1%
$ 8 per $100	or	8% per year 14.8%
$10 per $100	or	10% per year 18.5%
		1% per month 22.2%

If charged only on unpaid amount owed:

If Charged:	Simple Annual Rate is:
3/4 of 1% per month on unpaid balance 9%
5/6 of 1% per month on unpaid balance 10%
1% per month on unpaid balance 12%
1¼% per month on unpaid balance 15%
1½% per month on unpaid balance 18%
2½% per month on unpaid balance 30%

GUIDES FOR THE WISE USE OF CREDIT

◆ Shop for the lowest credit cost—in dollars and true annual interest rate.

◆ Be absolutely certain that you will be able to meet the financial obligations you are assuming.

◆ Use credit for major expenses only.

◆ Read your credit contract thoroughly before signing it.

◆ Never sign a contract that contains blank spaces within the printed text.

◆ Determine whether immediate possession of the item you wish to own is worth the extra cost of the credit.

◆ Make certain that not too large a portion of your discretionary income is allocated for credit payments.

◆ If you require a loan, offer the best security possible so as to benefit from the lower rate of interest.

◆ Steer clear of unlicensed lending agents.

◆ Borrow the absolute minimum required to meet your needs, not the maximum that the lender offers.

◆ When buying on credit be just as discriminating about the quality of the merchandise as you would be if you were paying cash.

◆ Pay off existing debts before taking on new ones.

◆ Be sure you are fully informed regarding all additional charges.

◆ Obtain complete information about the lender's policy in the event that you may not be able to meet every payment on time.

HOW DOES CREDIT AFFECT OUR ECONOMIC AND SOCIAL PATTERNS?

Credit has served to increase demand and consumption of goods and services. In this way it has stimulated our economy's growth, but it is a mixed blessing nevertheless. The overall benefits filter down to individuals and permit them to enjoy a better way of life. Consumers are able to enjoy goods and services while they are paying for them. However, credit also has led to abuses. The ready availability of credit has become an irresistible lure to many prospective buyers. The opportunity to obtain goods so painlessly often overrides the undeniable fact that ultimately payment must be made in an amount larger than if they had been purchased for cash. All too often families become thoroughly entangled in hopeless debt because of their failure to equate the credit they have obtained with their ability to pay for it. Credit becomes a way of life.

This attitude is aided and abetted by sellers of goods and services. Credit becomes an effective weapon in their campaign to stimulate sales. One of the greatest attractions to make a buyer succumb to temptation is the phrase "no down payment." Many of the nation's leading retail merchants are quick to admit that they make a greater profit on the credit they offer than on the goods they sell. A credit sale is always more profitable than a cash sale.

Credit arrangements are usually couched in vague and technical terms which bewilder the average buyer to the point where he is content with the answer to one simple question: "How much will this cost me each month?" Such techniques as the add-on, discount, simple interest, unpaid balance, per month and per year, lead to hopeless confusion on the part of the consumer even if he is intrepid enough to begin wading through the contract's fine print. In addition, the buyer of credit is confronted with charges of various types which add considerably to his cost. One in particular which has become a major factor leading to sharp increases in the cost of obtaining credit is credit life insurance. In some cases, charges are made for the insurance even though none is provided.

During the post-war period the Federal Reserve System and most of our nation's economists agreed that allocation of more than 13 percent of take-home pay for credit obligations constituted a potentially dangerous financial condition for the average family. In 1966 the nation's families were spending approximately 15 percent of their disposable income for credit. That same year the president of CUNA International (The Credit Union Movements Organization) indicated that personal debt should be kept below 20 percent of take-home pay. In a growing economy this expenditure can be absorbed by growing income. There is also a tendency to further increase credit obligations. Some persons even go so far as to mortgage their next year's income. Any of these people who are over extended in terms of credit and who might suffer even a slight setback in income, run the risk of seeing their way of life destroyed. There might not be "more where that came from."

Estimating the limit of credit obligations in terms of an arbitrary percentage of disposable income is not meaningful since the range of incomes varies so widely. It should be obvious that a person with a $25,000 annual income can probably assume a 20 percent credit obligation. For a person earning $5,000 a year, such an obligation would be an impossible burden. Credit should be utilized only if payments can be made from discretionary income without disturbing the expenditures for basic necessities.

To summarize the whole matter of consumer credit, let us agree that credit has been and continues to be a powerful stimulus to our country's economy. At the same time, credit can have negative effects, especially if it gets out of hand. It can actually overstimulate buying at a time when the economy is becoming "overheated." We must never permit credit to become an evil dragon. Buying on the installment plan and using the other forms of credit transactions have all become part of the American way of doing business. Consumers in the final analysis must decide for themselves how to best utilize credit so that it will continue to be a positive force capable of helping them to achieve a higher level of living rather than a negative factor always ready to betray them. Let credit be your servant not your master.

CONSUMER UNDERSTANDING CHECK

1. Why do you think that the use of credit has spread faster in this country than in other parts of the world?
2. Credit leads to extravagance. Explain what is meant by this statement.
3. Why was the use of credit sharply restricted during World War II?
4. The person who buys on credit or shops for a loan is a poor money manager. Discuss the validity of this statement.
5. In recent years increasing numbers of teenagers have been using charge accounts. How is this both good and bad?
6. Determine the true annual interest on a $1,000 loan from the various lending institutions in your community. Do the interest rates vary? Why?
7. Do you think you would be able to qualify, using the criteria of the three Cs, for a loan of $100?
8. Your father has purchased a refrigerator which cost $375.00. He made a down payment of $50 and has signed a credit agreement to pay $24.50 a month over an 18 month period of time. What is the true annual interest rate that your father will be paying?
9. Why is it usually easier for a person to obtain credit a second or third time than the first?
10. How do federal, state and local governments buy credit?

10. deciding
where to live

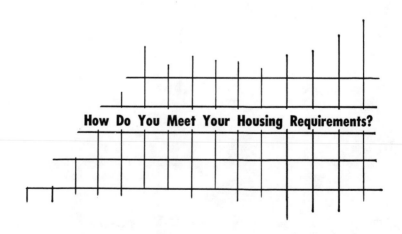

How Do You Meet Your Housing Requirements?

SOME BASIC CONSIDERATIONS

Whether an individual decides to rent an apartment or buy a house or apartment, he must first come to grips with the basic elements of the housing problem—the financial aspects, the career outlook, age, marital status, size of family and special personal requirements (a person suffering from arthritis would most likely require a dwelling at or near the ground level). One's living quarters set the pattern for daily activities because the home becomes the focal point around which work, play and relaxation revolve. For this reason along with many others that are equally persuasive, living quarters should be selected in such a way that all who are to share them will be satisfied and happy with the choice.

Through use of a budget every individual or family can accurately estimate the amount of money that should be spent for housing. Regardless of the type of housing to be selected, how much money you can afford to pay is the first consideration. You should not spend for shelter such a large proportion of your disposable income that you will have to reduce your spending for other necessities. A good general guide would be the following: monthly shelter costs should not exceed one week's take-home pay. This may vary slightly but should be viewed as a maximum figure—not average or minimum.

Your job or career is a very firm factor which will determine the type of dwelling you chose, whether you will rent or buy it, and its location. A young lawyer, twenty-seven years old, who has recently married has a firmer base on which to make a housing decision where permanence enters the picture. If he can afford to make a substantial downpayment, he might do well to consider purchasing a cooperative apartment or his own home. On the other hand, a young man who marries while attending evening high school and who, at the same time, has to support his wife and baby by working as a checker in a supermarket during the day, cannot possibly consider home or apartment ownership. In the first place, he simply can't afford it. Secondly, and hopefully, the job he presently holds will not be permanent. With additional training this young man can hope to increase his income and relocate, if necessary. His housing must be placed in the same temporary category as his job.

Most people prefer to select housing that is convenient to their place of employment either because of the existence of good public transportation or direct access roads which make automobile travel easy. Location has another important aspect as well—the dwelling should be so situated that the family living in it can avail itself of adequate shopping, recreational, educational and religious centers. It should be pointed out that the millions of Americans who prefer to live in suburban areas make a sacrifice in point of time spent commuting back and forth from work. But they make the sacrifice in order to reside in an area that meets all other requirements. After all, it is exceedingly difficult to find a location that is pleasant, convenient to your place of work, near stores, school, churches and recreational facilities. You usually have to make a compromise somewhere along the line. We've attempted thus far to show you that there are certain general considerations that every person or family planning to secure housing must weigh very carefully. And this must be done before any thought is given to the type of dwelling desired.

WHAT DO YOU CHOOSE—APARTMENT, COOPERATIVE OR HOUSE?

Like foods, there is no arguing when it comes to tastes and preferences in the area of housing. A private house can be a blessing for some people and a curse for others. There are millions of people who would never tie themselves down by house ownership, but derive full satisfaction from renting an apartment. There are also those who feel that be it ever so humble, there's no place like your own little home—and they'd rather fight than switch.

No type of dwelling is superior in every sense. Each has advantages and disadvantages—the apartment, the cooperative or the private house. And each must be evaluated comparatively with full consideration for the individual needs of the person or family concerned. It must be made emphatically clear that no one type of housing can meet all needs.

You should never move from one location to another without devoting the most serious kind of attention to the factors involved in

Apartment House

Private House

Garden Type Apartment

Trailer

A major decision—where should you live?

·**197**

your choice. Whether you elect to remain in an apartment or a house for a short while or a relatively long period of time is not as important as the choice of the dwelling itself. One's well being, emotional satisfaction and social status are all affected by the choice of a home.

What considerations are involved in the decisions we make concerning a place in which to live?

INCOME

Income is the most decisive factor, since it will determine the kind of home you can or cannot obtain. If your circumstances are such that you cannot make a free choice, you must find a dwelling that fits your income, and you will do well to disregard almost every other factor. A man whose take-home pay is $60 a week can hardly expect to afford to purchase even the smallest house. Therefore, he must set his sights on the rental of an apartment which will cost him about $60 per month. Apartments at this price level are few and far between.

Once your income climbs above minimal levels. income is not the deciding factor. Selection then revolves around other considerations.

LOCATION

It is obvious that a person must reside within commuting distance of the place where he works. For some, this might extend to as much as three hours of travel a day. Most people, however, prefer to spend much less time traveling to and from work. Therefore, using your place of work as a start, you should begin to look for your housing in a neighborhood or community that is within the travel radius you consider to be acceptable. Let us consider the case of a young aeronautical engineer who is being transferred from Long Island to Los Angeles because he has been given a promotion in his company. He is married and has two young children. He is faced with the important immediate problem of selecting a new residence. Where will he locate? He can choose any one of a dozen communities. He can live near the ocean, at Santa Monica or down at Laguna Beach. He can look north to Ventura, east to the San Fernando Valley or southeast to Pasadena. He can even live in Los Angeles itself. If he happens to like nature and appreciates the beauty of tall cactus plants and the romance of a desert, he has a choice of Woodland Hills (lots of sand—75 miles from Los Angeles). Bear in mind that, in general, the farther you go from the city the more satisfactory the dwelling you can get for your money. This applies both to renting and buying. Of course, when a person chooses to travel long distances each day to get to and from his place of work, he may save in one sense and lose in another. First, the cost of commuting can be considerable. And secondly, the time consumed in travel represents an increase in cost as well. Time spent in this fashion is lost for good—it can never be recaptured.

NEIGHBORHOOD

Your selection of a neighborhood should hinge on the conveniences you feel you want. Here again, individual tastes will vary, though the neighborhood must provide convenient shopping and a suitable variety of services. The young engineer we have just described must invest in two automobiles if he decides to live in Woodland Hills, California. One car is an absolute necessity for the family breadwinner and the other is for his wife's convenience. She would be a prisoner in her house without it. However, if he selected Hollywood he could do without a car—public transportation is adequate and the cost far less than that of purchasing and maintaining two automobiles.

SCHOOLS

Schools are a vital factor for families. It cannot be emphasized too strongly that persons who anticipate settling in a new neighborhood must be farsighted. They must look ahead to the time when their children will be attending elementary, junior and senior high school. The schools being considered in the community should be studied with care in order to determine whether the persons responsible for the schools, The Board of Education, the administrators, the teachers and the citizens themselves have a forward-looking philosophy toward education. Answers to these questions should be available and reassuring before a decision is made:

(a) Are the educators receptive to helpful and constructive criticism?

(b) Are the policymakers and adminstrators alert and on their toes, ready to meet any challenges that might arise?

(c) Does the public support the teachers and the administration?

(d) Is the physical school plant adequate and conducive to good educational achievement?

FAMILY

The individual family pattern should determine the size and type of dwelling. A family of four, with a twenty-three year old son who is working after having completed college and an eighteen year old daughter who is about to begin college out of state, must seek shelter that meets immediate requirements as well as future needs. Naturally, their requirements will differ from those of a family of five persons, two of which are children attending elementary school and the third member, the grandmother, 71 years of age. Each family must determine the direction of its efforts to obtain the shelter that will be most economical, most suitable and most flexible. Choice of dwelling must meet the immediate, daily requirements already listed.

CAREER

If a person's business or profession is of such a nature that he or she can expect to experience satisfaction and profit from remaining in or near the same community, then ownership of a dwelling is warranted. As a matter of fact, the public spirited, interested citizens of most suburban and rural communities are homeowners whose business and professional practices are located in the same community. The young salesman who goes to work for a national food company faces a different problem. Promotions in the future may require him to relocate many many miles away. Home ownership might not be indicated in his case since, with very short notice, he may be obliged to move. A better paying position may suddenly develop in another area, or he might be transferred to another state.

The knock of opportunity should not be disregarded in favor of home ownership.

So much for the various factors which will have a bearing on where to live and whether a house or an apartment will be the answer. It is now time to take a look at the choices of dwellings that are available. Each has specific merits and disadvantages. To make a wise decision relative to securing a place to live takes as much understanding and knowledge as do all other areas which affect our lives as consumers.

APARTMENTS

For our purposes, an apartment is defined as a dwelling of one or more rooms which a person obtains for use for a specified period of time at a specified regular payment (rent). Apartments that can be purchased, commonly called cooperatives, will be discussed later.

A major advantage of living in a rented apartment is that one retains the freedom to relocate if the occasion arises. One's commitment to the apartment is limited only by the terms of the contract generally signed with the owner. In addition, the tenant's responsibility usually is limited to his rental cost without any further work as to maintenance or repairs. Renting an apartment does not require the investment of large sums of money and one can estimate quite accurately how much his shelter will cost when he budgets his money. For these reasons, many people prefer to live in rented apartments which are found in small two, three or four family houses as well as in the large apartment houses which characterize urban society. There are certain individuals who live in apartments for reasons other than those cited above, including elderly people who are not physically capable of maintaining a private home, individuals or couples without children who have no need for a private home, and persons who are newcomers to an area and prefer to become acclimated before making a permanent choice.

Let's not lose sight of the many persons who would enjoy owning a home of their own but who, for financial reasons, find this dream impossible to realize.

Life in an apartment has its drawbacks too. In the first place, one finds himself living in close contact with other families, thus limiting the degree of privacy. Then too, apartment house owners frequently impose restrictions to which tenants must conform. They may include prohibition of children, pets, or playing the radio, TV or musical instruments after a prescribed hour. In some instances tenants may not have the pleasure of using certain types of appliances because of the landlord's restrictions. Air conditioners, washing machines and outdoor TV antennas have frequently been banned by landlords. Other apartment house owners levy additional rental charges for the privilege of installing certain appliances.

A major disadvantage often disregarded by those who elect to live in apartments is the fact that after years of paying rent one has no equity. In other words, if you live for ten years in an apartment that has a monthly rental of $175, you will spend $21,000 over the ten year period, assuming that the rental is always the same. This money will have been spent and no part of it can ever be recovered by the tenant. Apartment rental does not have the investment benefit of ownership.

COOPERATIVES

In recent years cooperative apartments have become increasingly popular. Such apartments are owned by the tenants who mutually share in the responsibilities and obligations as well as all maintenance costs. Cooperative apartments like private houses represent a major investment. For that reason, most cooperatively owned buildings are obtained through a mortgage which permits gradual payment of the cost. This cost should not be confused with rent. The standard cooperative has one mortgage for the entire structure. An innovation in cooperatives, however, is the development of the *condominium*. This new type of cooperative provides for individual mortgages to cover each resident's dwelling, thus eliminating the mutual responsibility factor which characterizes the standard cooperative.

Let's assume that you decide to buy a six-room apartment in a twenty-unit cooperative building. If only eighteen of the twenty apartments are purchased, the cost which normally would be spread among twenty families (if all apartments had been sold) must be borne by eighteen families. Thus, their financial responsibility will be increased. So it becomes apparent that purchasing a cooperative apartment carries some risk. Ownership of a condominium apartment eliminates such risk, however. If an apartment is vacant, the institution holding the mortgage on it is responsible for all payments. For this reason, when we discuss the advantages and disadvantages of cooperatives we shall include condominiums along with standard cooperatives.

Do cooperatives have advantages? By all means. The very term cooperative is associated with ownership. Therefore, when you buy a cooperative apartment you have the pride of ownership plus the benefit of ownership investment. One begins to build equity. Should you decide to sell at a subsequent date your share of the cooperative will return to you, at the very least, a portion of your investment. Additional benefits are realized because interest expenses resulting from your mortgage obligation are deductible from your federal income tax as well as from some states' income tax. You enjoy, also, an equal voice in the management of the affairs of the cooperative. For example, if you are the owner of a cooperative apartment in a building that contains 24 other cooperative units, you will have an equal share in the decision as to whether or not a landscape gardener should be employed to maintain the grounds. Your voice has equal weight regardless of whether your apartment consists of one room or eight. Last but not least, is the fact that all other advantages of apartment living also apply to cooperatives.

Now for the negative side, let's cite some of the disadvantages. First, ownership of a cooperative does not provide the flexibility and freedom of a rented apartment. Should the need for relocation develop, it could be difficult to find a buyer for your cooperative apartment at that particular time. And even if there were a buyer he might not be willing to pay the price you legitimately request. It is also possible that in times of declining real estate prices you might find it impossible to attract any buyers unless you would be willing to take a substantial loss. Ownership of a cooperative entails responsibilities and obligation that you should be aware of and willing to undertake. Occasionally, they may be unpleasant and time consuming.

MOBILE HOMES AND TRAVEL TRAILERS

Most of us are familiar with the common summer sight of trailers being towed by cars on the highway. Whenever you spot a trailer, you are seeing a portable shelter. The travel trailer has a maximum dimension of eight feet in width and twenty-eight feet in length. Quite often trailers are used by construction workers and by other persons whose jobs require them to be constantly moving about the country. Actually, such workers save money by carrying their homes with them.

The mobile home, however, has dimensions considerably larger than those of the travel trailer and often extends to twelve feet in width and from thirty to fifty feet in length. Such homes must be transported by special truck carriers. Normally mobile homes are set up on a semi-permanent basis in trailer parks located throughout the country.

All the comforts of home on wheels.

Travel trailers and mobile homes represent the ultimate in flexibility, since they can easily be relocated anywhere without difficulty. What is more, they do not depreciate in value as readily as some more fixed types of shelter. They are in great demand. The purchase price normally includes all furnishings and equipment. Of course, one must enjoy this type of living.

HOUSES

As has been already stated, the purchase of a house, whether new or old, will be for most people the largest single purchase in their lifetime—the realization of a fond ambition. Since a house is expensive, one has to exercise extreme caution in selecting it and must consider carefully all the economic and social factors involved in its acquisition.

Owning one's own home represents a special achievement for the fortunate ones in this category, as well as a kind of social anchor which serves to firmly root homeowners in the community.

HOW DOES ONE ACQUIRE A HOUSE?

Though the traditional arguments for owning one's own home are appealing and persuasive, it should be recognized that the purchase and maintenance costs of a house are greater than the total cost of maintaining an apartment with comparable living facilities. Because the purchase of a house is a serious step, one should take it only after he has solved successfully most if not all of the problems which are treated in the rest of this section on housing.

Consider at this point the alternative to purchasing a home— renting one. In some parts of the country it is relatively easy to rent a house that is either furnished or unfurnished. This possibility should be considered before you arrive at a definite conclusion to buy. Buying a home can be the host to all kinds of problems. You should be aware that it is a complex venture, differing greatly from any other type of shopping experience you have ever had—not only from the standpoint of cost, but also because it sets a pattern for your way of life.

CAN YOU AFFORD TO OWN A HOME?

To answer this fundamental question you should examine your budget in order to determine how much of your disposable income can be spent on housing. As we said before, don't look for a Rolls Royce when all you can afford is a used compact car. Be realistic.

By investigating the prevailing price levels of houses in the community in which you are interested you will be able to determine whether your financial situation will allow you to buy a home there. There are several rules of thumb or guidelines that can be used to help the prospective buyer:

> ◆ One should not pay a price for a house which is more than $2\frac{1}{2}$ times one's annual income. Preferably, to be on the safe side, the price should be no more than twice one's annual earnings. Of course, this suggested limit may be exceeded in the event that an increase in earnings will become a reality shortly after the house is purchased.

> ◆ Total monthly costs should be no more than one week's take-home pay. If one's income fluctuates from one pay period to another, the income for a full year should be averaged so that a fairly accurate weekly figure can guide the prospective purchaser.

> ◆ One week's take-home pay should equal one percent of the purchase price of the house.

These guides are not intended to assure a person who is thinking of buying a house that if he meets the minimum financial requirements he will be on thoroughly safe ground. If you have to make drastic economies in food, clothing, education or other basic expenses, it might be foolhardy to delude yourself that home ownership is for you. In addition, individual family circumstances might also rule out the practicality of owning a home. For example, chronic illness, having children who are approaching college age, or providing for a large number of dependents are typical obstacles that put a big dent in the dollar you need for housing.

FHA VALUE	DOWN PAYMENT	MAXIMUM MORTGAGE	monthly payments		
			20 yrs.	25 yrs.	30 yrs.
$15,000	$ 450	$14,550	$104.05	$ 93.31	$ 86.48
15,500	500	15,000	107.27	96.19	89.16
16,000	600	15,400	110.13	98.76	91.54
16,500	600	15,900	113.71	101.97	94.51
17,000	700	16,300	116.56	104.53	96.89
17,500	700	16,800	120.14	107.74	99.86
18,000	800	17,200	123.00	110.30	102.24
18,500	800	17,700	126.58	113.51	105.21
19,000	900	18,100	129.43	116.07	107.58
19,500	900	18,600	133.01	119.28	110.56
20,000	1000	19,000	135.87	121.85	112.94
20,500	1100	19,400	138.74	124.41	115.31
21,000	1200	19,800	141.59	126.98	117.69
21,500	1300	20,200	144.46	129.54	120.07
22,000	1400	20,600	147.31	132.11	122.45
22,500	1500	21,000	150.18	134.67	124.82
23,000	1600	21,400	153.04	137.24	127.20
23,500	1700	21,800	155.89	139.80	129.58
24,000	1800	22,200	158.76	142.37	131.96
24,500	1900	22,600	161.61	144.93	134.34
25,000	2000	23,000	164.48	147.50	136.71
25,500	2100	23,400	167.34	150.06	139.09
26,000	2200	23,800	170.20	152.63	141.46
26,500	2300	24,200	173.06	155.19	143.85
27,000	2400	24,600	175.92	157.76	146.22
27,500	2500	25,000	178.78	160.32	148.60
28,000	2600	25,400	181.64	162.89	150.98
28,500	2700	25,800	184.50	165.45	153.35
29,000	2800	26,200	187.36	168.02	155.74
29,500	2900	26,600	190.22	170.58	158.11
30,000	3000	27,000	193.08	173.15	160.49
30,500	3100	27,400	195.95	175.71	162.86
31,000	3200	27,800	198.80	178.28	165.24
31,500	3300	28,200	201.67	180.84	167.62
32,000	3400	28,600	204.52	183.41	170.00
32,500	3500	29,000	207.38	185.97	172.38
33,000	3600	29,400	210.25	188.54	174.75
33,500	3700	29,800	213.10	191.10	177.13
33,700	3700	30,000	214.54	192.39	178.32
33,800	3800	30,000	214.54	192.39	178.32

Absolute minimum down payments required

Never count on income from a second job or overtime pay when figuring your financial situation in relation to home ownership. One can never be sure of such income, hence you should not rely upon that type of assistance. It is also recommended that the income of a wife who is working be examined to determine whether it is safe to rely upon such assistance over a long-term period.

Another very important recommendation (so many people are unaware of this danger) is that you should not plan to buy a house unless you have some cash to serve as a down payment. It is unwise to lend a receptive ear to the temptation of a "no down payment" home deal. This warning is sounded especially for young families whose cash is very limited. It should be borne in mind that in all instances where long-term large mortgages are secured, the money paid out in interest will exceed the amount of the loan itself. How many people realize that a $16,000 mortgage at 6¼ percent for 30 years will cost about $19,000 during that period of time? In other words, you would have to pay back $35,000 for $16,000. Cash is important also for the many incidental expenses that one encounters after he takes possession of a house. The well should never be permitted to run dry.

WHICH HOUSE DO YOU BUY?

Once you have decided that you can afford to buy a house you are then ready to tackle the next phase—determining which house to buy. There are many types, sizes and styles from which to select, but your choice will have to be based upon your family's needs and preferences. You will have to supply answers to such questions as:

1. How many rooms?
2. A new house or an older house?
3. What floor plan is best?
4. How large should the plot be?
5. Split-level, two-story or ranch house?

6. Type of exterior—brick, wood, stone, shingle, stucco?

7. Type of plumbing?

8. Type of heating system?

9. Is a basement necessary?

10. Is a garage needed?

11. Is the electrical system adequate?

12. Is there adequate storage space?

13. Is the general appearance attractive?

14. Does the house give you a good feeling?

Once you get the feeling that a house you've inspected looks promising on the basis of having met most of the criteria outlined above, the next step is to employ the services of a qualified contractor or engineer in order to satisfy yourself concerning the quality of construction and the condition of the house. The small cost involved will prove to be a trifle compared with the enormous amount of money loss and heartaches that an unwise purchase can cause.

WHERE DO YOU BUY?

When you buy a house you buy a piece of the neighborhood. This is another way of saying that location is of paramount importance. The prospective buyer should consider a neighborhood in terms of the following:

1. *Appearance of the area.* There should be no evidence of deterioration, and the dwellings should be well kept.

2. *Zoning regulations.* One should find out whether the area is zoned exclusively for residential use and whether special restrictions exist (minimum plot size, design of homes, etc.).

3. *Traffic flow.* Are the houses sufficiently protected from heavy

traffic but at the same time convenient to major traffic arteries?

4. *The fiscal health of the community.* It is always wise to inquire into the fiscal policies and records of a community before committing yourself to a contract. Make certain that you know the prevailing tax rate, the basis for valuation of the community's property, future plans that may affect the tax rate, as well as the general financial soundness of the local government.

5. *Public and utility services.* Are the police and fire departments adequate to render protection to residents of the community? You should also evaluate such services as the collection of refuse and snow removal. Determine whether street lighting is adequate and whether sidewalks are maintained in good condition. By all means, find out whether sewers, gas and electric lines are properly located.

We feel an earlier suggestion is worth repeating. The selection of the community or neighborhood where a family will spend its time and its money must be based on other basic considerations in addition to the five we have just enumerated. These include the convenience and cost of commuting to work, the existence of convenient shopping facilities, recreation, churches, schools and other facilities.

A word to the wise: if you have to choose between a more modest house in a superior community and a more elaborate house in a more average community, decide in favor of the former. The fringe benefits and the intangible values will more than make up the difference.

WHICH ONE DO YOU BUY—A NEW HOUSE OR AN OLD ONE?

Since purchasing a house involves very personal preferences, you alone can make the decision. All that anyone can do for a prospective buyer is to present all the facts so that he may be able to arrive at his decision after having been fully informed.

It would be impossible to compare accurately one specific older house with a specific new house since both have advantages as well as disadvantages. The buyer has to weigh carefully the unique merits of each before making his final decision. People who favor new houses point to these advantages:

◆ Everything is brand new and in the best condition. Maintenance costs naturally will be lower in the early years. What a proud feeling one has when he moves into a brand new house!

◆ New houses often can be purchased with smaller down payments.

◆ A new house has modern equipment and is designed to provide maximum utilization of space.

◆ New houses are easier to decorate since all painting and decorating plans are approved to suit the buyer's tastes.

◆ The exterior of a new house can be landscaped to suit individual tastes and requirements.

People who favor purchasing an older home are equally emphatic about the advantages that a substantial house of seasoned vintage offers.

◆ The older house is often more sound from the standpoint of construction than a new house.

◆ Older houses tend to be more spacious.

◆ Older houses often include those "extras" that most new houses lack—for example, full landscaping, fixtures, built-in book shelves, fireplaces, wood paneling, etc.

◆ Older houses are located in neighborhoods that are already established. The facilities are already there and paid for.

◆ When you are in the market for an older house you have a wider selection from which to choose.

A brand new home makes one swell with pride.

There are definite advantages to be gained by acquiring a well-constructed, comfortable, older house.

Courtesy Peter Fornaby, Realtor

It must be emphasized that age itself is not a virtue. Equipment wears out with age and houses do deteriorate with the passage of time. If an older house is not in good condition structurally and many costly repairs are required, what might seem like a reasonable asking price could ultimately become a very high one—the old house might prove to be much more expensive than a new one. Therefore, the condition of an older house is of the utmost importance. Look before you leap! Have a qualified appraiser examine the house before you enter into negotiations.

HOW DO YOU PAY FOR A HOUSE?

Buying a house is not like buying a pair of shoes or a suit. Very few people are fortunate enough to have saved enough money to purchase a house for cash. As a matter of fact, well over 90 percent of all houses are bought with a mortgage of some kind. A mortgage is in reality a loan made specifically for buying a house and may be one of three varieties: Federal Housing Administration (FHA) insured loans; Veterans Administration (VA) guaranteed loans, and conventional loans or mortgages. All three types of loans may be obtained through banks, savings and loan associations and other lending institutions.

If you can qualify for a FHA or a VA loan you will be able to purchase a house by making a smaller down payment and obtaining a longer-term loan than if you have to seek a conventional mortgage. In any case, it is still to your advantage to make as large a down payment as you can since finance charges for mortgages are heavy over the years.

SHOPPING FOR A MORTGAGE

These days it is not easy to obtain a mortgage since credit has become tight. Interest rates on mortgages have gone up from 5 and $5\frac{1}{2}$ percent to as high as $6\frac{1}{4}$ percent (March, 1966). And this rate is for prime borrowers—persons whose credit rating is superior because of the positions they hold and their ability to assume the responsibilities of the debt. Other people are paying as high as 8 percent for home loans. So it is more important than ever for the mortgage hunter to shop around with the diligence and energy of the proverbial beaver. The savings he stands to achieve are worth the time and effort he spends in shopping for a home-loan at the most favorable interest rate and terms.

Here's a valuable shopping guide for the person who is in the market for a home mortgage.

1. Check every source for the lowest possible interest rate. Your local commercial banks, savings banks, savings and loan association, life insurance companies and mortgage investment companies are all good possibilities. A difference of just 1 percent in interest rate can amount to a saving of almost $3,000 on a twenty-year mortgage of $20,000.

2. Once you have decided which lending institution appears to offer you the most favorable terms, set your down payment at the highest possible amount and elect the shortest term for repayment of the loan that is consistent with your housing budget. The longer you take to pay off a mortgage the more interest you have to pay. Interest charges at the full rate continue as long as any portion of the loan is still outstanding. Note that if you obtain a $20,000 mortgage at 6 percent for a 30 year period you will pay almost $9,000 more than if you take out the same loan for a 20 year period. One can save over 60 percent in interest charges by electing the shorter term—if he can afford to do so.

	10 yr.	15 yr.	20 yr.	25 yr.	30 yr.
6 %	222.05	168.78	143.29	128.87	119.92
6¼%	224.57	171.49	146.19	131.94	123.15
6½%	227.10	174.23	149.12	135.05	126.42
6¾%	229.65	176.99	152.08	138.19	129.72
7 %	232.22	179.77	155.06	141.36	133.07

Monthly payments on a $20,000 mortgage.

3. Now look for the lowest closing costs. These amount to hundreds of dollars and should be considered as expenses to be added to interest payments. It is wise to protect one's self by insisting upon a "prepayment" clause without penalty. Both VA and the FHA mortgages require that lending institutions include this provision automatically. Another feature that is most desirable is known as the "open end" provision. This gives the borrower the opportunity to increase the amount of the mortgage if the need arises, with the added cost spread over the remaining period of the mortgage.

HOW DO YOU LEGALLY PROTECT YOUR INVESTMENT?

Never enter into negotiations for the purchase of a house without the benefit of legal advice and assistance. The purchase of a home is definitely not a do-it-yourself operation.

The first document you will sign after you have selected your home is the sales contract. This contract sets forth the legal obligations of both parties—the buyer and the seller, and also describes the conditions of sale. Usually the payment of a small sum of money is required as evidence of good faith. The buyer should insist that the contract include a statement to the effect that he will have his payment refunded in case a mortgage cannot be obtained. Naturally, a buyer who signs a contract and then fails to live up to the agreement, will forfeit the amount of the payment he has made. When both buyer and seller sign the contract it becomes a legally binding agreement that commits the former to the purchase of the house and the latter to its sale.

Before the buyer proceeds beyond the signing of the sales contract, he will arrange to have his lawyer or the lending institution that has agreed to offer him a mortgage institute a title search. This is necessary to assure the buyer that the seller actually owns the property he is seeking to sell and that no claims against the property are in existence. *Title* is another word for ownership, and the written evidence of that ownership is called the *deed*. The deed, however, is not sufficient to give the buyer clear title to the property.

....19........

Received from.. Purchaser,

residing at ....

the sum of $..as a deposit and on account of the Purchase Price of

SUBJECT TO THE FOLLOWING TERMS AND CONDITIONS:

The Purchase Price is $.., payable as follows:

$.................................., (including present deposit) on the signing of a formal contract as adopted by title

companies on..19........ at......................M., at the office of...

....

$..on the delivery of the deed to said premises on ....19........

at.................M. at the office of..

$..................................., ...

The formal contract of sale as provided for herein shall be drawn by the attorney for the seller and approved by the attorney for the purchaser.

The Seller recognizes   as the Broker who brought about this sale and agrees to pay the usual commission.

This deposit is accepted subject to the approval of the Seller.

....
Broker

THE ABOVE TERMS AND CONDITIONS ARE HEREBY APPROVED AND ACCEPTED

....
Purchaser   Seller

An offer to purchase which becomes a binder when accepted by both buyer and seller.

216·

Therefore, it is necessary that he obtain a title guarantee policy. This will insure that the title insurance company will defend you and assume all costs and responsibility to the full amount of the policy in the event that the owner's title is ever questioned.

The buyer's attorney should read all documents pertaining to any phase of the transaction in order to protect the interests of his client.

WHAT COSTS ARE INVOLVED IN OWNING A HOUSE?

It's not the initial cost but the upkeep. In estimating the cost of buying a house too many people call a halt to their calculations once they have determined they can make the down payments and the monthly payments on the mortgage. They seem woefully ignorant of the many extra costs that really mount up and add substantially to the total expenditure. There is no question that paying for a house exceeds the cost of living in an apartment. It is very easy to substantiate this by pointing out that even after the mortgage has been paid and the house is free and clear, the owner's cost will run anywhere from $\frac{1}{3}$ to $\frac{1}{2}$ of the costs while the mortgage is being amortized.

Every buyer should be prepared to spend per year approximately $1\frac{1}{2}$ percent of the purchase price of the house for maintenance and repairs. As the house gets older, this amount will increase to approximately $2\frac{1}{2}$ or 3 percent. Failure to spend money for necessary repairs will result in deterioration of the property with a corresponding decrease in the investment value of the house.

Let's consider some of the basic expenses that every homeowner faces after he takes possession.

- Fuel—oil, gas or electricity.
- Utilities—these costs will be much higher than those incurred by persons who live in apartments. Appliances will be more numerous, and the space of a house will also affect the costs.
- Taxes—real estate, school, sewerage system, special assessments.
- Garbage removal costs.
- Insurance—fire, theft, personal liability.

◆ Repairs—plumbing, electrical, carpentry, roof, painting, etc.
◆ Increased furnishings costs—it usually costs much more to furnish a house than an apartment.
◆ Tools—the do-it-yourself pattern requires expenditures of money for hand tools and other basic equipment necessary for making home repairs.
◆ Care of grounds—these costs can be considerable. If one has to hire a gardener the price of keeping a lush green lawn can skyrocket.

Let's look in once again on our good friend Ernest Colville. Since we last met him he has been promoted to a higher position in his company and now receives an annual salary of $12,000. His monthly take-home pay amounts to $800. Since his new position required him to move to a new community, he has once again taken the plunge. He has bought an attractive older home for $21,000.

It wasn't easy for Ernest to acquire this home. In fact, he had to use the bulk of his savings in order to make a cash down payment of $7,000. He has obtained a $14,000 mortgage at $6\frac{1}{4}$ percent interest rate for a twenty year period. He is a prudent man by nature and not likely to waste his hard earned money. Nevertheless, his monthly expenses will be far from light. Take a look at them.

1.	Mortgage	$105
2.	All taxes	50
3.	Fuel	20
4.	Gas and electricity	15
5.	Telephone and water	10
6.	Garbage removal	2
7.	House insurance	9
8.	Tools	10
9.	Grounds	10
10.	Maintenance	20
	Total	$251

So each month Ernest Colville spends a little more than $2\frac{1}{2}$ percent of his annual take home pay to live in his newly acquired "dream house."

A bit of sound advice that every prospective home purchaser should follow religiously is this: watch your step and figure all costs *before* signing the contract. Remember that all those glowing promises fade beyond the horizon once the ink on the contract dries.

ARE THERE FINANCIAL ADVANTAGES TO OWNING YOUR OWN HOME?

There certainly are advantages, provided you can afford to buy and maintain a home. As was stated earlier, home ownership permits a person to build equity. Even if prices fell and one had to sell his property during a period of depressed prices he could recover some portion of what has amounted to forced savings. Another advantage is realized when you prepare your income tax returns. Interest expense, or the amount of interest you pay on your mortgage, is a deductible item. This is particularly beneficial during the early years of home ownership since that is the period when lending institutions levy the bulk of the interest charges. Their profit comes first.

It should be pointed out here that property taxes are also deductible from one's income taxes. And another advantage of home ownership is that tax-free feature of the profit that one might realize in the event that he is fortunate in selling his house for a higher price than he originally paid. It should be noted, however, that this benefit is applicable only if the seller buys another house within one year.

All in all, a house qualifies as a good investment. Many people have used investments in sound homes as protection against inflation with excellent results.

In looking at either apartments or houses to rent or buy, there are both [g]eral and specific points to consider (such as those included in the chec[k] below) to help you decide whether the facilities will meet your requireme[nts]. Answers to many of the questions can be found through careful inspect[ion], trying out equipment and plumbing, and by asking questions of the occup[ant], owner, or other person in charge. Questions of a technical nature to which [you] would like the answers may require the help of an expert. *To use the check[list],* make a check opposite each point that is adequate for your needs, omit[ting]

Exterior

- Is the character of the community:
  to your liking? _____
  convenient for your activities? _____
- Is the style of the dwelling:
  attractive? _____
  in keeping with others in the area? _____
- Is exterior construction in good condition? _____
- Are major views pleasant? _____
  Is there sufficient:
  daylight? _____
  sunlight? _____
- If there is a yard, is it large enough for:
  a play area? _____
  outdoor living? _____
  a garden? _____
- If it is a house, is it located to take best advantage of:
  sun? _____
  wind? _____
  shade? _____
- Is property fenced in or enclosed with shrubs for children's safety? _____
- Are the dwellings far enough apart to provide the privacy you want on either side, as well as at the back of the house? _____
- Is yard landscaped, with lawn and shrubs in good condition? _____
- If there is a well instead of a public water system, are the following adequate:
  depth of well? _____
  quantity of water? _____
  flow of water? _____
- If there is a septic tank instead of a municipal sewer system, is it:
  adequate in size for your family? _____
  properly installed? _____

- Are there improvements on the lot, such as:
  sidewalks and streets? ___
  grading? ___
  utility connections? ___
- Are there parking facilities, such as:
  a garage or carport? ___
  24-hour parking on street or in an alley? ___

Entrance

- Are entrances well lighted? ___
- Is there a side or rear entrance for deliveries? ___
- Is there an outside entrance for fuel deliveries? ___
- Is the entrance to inside hallway kept locked? ___
- Are there locked mailboxes? ___
- Are there facilities for accepting packages when you are away? ___
- Are hallways and stairways well lighted and clean? ___
- Is there elevator service that eliminates climbing steps to the apartment? ___
- Are there adequate fire escapes? ___

Interior

- Are the following in good condition:
  windows and doors? ___
  floors, walls, and ceilings? ___
  roof and gutters? ___
  porches, including railings? ___
  steps? ___
- Is insulation adequate? ___
- Are walls and floors insulated against noise? ___
- Are electric outlets where you will need them for:
  lamps? ___
  radio and television? ___
  large appliances? ___
  small appliances? ___

se which do not apply to the property at which you are looking. Then
luate the importance to you of the points you have left unchecked. You
bably will not find any one location that will measure up to your standards
all respects, but if the features most important to you are included, per-
s you can afford to overlook the less important items. Applying this check-
to each house or apartment in which you are interested may give you a
is for making an intelligent decision, and may save you from dissatisfac-
and unnecessary expense later on.

---

e current adequate for all pur-
s and appliances?

ere is a basement, is it:
ell ventilated and dry?
ell lighted?
thout hazards, such as low
ams, exposed pipes and wires?

nent

eded, are the following provided
ll windows:
ades or blinds?
rm windows?
reens?

the following adequate and in
condition:
umbing?
ating unit?
chen appliances?
ndry appliances?
ter heater?
e all of the above operating sat-
actory?

eded, is there a place for storing:
reens?
rm windows and doors?
tdoor furniture?
rden and yard tools?

there facilities for disposal of
age, such as:
incinerator?
poser in kitchen sink?
y garbage collection?

ere telephone service?
you have a telephone installed?

you have an outside aerial for
sion?

ere a charge for plugging into a
mon aerial?

Arrangement of space
- Can the rooms be adapted to your needs?
- Are rooms and wall spaces large enough for your furniture?
- Is amount and arrangement of work space in kitchen satisfactory?
- Is there space for laundry purposes?
- Is placement of bathroom convenient to all areas of house?
- Are closets, cabinets, shelves and all other storage spaces adequate for your needs?
- Are windows well placed for satisfactory ventilation in all rooms?
  If not, are there fans or an air conditioning system?

Responsibility for maintenance when renting
- Is the person responsible for upkeep and taking care of complaints easy to get in touch with?
  Is he:
    the owner?
    an agent?
    a representative of a management firm?
- What maintenance costs are included in the rent, such as for:
    electricity?
    gas?
    water?
    telephone?
    repairs and replacement?
    decorating?
- If needed:
    will the landlord make repairs?
    decorate completely before you move in?
- Is window washing taken care of by the management?
- Are you offered a written lease?

CONSUMER UNDERSTANDING CHECK

1. What factors affect the value of a house over a period of time?
2. Housing costs differ in various parts of the country. Why?
3. If you were going to purchase a home of your own, what features inside and outside of the house would you look for?
4. What are the advantages and disadvantages of:

        (a) A cooperative apartment
        (b) A condominium apartment
        (c) A rented apartment

Which type would you choose? Why?

5. If a man earns $225 a week, what is the maximum amount he should plan to spend for a house? Determine the approximate costs for owning and maintaining such a house in your own community.
6. In what ways does apartment living differ from living in one's own house?
7. Why is it important to determine the actual interest rate of a mortgage rather than just the monthly carrying charge?
8. Examine the advertisement below very closely. It is fairly typical of the kind of advertisement one will find in any newspaper. What other information would you wish to obtain before considering this house?

SPLIT LEVEL
3 bdrms, den, playrm, 1½ bths,
heated gar, walking distance to
station, hi $30's, by owner

9. A young couple with two small children must decide between renting an apartment for $150 a month and buying a modest home in the suburbs which the real estate agent claims can be "carried" for $131.80 a month. What hidden costs does this sales pitch fail to bring out in the open?
10. List six different types of individuals or families who would prefer apartment lving to living in their own homes?

11. insurance
and social legislation

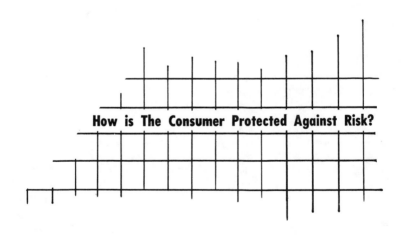

How is The Consumer Protected Against Risk?

INSURANCE AND SOCIAL LEGISLATION

HOW IS THE CONSUMER PROTECTED AGAINST RISK?
HOW DID INSURANCE DEVELOP?

Research reveals that life insurance had its beginning in the time of ancient Rome where the *collegia*, or Roman societies, paid for the burial of their members who died. We find that at a later period, the Middle Ages, the craft guilds did essentially the same thing and even went so far as to assist their members who were in financial distress or who were too old to engage in any kind of work.

What is now considered true life insurance developed as trade expanded in Western Europe. It became the outgrowth of marine insurance because merchants decided to insure the ships' masters as well as the cargoes of their ships. In America, too, the early emphasis was upon marine insurance. As early as 1721 there is record of an insurance office having been opened in Philadelphia. As cities developed along the Atlantic seaboard, fire insurance made its need felt.

In the United States life insurance appeared on the scene before the Revolutionary War. The first company, begun in 1759, is still in existence and is known as the Presbyterian Minister's Fund. Today there are more than 1,550 life insurance companies in this country. Some are large enterprises and others are of lesser size. However, all together they handle life insurance policies in the amount of slightly less than $800 billion, including ordinary, group, industrial and credit policies.

WHAT PURPOSE DOES INSURANCE SERVE?

Every minute in our daily lives we face a succession of risks. Very few people are so secure financially that the sudden occurrence of theft, fire, death, accident or illness can be borne without serious consequences. Thus, insurance has become the tool created by people themselves for the purpose of shifting probable loss from the individual to a group. Insurance permits the achievement of economic security through a system of periodic payments to an insurance company which extends protection in return. The underlying principle of insurance is that if a large enough group participates in a risk-sharing plan the probability of disaster striking a majority or all of those participating at the same time is virtually nonexistent. Therefore, the insurance company is enabled to reimburse those who do suffer loss and, at the same time, is able to retain the balance of funds as a continuously growing reserve. In fact, the insurance company has as its goal the achievement of a profit as the reserve reaches the proportion where mathematically computed risk cannot affect its stability. The larger the group that participates, the lower will be the cost of insurance to the individual and the smaller the risks for the pooled resources of the insurance company.

In simple terms, when an individual buys insurance against any kind of hazard he is in reality substituting a small known expenditure for protection against risk of a large uncertain loss.

Of course, it is unwise to attempt to insure one's self against every conceivable type of risk. The small losses can be absorbed by the individual. The major risks such as death, fire, theft, personal liability, accident and health are so great for every one of us that insurance against all of them is a necessity. Insurance must never be regarded as a luxury. Quite the opposite—it is an absolute necessity. This is particularly true in cases where people have dependents or heavy business and professional responsibilities.

Insurance carries with it not only protection against financial loss, but also psychological benefits in that those insured enjoy peace of mind. The assurance that one's risks are minimized engenders security which is important for emotional well-being.

WHAT ARE THE BASIC TYPES OF INSURANCE?

Insurance serves as a protective shield in a variety of areas. Individuals, families, industry and institutions make extensive use of insurance to minimize financal loss that could result from the inherent risks to which every person is subject. Insurance may be broadly classified as follows:

(a) *Risks to persons:* death, accident, sickness, permanent disability, old age and loss of employment.

(b) *Property risks:* fire, riot and civil revolt, malicious mischief, vandalism, natural disasters, transportation, defective legal titles, theft, water damage, mysterious disappearance and marine.

It is safe to say that a person can be insured against possible loss due to any conceivable risk. A concert pianist can obtain insurance for his hands, a dancer for his limbs, a circus company for its trained animals, a movie star for her face, a producer of an outdoor theatrical production against inclement weather. Lloyd's of London, the world's leading group of insurance in terms of scope of protection, will underwrite a policy for every risk that can be identified.

Since the kinds of insurance that we can purchase to protect ourselves, our dependents, and our worldly goods are limitless, it will serve a good purpose to become familiar with the important types of insurance that provide this valuable protection.

LIFE INSURANCE

Life insurance is protection against economic loss to a person's dependents or to his estate as a result of death. There are four basic types of life insurance policies: *ordinary or straight life, limited payment, term* and *endowment.* They differ essentially in terms of whether the protection is permanent or temporary and the extent to which savings may accumulate.

1. *Ordinary life,* also known as *straight* or *whole life.* The face value of the policy is paid only when the person insured dies. The premium rate is higher than the rate on a term policy but is lower than the rate on any other permanent policy, and depends on the age of the individual at the time the policy is purchased. The premium rate remains the same year after year. This type of policy builds a cash value which increases the longer the policy remains in force. In addition, this policy builds up a loan value. You can borrow against its value and continue to be insured. Should you decide to give up the policy, you can take the cash in one lump sum, as income, or as paid-up insurance. Naturally, the cash value is based on the number of years during which payment has been made.

If the insured person dies, the beneficiary is paid the face value. If there is a loan outstanding at the time of death, the amount of the loan will be subtracted from the value of the policy and the beneficiary will receive the difference.

2. *Limited payment life insurance.* This type of life insurance differs from straight life in several ways. Sometimes called limited payment insurance, these policies provide for the premiums to be paid in a limited number of years—10, 20, or 30 years. This means that the premiums will be higher than for straight life. But the higher premiums have the advantage of providing higher cash values within a shorter period of time.

The higher premium feature may be a disadvantage, however, in cases where maximum protection is required since the same number of dollars buys less protection than if the money were spent to buy a straight life policy.

3. *Endowment policies.* In such policies the face value is paid to the insured person if he is alive when the policy matures. The insured has the choice of receiving his money in one lump sum, or in installments. If he dies while the installments are being paid, his estate is entitled to the remaining portion.

Premiums are paid for a set number of years or up to a certain age. This feature increases the cost. Thus, endowment policies cost more than any other type of life insurance. As with limited payment life insurance, this type of policy is not ideal for a person who requires maximum protection at the lowest rate.

4. *Term insurance.* Here we see insurance that offers the lowest cost protection for specified periods of time. One can buy a term policy for 1, 5, 10 or more years. After the term expires, the policy is no longer in force. Some term policies may be renewed at a higher premium, of course. Renewable clause policies make it possible to obtain the same protection without having to undergo a physical examination at the time of renewal. Some companies will not renew term policies after a person reaches 50 or 60 years of age.

Term insurance has no cash or loan value. For this reason, persons who can benefit from insurance providing a savings element, which is a feature of permanent life insurance, should not favor a term policy. Over the years, term insurance tends to be expensive. For young people with immediate need for inexpensive insurance, however, it continues to be an ideal type.

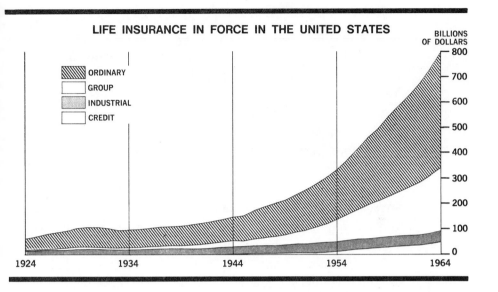

LIFE INSURANCE IN FORCE IN THE UNITED STATES

BILLIONS
OF DOLLARS

ORDINARY
GROUP
INDUSTRIAL
CREDIT

800
700
600
500
400
300
200
100
0

1924   1934   1944   1954   1964

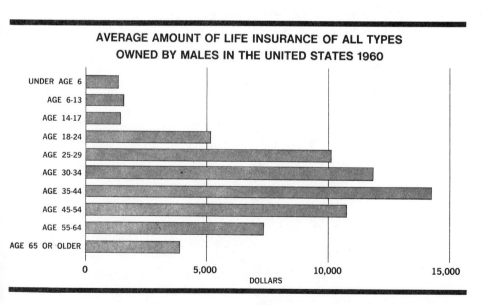

**AVERAGE AMOUNT OF LIFE INSURANCE OF ALL TYPES
OWNED BY MALES IN THE UNITED STATES 1960**

UNDER AGE 6
AGE 6-13
AGE 14-17
AGE 18-24
AGE 25-29
AGE 30-34
AGE 35-44
AGE 45-54
AGE 55-64
AGE 65 OR OLDER

0   5,000   10,000   15,000
DOLLARS

There are at least six ways through which the consumer may obtain life insurance. They are:

(a) *Group life insurance.* Large groups make it possible to have group life insurance issued for their members. They are usually the employees of a business or of the government. No medical examination is required and the cost is moderate. Very often the employer pays part of the cost. It is usually term insurance, and the protection ends when the employee leaves his position. Provisions do exist for term insurance to be converted to a permanent life insurance provided certain conditions are met.

(b) *Life insurance companies.* Most life insurance policies are sold through such companies. A medical examination is generally a requirement. Premiums may be paid annually, twice a year, quarterly or by the month.

(c) *Industrial insurance.* Industrial insurance policies are usually small ones, a few hundred dollars to a thousand dollars. Premiums are collected weekly or monthly by an insurance agent. Because of the extra cost involved in the collection of premiums and the bookkeeping, this kind of insurance is costly.

(d) *Fraternal organizations.* The many social and fraternal organizations that exist offer ordinary life insurance to their members.

(e) *Savings bank life insurance.* In some states mutual savings banks are authorized to sell life insurance. All types are sold at lower cost because agents' commissions do not have to be paid.

(f) *Armed forces life insurance (G. I.).* At various periods in the nation's history members of any of the armed forces have been able to purchase life insurance at very low cost. Veterans should carry as much insurance of this type as they possibly can since no insurance company can ever offer so much protection for so small a cost.

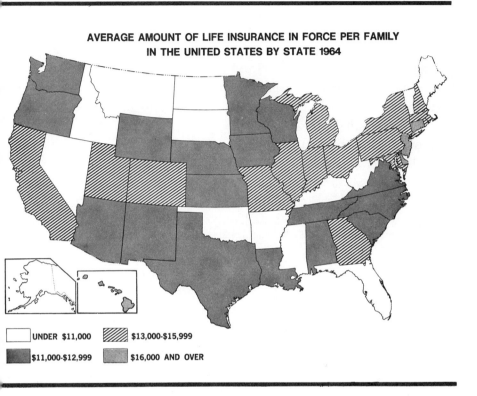

AVERAGE AMOUNT OF LIFE INSURANCE IN FORCE PER FAMILY IN THE UNITED STATES BY STATE 1964

| UNDER $11,000 | $13,000-$15,999 |
| $11,000-$12,999 | $16,000 AND OVER |

LIFE INSURANCE AND DISPOSABLE PERSONAL INCOME PER FAMILY IN THE UNITED STATES

Year	Life Insurance Per Family	Disposable Personal Income Per Family	Year	Life Insurance Per Family	Disposable Personal Income Per Family
1930	$2,800	$1,900	1956	$7,600	$5,400
1935	2,400	1,400	1957	8,300	5,600
1940	2,700	1,700	1958	8,800	5,700
1945	3,200	3,200	1959	9,500	5,900
1950	4,600	4,100	1960	10,200	6,100
1951	4,900	4,400	1961	10,800	6,300
1952	5,300	4,600	1962	11,400	6,500
1953	5,800	4,800	1963	12,200	6,700
1954	6,300	4,800	1964	13,300	7,200
1955	6,900	5,100	1965	14,700	7,600

Sources: Spectator Year Book, *Institute of Life Insurance and U.S. Department of Commerce.* "*Families" here include the units defined by the Bureau of the Census as families, subfamilies and unrelated individuals, and numbered 60,151,000 in 1964.*

This type of insurance, also called disability insurance, offers protection against loss of income arising from accident or illness, and also covers expenses that are incurred as a result of accident or illness. The expenses covered by such policies include hospital, surgical and medical costs. Hospitalization insurance covers hospital charges to specified maximum amounts and medical and surgical coverage insures a person against doctors' bills in connection with hospitalization. Expanded policies offer medical insurance for preventive care and routine office or home visits in addition to the basic coverage which centers about hospitalization. For example, major medical insurance plans are designed to cover those areas of risk which regular health and accident policies do not cover. The policies are written with a deductible clause, which means that the insured person assumes a certain portion of the cost of medical treatment or hospitalization before the insurance becomes effective. Normally, basic hospitalization coverage will reimburse the insured person for the amount deducted. Since accident and health insurance policies vary greatly as to specific coverage limits as well as cost of the protection they offer, the prospective buyer will find it advantageous to learn all he can in advance so that he can identify the kind of protection that best meets his own particular requirements.

Industrial and professional group insurance plans have become increasingly popular in recent years. They extend to members of industrial or professional groups health and accident protection through policies that are written through the organization to which the members belong. No outsiders may receive such protection. The premiums are paid by the individual directly to the company and tend to be considerably lower than for policies sold to individuals. Moreover, such policies tend to offer a more liberal range of coverage.

There are now available various insurance plans which provide accident or illness income benefits. If the insured through illness or accident is temporarily or totally disabled and is prevented from working, he may receive payments for a specified period of time. Provisions vary greatly, of course, as do costs of such policies.

FIRE INSURANCE

This type of insurance is necessary to protect your home as well as its contents. The standard fire policy protects the insured against loss through fire or lightning. In addition, one may obtain extended coverage at extra cost which protects against other risks such as water damage, wind and snow, smoke, explosion, riots and a host of others. The insured receives assurance when he purchases a fire insurance policy that if the building he insures is partially or totally destroyed by fire he will be reimbursed for the costs required for repairs or replacement.

Fire losses in the period 1953-1962 amounted to $10,357,000,000. Not all losses were covered by insurance.

Coinsurance is an important feature of most fire policies. Normally such coinsurance is stated at a rate of 80 percent of the valuation of the property to be insured. Thus, if a house is valued at $25,000 the maximum insurance that may be obtained under coinsurance will be $20,000. In the event of total destruction of the property through fire, the insured can recover only that amount. If the loss is under that amount, the financial burden is shared between the insurance company and the insured on an 80-20 basis. In other words, if the fire damage amounted to $10,000, the insured would recover $8,000 from the insurance company.

People who own their own homes very often make use of the so-called "home owners package" or personal property floater policy. This type policy does away with the need for separate policies covering fire, extended-coverage, theft, and water-damage insurance. Even included is coverage for jewelry, furs and other valuables such as pictures and works of art. In reality the contract is an all-risk policy that covers the insured as well as all members of the family who reside in the home whether they are inside or outside the dwelling on which the policy is written at the time of loss or accident.

THEFT INSURANCE

It is possible to purchase insurance providing protection against loss due to theft, burglary and robbery. You can insure personal property and household effects against theft while they are in your home, and you can also insure items against loss that are not on the premises. Policies provide for protection in the event of loss by actual theft, mysterious disappearance, or similar causes. Broad form personal theft insurance affords truly an umbrella-like protection covering hundreds of possible types of loss.

LIABILITY INSURANCE

Home owners, store owners and owners of business enterprises both large and small have always been vulnerable to liability claims and lawsuits. A person may fall on the floor after entering a store and if he fractures his ankle or suffers other injuries, the owner of the store might very well find himself the defendant in a negligence case. It is not uncommon for customers to file claims against store owners, employees against employers and even house guests against their hosts and hostesses. To receive protection against the hazards involved, liability insurance policies are purchased by those who seek to obtain peace of mind and freedom from financial loss. Some of the common forms of liability insurance are: automobile, landlords and owners, physicians, hospitals and dentists and manufacturers and contractors. Premiums on liability policies are generally low.

AUTOMOBILE INSURANCE

All operators of automobiles, whether they are privately owned or vehicles used in commercial enterprises, such as taxicabs or delivery trucks, should have protection from the liability resulting from owning, operating or maintaining an automobile or any type of gasoline or diesel-operated vehicle. Even though only three states (New York, Massachusetts and North Carolina) make such insurance mandatory, no responsible person should set foot in a car unless it is properly insured. Automobile insurance is so vital that everyone should become thoroughly aware of the features that a good policy should include.

Insurance can lessen the pain, anguish and expense resulting from accidents.

Bodily injury. This is insurance covering injury to other persons. Minimum coverage is $10,000 for one person with a maximum of $20,000 for two. The maximum coverage can be $1 million per person and $3 million for the entire accident. The protection offered by a policy with higher coverage is very inexpensive. For that reason it is recommended that the individual who drives or owns a car should obtain bodily injury insurance of the $100-$300,000 as a minimum, if possible. In states that require automobile insurance, the bodily injury feature is mandatory.

Property damage. Property damage insurance protects the insured against losses incurred to property belonging to persons other than himself. Of course, this loss must be a result of an accident involving the insured person's automobile. Such loss may take the form of damage to another automobile, a building, a fence, a public utility pole, landscaping, etc. The usual amount of property damage coverage is $5,000. However, it is advisable to consider protection based upon a higher figure. For a very slight increase in premium you can obtain $25,000 worth of protection. Property damage insurance is also mandatory in states requiring automobile insurance as a prerequisite for driving.

Uninsured motorist. This protection is mandatory in the three states mentioned previously and is also available to automobile owners in all states. It is insurance against three specific types of risks: (1) motorists who are not insured—either from another state, or driving illegally without insurance, (2) hit and run accidents, and (3) accidents caused by drivers of stolen cars. Premiums paid for this kind of protection are pooled in a fund under the administration of the state governments. Therefore, claims arising from accidents in any of the three categories described must be made to the state.

Comprehensive. Comprehensive coverage provides protection against fire, theft, acts of nature, vandalism, malicious mischief, and glass breakage resulting from acts of vandalism or malicious mischief. In fact, it provides coverage for all damages or losses which are not the result of an accident that occurs while an automobile is in motion. In some parts of the country, comprehensive insurance is available only with a deductible clause. For example, if a policy is written with a $50 deductible feature, it means that the insured will be responsible for the first $50 of any loss that might occur. Thus, if your car suffers damage as a result of fire and the cost of repairs is certified to be $210, under such a policy the insurance company is obligated to reimburse you for $160 and no more.

Fire and theft. A strong recommendation for comprehensive coverage must be made at this point in our discussion. The rates are moderate, yet the protection extensive. By all means consider buying a comprehensive policy rather than one that merely provides protection against fire and theft. Of course, if you purchase a new or a used car through the use of credit, the lending institution will require fire and theft coverage to protect the investment.

Collision. If you wish to protect your own automobile against the risk of damage resulting from an accident, collision insurance is the only insurance that you can buy for this purpose. It is sold on a deductible basis only. Such protection is relatively expensive, although the higher the deductible amount, the lower will be the premium. It is considered unwise to carry collision insurance on an old automobile (four years old or more) since the cost of such insurance will become excessive in terms of the market value of the vehicle itself.

Medical payments. This coverage protects the insured and all passengers in his automobile for medical costs that might result from an accident. Insurance protection is not extended to persons outside the vehicle, however.

Towing and labor costs. Accidents frequently result in damage to vehicles whereby towing and related services become necessary. Costs for all these required services can be met through this insurance feature.

TITLE INSURANCE

Because a person buying property must be assured that the previous owner of property actually has full and clear title to the property he is offering for sale, it is necessary to have title insurance. A title insurance company will make a thorough investigation of the title to be insured and will offer insurance against all claims that might conceivably arise. In this way the new buyer is thoroughly protected.

INLAND MARINE INSURANCE

The term inland marine is not very precise because it does not describe the kinds of coverage that such policies offer. However, it is difficult to find a better name since the comprehensive nature of this insurance extends to so many risks. Included in the great variety of forms of this type of insurance are: (a) transportation floaters, (b) parcel post policies, (c) jewelers' block policies, (f) furriers' customers floaters, (g) commercial property policy, (h) personal property floaters. Actually, all forms of inland marine insurance are extensions of marine insurance. All possible risks of this type are covered.

CREDIT INSURANCE

Sometimes called consumer-credit insurance, this type of insurance has become popular in recent years as the use of consumer credit has grown rapidly. Credit life insurance is now a feature of many installment debts and personal loans. FHA mortgages require credit life insurance as part of the mortgage package and charge ½ of one percent for such coverage. At the present time over $50 billion worth of credit life insurance is outstanding. All of it is term insurance and decreases in value as the outstanding obligation shrinks.

CONSUMER BENEFITS FROM SOCIAL LEGISLATION

"All during the twentieth century, and especially since the Thirties, government has been playing an increasing role in areas of economic security where large numbers of people had little or no protection under voluntary measures. The first major step in this direction was taken early this century when a number of states passed laws obliging employers to compensate their workers for job injuries. During the Twenties and early Thirties, many states established public welfare programs, especially to protect the families of workers who died, and a few states passed unemployment insurance laws.

"In more recent years, most of the expansion in this area has been at the Federal level. The Federal government's commitment to promoting economic security was one of the key principles of the New Deal. Most of its programs have been retained and expanded during later administrations, and are meant to provide a minimum of income for families while also helping to keep the national economy on an even keel in times of economic trouble.

"The majority of these government programs are entirely or partially financed by special Federal taxes. However, with the exception of Old Age, Survivors, and Disability Insurance (OASDI) and the veterans programs, administration is left up to the individual states."[17]

Social insurance, regardless of the specific type, has one basic purpose—to spread the cost of a misfortunate event throughout the community, the state or the nation so that no one individual will be crushed by economic setbacks. Thus, reasonable financial security becomes possible when social protection exists. Modern life has brought with its tremendous social advancements, increased insecurity as well. Rapid technological and scientific advancements have created unemployment, and changes in society have tended to make the average man feel at times that he is all alone, exposed to the hand of fate. Thousands of citizens have suddenly had their jobs cut out from under them by forces beyond their control—business establishments moving out of the country, mergers and consolidations, or drastic alterations in product emphasis. Even now, as this book is being written, automation has affected the employment pattern of virtually all industries. The number of victims is estimated by some to be as much as 40,000 a week. Fortunately, in good times, most persons in this category go on to find employment in other fields. The plight of some 10,000 elevator operators in New York who lost their jobs since the end of World War II is an illustration of how misfortune can suddenly appear on the scene like a thief in the night. With the installation of self-service, automated building elevators, elevator operators were no longer needed. Certainly these operators could not be held responsible for losing their jobs.

As a nation we cannot afford to permit people to starve, to be without required medical attention, or to be without shelter at a

---

[17] *The Search for Economic Security*, Educational Division, Institute of Life Insurance, New York, 1965, pp. 56-57.

time when social and economic developments have produced an affluent society. Therefore, America has elected to provide a broad program of social insurance. From all indications, the future will see even further expansion of social legislation.

WHAT KINDS OF SOCIAL INSURANCE EXIST?

Until 1935 attempts in this country to solve the problems related to the hardships of unemployment were all tied in with private initiative. However, the crushing hardships brought about by the depression during the early 1930's instigated tremendous agitation for social action. There was need for relief on a large scale, for 14 million persons were without work. Added to that staggering number were millions of persons too old to work even if it had been possible to find jobs. So in 1935 the Social Security Act was passed to provide payments for retired workers. Later the provisions of the Act were expanded to include wives and dependent children. Employees and employers were required to defray the cost of this form of social insurance (Social Security Taxes) by contributing matching amounts. As of 1966, this figure amounted to 4.2 percent of the first $6,600 of earnings. This figure will increase each year until 1970 due to new legislation which has incorporated medicare into the Social Security program.

The Social Security program attempts to provide protection in four different areas: (1) old age, (2) survivors, (3) disability, and (4) medical care. Nine out of every ten workers (and their families) are protected under Social Security.

No one is fully insured with credit for less than 1½ years of work and no one needs to work more than 10 years to be fully insured. However, having a fully insured status means only that some benefits are payable—it does not govern the amount of those benefits. The amount will depend on your average earnings over the 10-year period.

Percentage of United States Population*
With Some Form of Health Insurance Protection

1940-1964

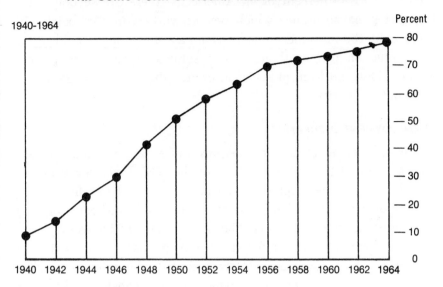

*Population consists of the total civilian population.
Source: Health Insurance Council and U.S. Department of Commerce, Bureau of the Census.

OLD AGE, SURVIVORS, AND DISABILITY INSURANCE
(000 Omitted)

Year	Persons with Wage Credits Year-End*	Person Employed with Coverage in Effect**	Employer and Worker Taxes in Year	Persons Fully Insured Year-End	Persons Receiving Monthly Benefits Year-End	Monthly and Lump-Sum Payments in Year
1940	44,800	26,800	$ 637,000	24,200	222	$ 35,354
1945	72,400	42,000	1,285,486	33,400	1,288	273,885
1950	82,400	38,700	2,670,771	59,800	3,477	961,094
1955	98,200	54,700	5,713,045	70,500	7,961	4,968,155
1960	109,100	59,100	11,876,220	84,400	14,845	11,244,795
1961	110,900	59,500	12,322,971	88,500	16,495	12,748,726
1962	112,700	60,800	13,105,002	89,900	18,053	14,461,461
1963	114,900	61,700	15,640,067	91,400	19,035	15,426,776
1964	117,000	63,100	16,842,824	93,000	19,800	16,223,079

*Persons who have ever had covered earnings.
**Annual average of employed persons in labor force with coverage in effect, based on selected weekly averages.
Source: Social Security Administration, U.S. Department of Health, Education, and Welfare.

Courtesy Institute of Life Insurance

Besides Social Security, which we have pointed out as providing protection to 90 percent of all Americans, there are several other forms of social insurance which benefit workers in our society. In every case, the insurance concept is apparent—money is paid in for the protection just as though the insurance were of the private variety. Thus, no form of social insurance should be regarded as a hand out or charity.

UNEMPLOYMENT INSURANCE

Unemployment insurance operates under a joint federal-state arrangement. It too was a provision of the 1935 Social Security Act in order to provide income for a worker who had lost his job for reasons over which he had no control. In most states contributions are made solely by employers. The rate of the contribution is based on the experience factors for the company and the industry. In industries where slack periods are frequent, the rates are higher than for an industry whose employment record reveals stability (the insurance industry itself, for example). In construction work the employer will pay a relatively high rate because of seasonal fluctuations.

There are limits to the number of weeks during which an unemployed person can collect his insurance. The amount of insurance is also limited by state law.

MEDICARE

The medicare amendment to the Social Security Act became effective on July 1, 1966. For a monthly payment of $3 individuals currently receiving social security benefits under the old-age provision are entitled to medical and hospital care. This medical insurance covers a great many health care costs, but not all. Prescription drug costs are not covered, for example. But it will pay $4 out of every $5 of physicians' bills. According to the *hospital insurance* feature of medicare, every eligible person will be covered. Most hospital costs will be paid under this arrangement.

WORKMEN'S COMPENSATION

All states have enacted workmen's compensation laws which constitute another type of social insurance. Workers are protected against loss of income arising from accidents or sickness. The provisions of the laws vary from state to state and in some states employers are not required to make contributions. However, if an employee in such a state is injured or falls ill, and his employer is not insured, the employee can sue for compensation. The accident or illness must result directly from the nature of the employment and cannot be covered under workmen's compensation if they occur away from the place of employment. The disabled worker will receive compensation for as long a period as he must remain away from his job. In some states it is even possible to receive compensation for life in case of total disability arising from an accident or an illness related to employment. If the injury or illness results in the death of a worker, his wife and children are entitled to compensation. In industries where chances of accident are great, the rate of insurance will be high.

DISABILITY BENEFITS INSURANCE

In some states this type of insurance is required of all business establishments with one or more employees. It is similar to workmen's compensation but by contrast applies to injury or illness resulting away from the place of employment and not attributable to the work. Both employer and employee make contributions. Benefits are smaller than those received under workmen's compensation insurance.

HOW SHOULD YOU BUY INSURANCE?

Just as with every other kind of service or goods that we buy, shopping for insurance of the proper type, in the amount desired, and for the amount of money you can afford, is a complex undertaking. The consumer of insurance cannot easily determine the proper blend of the three insurance problems that confront him. He is usually quite naive, for though he may know what he likes, he is probably not sufficiently informed to know if it is good for him. In the insurance field one must be extra cautious.

The first consideration should be how much you can afford. Using this as a starter it is possible to adjust your insurance program so as to cover the greatest and most important risks first. When you find that you have to stretch your insurance dollar, buy term insurance to achieve maximum protection for a temporary period of time. It will be cheaper. When in the market for automobile insurance, purchase those coverages that are mandatory plus those that will ensure continuous operation of your car.

When you are squeezed by a limited budget, you will have to assume many of the risks that others with greater resources can cover with insurance. In one sense, by so doing you'll be insuring yourself. If possible, obtain all the insurance you can through a group plan or an organization. The cost to you will be much less that way. Moreover, there's the other possibility, as well, that by this method of getting insurance you'll even be able to increase your coverage.

When you are planning to buy life insurance, don't overlook the bargains that are available in savings bank life insurance (if permitted in your state) or in policies sold through credit unions or the armed forces.

In conclusion, it is suggested that if you're in the market for insurance, regardless of the form, you give some thought to the following six recommendations:

◆ Check the reliability of the insurance company with which you plan to deal. Determine whether it is licensed to do business in your state.

◆ Ascertain the reputation and reliability of your agent.

◆ Arrange to pay premiums either annually or semi-annually. You save money that way.

◆ Review very carefully the conditions stated in the policy you are considering. Make certain it contains all the protection you want.

◆ Compare similar policies from a variety of sources.

◆ Don't join the ranks of those who are insurance rich but money poor.

CONSUMER UNDERSTANDING CHECK

1. Medicare will provide insurance against hospital and medical costs for persons over 65 years of age. Who will shoulder the burden for this insurance service? How will society beneft?

2. In what ways do Social Security and Unemployment Insurance aid the economy in periods of economic recessions or depressions?

3. It is customary to insure a dwelling or a place of business for an amount greater than the purchase price. Why is this done?

4. How does workmen's compensation insurance differ from disability benefits insurance?

5. What type of life insurance policy provides maximum protection at a minimum of premium outlay? Are there any disadvantages in such a policy?

6. How would an insurance company compute the premium rate for a policy insuring the face of a famous movie star?

7. Some people maintain that insurance is an ideal form of savings. Do you agree or disagree with this view? Why?

8. Which groups of people would profit most by purchasing each of the following types of life insurance?

   (a) ordinary or straight life
   (b) term
   (c) endowment
   (d) limited payment

9. If it would be financially impossible for you to carry "complete" automobile insurance, which of the seven features would you elect to eliminate? Why?

10. What are the reasons for not recommending the purchase of collision insurance for a five year old car?

12. putting your money to work

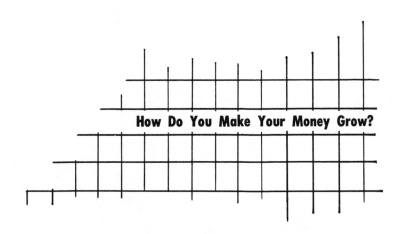

How Do You Make Your Money Grow?

WHY SAVE?

Everyone feels the effects of rising prices. One of the most popular complaints one hears is that money doesn't buy nowadays what it did fifteen or twenty years ago. And people talk about how hard it is to save.

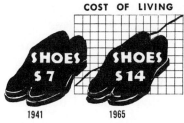

COST OF LIVING

SHOES $7 — 1941

SHOES $14 — 1965

It should be pointed out that among those who feel this way there is an uncomfortably large group still advocating the notion that it's better to spend freely than to put money away for the future. This group comprises the believers in the easy-come, easy-go philosophy —people conditioned by booming business conditions following World War II.

The old-fashioned habit of putting something away for a rainy day has for many never become part of their behavior, primarily because of the era in which they have been living. Unlike the lean period between 1929 and the beginning of World War II, when there was no extra money for saving, the post-war period has been characterized by (a) plentiful money everywhere due to sharply improved economic conditions, and (b) a tendency toward spending freely with little concern for building reserves for the future.

If you were born after 1940 you have experienced what might be termed living in a "loose money" era, a period when everybody seems to be affected by boom psychology. As the economy has continued to expand and improve with no serious interruptions, it would seem that many people have put aside all concern for "stormy days." But it must be made abundantly clear that the decade from 1929 to 1939 was a very lean period, one that taught Americans bitter and frightening lessons.

It is safe to say that those among us who experienced the "great depression," do not need to be shown the reasons for saving. The younger generation, on the other hand, will do well to give careful attention to the advice contained in this section.

Now let us examine the question of what saving is. While some people think it is old fashioned to save, be assured that it isn't. Saving has new implications and increased importance at the present time. Also, saving does not imply that you entertain no confidence in the future. Quite the opposite; if you save, it means that you hold visions of a better future, one with a store of increased opportunities, purchase of a home, some of the comforting luxuries that make life a little happier, or perhaps even a secure retirement.

To accentuate the positive it should be stated that the ability to save proves that you have mastered the art of managing money. Moreover, saving a portion of one's income in systematic fashion is proof that the saver can discipline himself or herself, and is further testimony that you are not likely to let yourself act on impulse. In other words, saving is proof of ability to control one's self.

Since it is customary to judge the success of any business enterprise by its capacity to make a profit and to accumulate reserves, it is logical for us to apply the same yardstick to our own financial operations. If we learn to manage our money successfully and we systematically add to our savings, we are then profiting from the application of sound business practices.

HOW DO YOU MANAGE TO SAVE?

It isn't hard to save; you just have to learn how to avoid falling for the argument, "Why knock yourself out trying to put away a few dollars? All you have to do is make more money; that's all there is to it." Of course, if you are a person who tends to live up to every dollar you earn, and you find that you can do no better than make ends meet, you *do* need help.

When we discussed budgeting in Section 8, you found that it isn't as remote as it seems to come up with surplus funds. Let's assume for the time being that your budget does place your income and expenses in some kind of balance. Isn't it just barely possible that with a very special effort you can succeed in cutting your daily expenses so that a little something will be left over? These three rules might help:

1. Saving should be a family affair in which all members of a family should pull in the same direction. If you walk twelve blocks to save the amount of the bus fare and your sister prefers to take a taxicab rather than walk six blocks, you're at cross purposes.

2. Save first, then spend. You should decide on a sum that you wish to put away and every time you receive your pay, whether you are paid weekly, twice a month or on a monthly basis, make a deposit in that amount. To be effective, saving should be regularly planned.

3. If you are easily tempted, use forced-saving techniques such as a payroll deduction plan for buying United States Savings Bonds.

Some individuals find that by depositing their entire income in their checking account they avoid difficulties. By doing this, and paying all expenses by check, they keep control on what goes in and out. It should be emphasized, however, that a checking account is not meant to be a substitute for a savings account.

Even if you acquire the knack of saving, and surplus funds begin to accumulate, the whole problem isn't solved. Now you have to determine what to do with your savings.

WHERE TO KEEP YOUR SAVINGS

The skill of the advertising industry can be seen all about us as it seeks to persuade you to employ your surplus money in one way or another. Here are but a few of the organizations that would like to attract your savings: insurance companies, savings banks, savings and loan associations, brokerage houses, our Government with its Savings Bonds, mutual funds, real estate interests, mortgage companies and commercial banks. And this is as it should be since the economic life of our nation is kept healthy by the established practice of the millions of citizens who put their savings to work. Business needs such savings in order to expand existing enterprises or to begin new ones. The Government also uses savings for domestic projects, improvements or for meeting its expenses.

A leak in the economy is stopped through credit

So you have quite a decision to make. Should you deposit your surplus money in a savings bank? Should you, on the other hand, invest it? If you invest your money, what investments should you select?

All groups that would like to use your money must pay you for the use of your surplus dollars. In general, they represent two kinds of investments: those that produce income and those that attempt to produce capital gains, that is, an increase in the money invested.

SAVINGS PRODUCE INCOME

If you can't save, you'll have nothing to invest. As was implied in Section 8, saving is putting away money from present income for use sometime in the future. What your goals are will have great bearing on your savings program. We know that the greatest incentive to save is provided when the purpose is established firmly in advance. It can be saving for an education, to buy a home or just to establish a bank account for use in emergencies.

Accepted thinking in the field of investing points to the desirability of providing for insurance and savings before thinking of investing for future income. In general, it is wise to provide protection for one's family through insurance equal to from three to four times your annual income. Thus, if a man earns $6,000 a year, he should make certain that his family is protected with life insurance totaling at least $18,000.

Savings should make it possible for a family to have funds for an emergency. It is recommended that such savings should equal from three to six times the family's total monthly income. For example, the family with an income of $6,000 ($500 a month) should have at least $1,500 in a savings account.

In the preceding section, the role of insurance in providing for family protection was discussed in detail. Now we shall consider how money can be held safely for future use while it earns a safe amount of interest.

SAVINGS ACCOUNTS

These can be opened in a bank with deposits of one dollar or more. A few banks require that initial deposits be higher. Withdrawals can be made whenever you wish, although banks can legally require at least 30 days notice. Interest is paid on deposits and is credited usually four times a year. Current interest rates range from 4 to 5 percent. You have a choice of *savings banks, commercial banks* and *savings and loan associations.*

BANKS

Before you select a bank consider the following:

◆ Does the bank insure deposits? In this country all banks that belong to the Federal Deposit Insurance Corporation insure deposits up to $10,000 for each depositor. Be sure to determine whether the bank you are considering is covered by this insurance.

◆ What rate of interest does the bank pay? Interest rates vary from bank to bank and in different parts of the country. Be sure to inquire whether the bank pays compound interest quarterly, semiannually or annually.

◆ What kind of bank is this? Is the bank a mutual savings bank, a commercial bank or a savings and loan association? You may think that all banks are alike, and that it makes no difference which one you select. But there are differences. Mutual savings banks (most savings banks are of this type) are owned by the depositors and specialize in savings accounts. They limit their investments almost entirely to mortgages and offer few services outside of providing for savings. Commercial banks have commercial and savings accounts and provide many other services, such as safe deposit boxes, personal and mortgage loans, traveler's checks and the sale and redemption of government bonds. Savings and loan associations are similar to mutual savings banks and generally pay a higher rate of interest than other savings institutions. Most of their funds are invested in high income-yielding first mortgages. Moreover, savings and loan associations are not required by law to retain as high a proportion of their assets in cash and government securities as are some other types of banks.

◆ Is there a limit to how much can be in a savings account? Although there is no legal limit, some banks do set a limit.

◆ Is money in an account available at any time? In most banks your money will be made available on demand. Legally, however, banks may require written notice in advance when a depositor desires to make a withdrawal. If a depositor wishes to withdraw a very large sum a bank might be likely to enforce this regulation.

GOVERNMENT SAVINGS BONDS

Government savings bonds are safe because they represent an obligation of the government. Should the bonds be lost, burned or destroyed accidentally they can be replaced by applying to the government. The good features of this type of saving are:

1. Government savings bonds are a very convenient form of saving. You can buy them or redeem them without charge. You can also purchase such bonds regularly through a payroll deduction plan at your place of employment or through your bank.
2. Considering the great safety of your money, the return on your investment is good. Recent legislation has raised the return on money invested in government savings bonds to a point where it is almost on a par with the rate paid by savings banks.
3. There is no risk of changing prices. Savings bonds have a specified redemption value depending on the length of time they have been held.

CREDIT UNION SHARES

Credit unions, which are cooperative associations formed to encourage saving on the part of members, do offer credit to members who need it. Membership is limited to persons who are employed in the same company or to persons sharing a common goal, social, professional or vocational. Credit unions are chartered by the state or Federal Government and the records of each union are examined at least once a year by the same authority that grants the charter. Credit union shares are purchased in five dollar units, and dividends are usually declared once a year. Deposits are not insured. Though there are somewhat greater risks involved in credit union shares, money deposited in credit unions very often earns more than if deposited in commercial or savings banks. Savings resulting from the economical operations of most institutions of this type as well as from their tax exempt status, are factors which permit credit unions to offer high earnings on savings.

Be sure to evaluate a credit union very carefully to determine how well it is managed, how its funds are invested and how adequate the reserve funds are. Also, investigate and ascertain how many of its loans are overdue.

WHAT ABOUT INVESTING?

It is often said that many consumers are poor shoppers when they seek goods or services. But their ignorance is negligible compared to that of many who try their hands at investing money. To be sure, there are saver-investors who are as knowledgeable and shrewd when it comes to investing as are the executives of prosperous corporations. But it should be emphasized again and again that too many investors are rank amateurs. They make costly mistakes. It has been estimated that between $150 and $200 million are lost every year by Americans who invest in "hot tips," phony business ventures and outright swindles. Thousands of families lose their savings each year by putting their funds in speculative business endeavors and the ever-present get-rich-quick schemes.

Almost as unfortunate is the picture posed by others who, so fearful of losing their life-time savings, have kept *all* their funds in fixed-income investments such as life insurance, government bonds, postal savings, or in savings accounts. Their money would, of course, be safe in any one or all of the above forms of investments. However, since 1940 the purchasing power of such funds has decreased by about 50 percent. In other words, the very meager earnings of funds invested in such fashion failed to permit the original principal even to hold its own as far as purchasing power is concerned. Inflation over the past 26 years has been too great. Therefore, as effective income-producing assets, the above would not rate high, especially if one's savings are substantial.

Wise investing involves protecting your money, of course. But it also implies employing funds in such a fashion so that you may receive a return in the form of interest, dividends, increase in value, rent, profits, or such income that will represent genuine growth of capital over the years.

Look at the problem in this light: if you are like the vast majority of Americans you are what we might call a defensive investor. You have modest savings to invest and you wish to accomplish this so that your chance of loss is kept to a minimum. Moreover, since you feel that you have had little training in the area of investing, you feel uncomfortable at the thought of spending too much time trying to make the right decisions. Persons in this category should be guided by these objectives:

1. SECURITY OF PRINCIPAL. The original investment should be safe and its return guaranteed. At the same time the purchasing power should be preserved and preferably increased. In times of rising prices such as we have been experiencing since World War II, preservation of purchasing power has been best accomplished through investments in common stocks, investment trust shares and in real estate. When prices tend to fall, then investments in bonds prove to be the better choice.

2. STABILITY OF INCOME. The whole concept of income is related to purchasing power. A 3 percent return from a bond may prove satisfactory when prices remain steady, but it is far from satisfactory during an inflationary period.

3. CAPITAL GROWTH. When taxes increase, the need to have your funds grow becomes especially important.

4. DIVERSIFICATION. Funds can be better safeguarded and income assured by spreading them among several different kinds of investments.

5. EASY MARKETABILITY. That means the ability to sell an investment at the prevailing price.

6. TAX BRACKET OF THE INVESTOR. Remember that your income tax bracket has a distinct bearing on your investments. For example, a low yielding tax exempt municipal bond is far superior as an investment for a person in the 60 percent tax bracket since income from such bonds is not taxable.

HOW SHOULD YOU INVEST?

In the final analysis, a sound investment is one that has good results even under difficult economic conditions. It would not be too difficult for the average person to make wise investment decisions if boom times went on for ever and real estate values went only one way—up. Since we cannot predict what the future holds for us, the best procedure is to study carefully and be guided by experience. Every person who is contemplating the investment of surplus funds should give much thought to such basic factors as how old he is, his family status, how much life insurance he has, how much he earns a year, the size of his cash reserve, his probable earnings over the next few years and his income tax bracket. He then must decide how large a risk he can assume and what his investment goals are. Clearly apparent is the fact that a young man can afford to take some risks in an effort to increase his capital while an older married man with several children cannot.

THE RISKS IN INVESTMENTS

Greedy people are very apt to be hurt the most by their investment ventures. They are the ones who try to get something for nothing or close to it, at any rate. *Let it be emphasized most forcefully that it is unwise to aspire to make too much too quickly.* Beware of investments that promise large returns. Remember, the higher the yield, the greater the risk. Not many years ago one saw advertisements describing attractive real estate bonds for sale in denominations of from $500 to $15,000 bearing interest from 8 to 10 percent. The names associated with the ventures fired the readers' imaginations and, as can be imagined, the "suckers" snapped up the bonds as fast as they could be printed. The end of the story is sad indeed, for few of the ventures were ever completed, and those that were lasted only a year or two. With bankruptcy, the investors lost all their money.

One can lose money in what may be termed a fairly sound investment. People who purchased stock of such reputable companies as American Telephone and Telegraph, General Motors and Standard

"Boiler Room" Swindlers Breed on the Public's Greed.

Oil of New Jersey before the stock market collapse of 1929 saw within a very short time their investment values dwindle to mere fractions of the amounts they spent for the stock. For example, the stocks of the three grade A companies described above crumbled in a three year period as follows:

American Telephone and Telegraph reached a high in 1929 of $310.25 a share and sank to a low of $70.25.

General Motors reached a high of $145.50 the same year and then sagged to $7.62 shortly thereafter. Standard Oil of New Jersey's stock suffered a similar fate when it declined from a high of $68.50 to a low of $3.37 a share. Excellent companies, to be sure, but the timing was poor. It took from 25 to 30 years for most stocks to regain their 1929 price level. Many are now at prices far higher than they ever were; others never made a comeback. During those dark days investors lost heavily in mortgages, real estate, municipal bonds and in practically every type of investment which up to that time had been considered of the gilt-edge variety.

You may well be asking yourself as you read this whether there is some fool-proof way of avoiding this risk. The honest answer is that there is none. But there are certain basic principles of investing and there are important guides that can provide valuable help to those who desire to put their hard-earned savings to work for them in profitable fashion. Consider first the two broad categories of investments described below.

FIXED-INCOME AND VARIABLE INVESTMENTS

First, know what you are investing for. There is a big difference, you know, between putting your money into a mortgage and buying shares of common stock. If you decide to put money into insurance, bonds, the savings bank, or preferred stock, you are putting your funds into what are called "fixed-income" investments. That means that the exact value of your investment is readily stated because the interest or dividend rate is fixed in advance. The value of the investment and the income it produces are theoretically most affected by changes in business conditions. Even with bonds and preferred stocks, the value can fluctuate and frequently does, but the income remains fixed. For example, the $5 preferred stock of the Gulf, Mobile and Ohio Railroad has fluctuated between $67.50 a share in 1959 to a high of $98 in 1963. The yearly dividend never deviated from the $5 amount, however.

On the other hand, when one places his money in common stocks, real estate or commodities, he is investing in "variables." In variable investments both the value of the money you put into them and the income you receive from the investments are subject to change as business conditions fluctuate. During periods of rising prices such investments assume a very appealing appearance. Profit possibilities are great. However, during periods of recession or depression, the opposite is true. Since such investments fluctuate, the risk is great. Profit possibilities are great and so are the chances of losing. Here's the proof. In 1941 a well constructed six-room private house could be purchased for 6 to 8 thousand dollars. Twenty years later the same house, though it had aged considerably, was worth according to prevailing prices from 3 to 4 times that amount. In one year, the price of Xerox Corporation's stock rose from $146.25 a share to a high of $434.50 (1963). In other words, one could have made a profit of almost 200 percent within a period of less than a year.

Such examples are not unusual because the trends of real-estate values and common stock prices has continued to be upward without serious interruption over the past 25 years. But one cannot predict the future. As an investor you must recognize that if you should find it necessary to raise cash at a particular time when price corrections have developed, the possibility always exists that you might have to sell at a loss.

A RECOMMENDED INVESTMENT PLAN

A good plan to follow is one that will provide investments of both types. However, since every person's situation is different, how much money to invest in the one type or the other will depend upon your special needs and circumstances. Since all of us need to have a sum of ready cash in the event of emergencies, all one's money should not be invested in "variables" that cannot be readily turned into cash with a fixed value. This is where fixed-dollar investments come in handy. It will pay you to have investments of this nature equal to from one-half to a whole year's income. Such funds may

Savings Certificates of Deposit pay a full 5% ANNUAL RATE on denominations of $2,500 or more.

REGULAR SAVINGS ACCOUNT

RATE ON SHORT TERM SAVINGS
STARTS EARNING IMMEDIATELY

4.50% a year

Anticipated for the quarter beginning April 1, 1966, based on the continuance of favorable earnings.

RATE ON LONG TERM SAVINGS

4.60% a year

Dividend declared for the quarter ending March 31, 1966, on long term savings (money on deposit since January 15, 1965).
Anticipated for the quarter beginning April 1, 1966, based on the continuance of favorable earnings, on money on deposit since April 14, 1965.

Your money earns 4.50% at Dry Dock.

4.60% a year

4.60% bonus rate declared for quarter ending March 31, 1966.
Anticipated for the quarter beginning April 1, 1966, based on the continuance of favorable earnings.

TERM INVESTMENT SAVINGS ACCOUNT
Starts Earning Immediately

Minimum Deposit: $500.
Money must remain on deposit until December 31, 1966 to earn the bonus rate.

Send for Booklet with Complete Details

Payment of future bonus rates will depend upon earnings for each quarter. If any withdrawal is made prior to December 31, 1966 (except accrued dividends), dividends on the entire account will accrue quarterly at 10% less than the lowest rate on savings for the current quarter.

be kept in a savings account or may be invested in U. S. Government bonds (Series E savings bonds or Series H bonds). A slightly higher rate of interest may be obtained from funds invested in corporation bonds or city, state or other types of local government bonds. Such bonds may be purchased through any bank or reputable broker. A feature which makes many municipal bonds attractive as investment media is the fact that the income you get from them is frequently exempt from the federal income tax. Hence, a 3¾ percent return from a tax-exempt bond could easily represent a yield of 5 to 6 percent depending upon one's tax bracket. It is a fact that persons in the upper income bracket seem to take advantage of the benefits offered by municipal bonds more frequently than people of the low or middle brackets. These bonds have excellent safety records. Even during the depression years, municipal bonds were considered second only to U. S. Government bonds from the standpoint of soundness of investment.

Now let's examine what is meant by investments in "variables." Whereas you are permitting a company or the government to borrow your money when you purchase a bond, when you purchase stock you are acquiring a share in a business. As a bondholder you are just a creditor. You receive a guaranteed rate of interest, but you have no voice in the affairs of the entity whose bond you own. The picture is a very different one when you purchase stock. You then become a partner and your fortunes will be affected by the degree of success that the company may enjoy. It will prove worthwhile to become thoroughly acquainted with the differences between preferred stocks and common stocks, the manner in which they are traded, and the factors that influence their value.

PREFERRED STOCKS

Preferred stocks have some of the advantages of bonds and some of the disadvantages also. If you buy a share of preferred stock you will receive a share of the company's profits in the form of a dividend. You are entitled to a dividend before any common stock holder can be paid a dividend. But if the company's business does not show a profit you run the risk of losing your dividend payment while the bondholder does not. The negative features of bonds also apply to some degree to this type of stock when we have inflation. No matter how great the rise in profits may be, as a holder of preferred stock you will always receive the same rate of dividend.

There are several clases of preferred stocks:

(a) Prior preferred stock, first preferred and second preferred stock. The names indicate the degree of preference which the preferred stocks have on claims for dividends.

(b) Convertible preferred stock. Such stocks have the same convertible features as bonds—that is, they may be turned in for other type securities.

(c) Participating preferred stock. Such stock has one of the advantages of common stock in the matter of dividend since the owners of such stock are permitted to participate with common stock holders in dividends up to a set amount.

Why buy preferred stock? One has in shares of high quality companies relative security of investment, a set yield as a dividend, and a chance to see his investment grow. Preferred stocks do increase in value. Of course, they also decrease under adverse conditions. The rate of rise and fall is smaller than in the case of common stocks, however. Study this illustration:

The common stock of General Motors rose from a low of $4\frac{1}{4}$ to $110\frac{1}{4}$ between 1936 and 1965. During the same period the cumulative preferred stock only rose 18 points—from $100 to $118.

Thus we see that in a sense preferred stocks permit the owner of them to enjoy both the advantages of fixed-income investments as well as the growth possibilities of variable investments.

COMMON STOCKS

As was stated before, shares of stock represent ownership interest in a business or property. The buyer of common stock shares cannot receive dividends until the bondholders and holders of preferred stock in the same company have received their guaranteed amounts of dividends. After the management decides how much money is available for payment of common stock dividends, that figure is then distributed on a set amount per each existing share of stock.

If there is no profit, and no funds available from previous years, holders of common stock are apt to lose out. That is one of the risks you take when you purchase common stock.

There are 1,066 stocks listed on the New York Stock Exchange and many more that are traded on the American Stock Exchange, the Boston Stock Exchange and elsewhere. One can readily follow the price fluctuations of common stocks by examining the daily quotations in the newspapers.

WHO OWNS COMMON STOCKS?

It is estimated that 20 million people own shares in publicly held companies. It is interesting to note that 51 percent of all stockholders are women.

Why did these persons purchase stock? Purely and simply to prevent the purchasing power of their dollars from dropping—that is the reason. Common stock prices tend to rise as prices rise. In other words, since inflation is with us all the time, wise investments in the common stocks of prosperous companies can prove to be an effective defense against eroding inflation. Consider this illustration. In 1940 you could buy a good automobile for well under $1,000. Today you need from 2 to 3 times that amount to buy a medium-priced car. If you had placed the thousand dollars in a savings bank, now you would have the same thousand dollars plus the interest earned over the years. However, $1,000 invested in sound common stocks in 1940 could easily be worth from 5 to 7 thousand dollars or even more today—enough to buy two cars.

To be sure, there are risks in owning stocks, because in a free economy such as ours some companies do very well, others make only a small profit, while some even lose money. But if you have the right outlook and exercise prudence, investing in stocks can be rewarding. Your temperament should be one of your guides. If you are the type who becomes jittery when share prices fluctuate, it is unwise to buy stocks. There also are those who, if their stocks go up 50 cents or a dollar a share, immediately begin to price motor boats and mink coats. When prices drop they fear another 1929. Don't be greedy. Unless you can afford to invest a portion of your discretionary funds in common stocks without worrying about meeting your living expenses, *DON'T BUY STOCKS*. The wise investments of small amounts of money in sound securities will generally prove to be profitable over a period of years. But BEWARE OF SPECULATION! You can get badly burned by it.

WHICH COMMON STOCKS SHOULD YOU BUY?

A simple classification of stocks according to risk can be made:

1. *Blue chip stocks:* These are securities of the leading corporations in the United States. They usually enjoy long records of paying dividends and have large amounts of capital. American Telephone and Telegraph, Standard Oil of New Jersey and General Motors are examples of blue chips. Banks, trust companies, pension funds and insurance companies invest their funds in such stocks.

2. *Growth stocks:* These are securities in companies that reinvest a large part of the money earned into their companies' operations. Such stocks show continued growth of sales and profits over the years. They also carry on extensive research leading to the introduction of new products. Companies engaged in the manufacture of chemicals, ethical drugs, electronics and missile components merit consideration for their growth in recent years—for example, Sterling Drugs, Boeing, Searle, General Telephone and Electronics and du Pont.

3. *Defensive stocks:* Companies whose fortunes vary little regardless of business conditions are in this category. Earnings tend to be stable in good times or bad. Industries that qualify in this group include gas and electricity, tobacco, food, and variety chain stores. Some well-known defensive stocks are: Public Service Electric and Gas, Consolidated Edison, Woolworth, American Tobacco Company and Safeway Stores.

4. *Speculative stocks:* All shares whose prices fluctuate sharply depending upon the business cycle, earnings and the emotional climate of the times can be classified as speculative securities. Dividend payments on such shares are often erratic. Most low-priced stocks attract speculators.

	Fuel	Other Operation	Maintenance	Total Operation & Maintenance	Depreciation
1965...........	$ 71,058	$80,284	$ 33,414	$184,756	$ 59,183
% of Revenue*	15.9	17.9	7.5	41.3	13.2
1964...........	66,638	69,341	30,970	166,949	56,857
% of Revenue*	15.8	16.5	7.3	39.6	13.5
1963...........	62,959	64,447	30,458	157,864	54,455
% of Revenue*	15.9	16.3	7.7	39.9	13.7
1962...........	58,982	60,957	28,646	148,585	51,584
% of Revenue*	15.6	16.1	7.6	39.3	13.7
1961...........	55,295	57,311	27,854	140,460	49,620
% of Revenue*	15.7	16.2	7.9	39.8	14.1
1960...........	53,282	57,094	28,064	138,440	44,882
% of Revenue*	15.7	16.9	8.3	40.9	13.3
1955...........	42,878	42,192	23,972	109,042	30,482
% of Revenue*	16.6	16.4	9.3	42.3	11.8

	Taxes	Total Operating Expenses	Shareholders (Dec. 31)	Earnings Per Share (d)	Dividends Per Share (d)	Dividend Pay-out Ratio %
1965...........	$90,912	$334,851	66,647	$1.78	$1.26	70.9
% of Revenue*	20.3	74.8				
1964...........	90,324	314,130	63,569	1.66	1.18	71.0
% of Revenue*	21.5	74.6				
1963...........	83,792	296,111	57,518	1.54	1.07	69.3
% of Revenue*	21.2	74.8				
1962...........	83,540	283,709	52,961	1.42	.98	68.9
% of Revenue*	22.1	75.1				
1961...........	78,187	268,267	52,106	1.22	.92	75.5
% of Revenue*	22.1	76.0				
1960...........	75,384	258,706	51,032	1.20	.86	72.1
% of Revenue*	22.3	76.5				
1955...........	58,984	198,508	37,687	.90	.56	62.2
% of Revenue*	22.9	77.0				

*Based on Total Operating Revenues plus Other Income.

A top quality stock's growth record over a period of ten years.

Buy blue chip stocks if you want a steady income and a fair chance of seeing your money grow without worry. If you seek better than average growth for your investment with a very small return while you wait for possible profits, growth stocks are the answer. For the very conservative person defensive stocks are best. And if you are like lots of others who experience a thrill just thinking of "making a killing," then try speculative stocks. You might be lucky and strike it rich. Then again you might lose your shirt.

LOOK BEFORE YOU LEAP

Before you invest any money in the stock of any company consider every point in this checklist. After you have gotten all the necessary information, then make your decision.

◆ What is the company's position in its industry?
◆ What product or services does it sell?
◆ Has the company made a profit over the years?
◆ Is the company making a profit now?
◆ What are the prospects for future profits?

- What are the company's assets and liabilities?
- How old is the company?
- How much is the dividend?
- Does the dividend look secure?
- What is the price range of the stock?
- Why do you think the stock is a good buy at its present price?

WHAT OTHER INVESTMENT POSSIBILITIES EXIST?

If you dislike taking chances and daily price fluctuations of common stocks give you an uneasy feeling, then mutual funds might be just right for you. This modern method of investing offers continuous professional management of your money. While risks are not eliminated through investing in mutual funds, they are considerably reduced because your money is placed in a broadly diversified list of selected stocks.

Many investment or mutual companies have achieved splendid records of growth. Some, of course, have not done as well. Yet generally speaking, mutual funds should be considered as conservative, prudent investments. This new form of investment has placed the small investor more or less on the same plane with the large investor. The man or woman with $25 or $50 a month to invest has expert managers to guide the placement of their funds.

Each small investor's money goes into a common pool, along with the money of all the other investors, and the pool is then invested by the people who manage the funds. Each investor in turn gets his proportionate share of the dividends paid by the securities the fund owns, and of profits the fund may get from the sale of stock.

Shares of a mutual fund are offered through a prospectus which includes information relative to the fund's objectives, policies, management, record, sales commissions and other information. Complete information about any of the well-known, reputable funds may be obtained from any stock broker.

REAL ESTATE—A "PROPERTY" OR GROWTH INVESTMENT

Many people have gotten rich over the years through purchase of real estate. But real estate is liable to fluctuate drastically in price.

What one pays for property in the present is no valid indication of what the value in the future will be. Real estate values can be depressed badly by any one or more of the following:

1. Aging of a neighborhood
2. Urban redevelopment
3. Construction of highways
4. Recessions
5. Government regulation of rent
6. Rezoning

Experience has shown that it is often risky to attempt to guess the pattern and direction of a city's or community's growth. Old neighborhoods become run down and property values shrink rapidly. Of course, during periods of prosperity when communities are growing, property that is well situated tends to rise in value. Housing shortages also cause property values to skyrocket.

The average small investor should think twice before investing his surplus money in real estate with the expectation that he is going to see his capital grow. Above all, he should not consider purchasing unimproved property (without buildings). In nine out of ten cases when vacant land is bought one is speculating, not investing.

Before investing in real estate, one should be sure that sound answers can be obtained for the following questions:

1. Is the location desirable?
2. Will it be easy to rent the property?
3. What rental will the property gross?
4. How much will it cost to repair the property each year?
5. How much are the taxes?
6. What net earnings can reasonably be expected from the property?

In this section the reader has been exposed to a generous sprinkling of investment opportunities. Whether a person has a large or small amount of money to invest, he can find in the investment media described many that will prove successful PROVIDED HE STUDIES HIS MOVES WITH GREAT CARE. Investing is serious business.

In conclusion, the best advice that can be given to anyone planning to invest his hard earned money is that contained in New York State Attorney General Louis J. Lefkowitz's pamphlet "A 10-Point Guide For The Careful Investor."

1. BEWARE OF TIPS AND RUMORS. These may come from well-meaning but uninformed amateurs. When you invest, consult someone with experience in the investment business.

2. BEWARE OF SO-CALLED "INSIDE INFORMATION." Nothing sounds better than "inside information"—yet, second only to outright fraud, it has cost investors more money than anything else.

3. WATCH OUT FOR THE PROMOTER IN A HURRY. The crooks are always in a hurry. They want to get your money before you have a chance to think twice. They'll urge you to buy fast "before the market goes up."

4. BEWARE OF PLUGS FOR A SPECIFIC STOCK. The legitimate broker doesn't high pressure you into buying any particular stock. He will recommend some stocks that he thinks are suited to your particular needs.

5. CONSIDER YOUR RESOURCES. Ask yourself if you can afford to lose the money you are investing if the investment fails.

6. DEAL ONLY WITH RELIABLE FIRMS. You can check their reputation through your local bank, the New York Stock Exchange, the American Stock Exchange and the National Association of Securities Dealers.

7. FIGHT THE TEMPTATION TO MAKE A QUICK KILLING. The legitimate broker offers no overnight rewards. He may tell you that most investors who have put their money into sound stocks have made a good return in the long run, but he will not pressure you into buying.

8. BEWARE OF HIGH PRESSURE TELEPHONE PROMOTERS. If an unknown salesman telephones to let you in on "the chance of a lifetime," ask yourself this question: Why doesn't he advise his friends or buy the stock himself?

9. BEWARE OF VAGUE ANSWERS TO QUESTIONS. A reliable broker will not be evasive. He will answer your queries with facts.

10. REMEMBER—the cautious investor is the best deterrent against fraud.

CONSUMER UNDERSTANDING CHECK

1. Why do investors tend to favor common stocks over bonds •during a rising economy?
2. What is meant by the statement that good common stocks often have helped their owners to keep in step with living costs?
3. If you were given $5,000 how would you invest that sum of money? Would you buy life insurance, place it in a savings bank, buy preferred stock or U. S. Government savings bonds? Why?
4. Why do investors in the upper income brackets favor municipal bonds?
5. How will the investment requirements of a young man differ from those of a man of 65 years of age who has just retired?
6. Which category of stocks among the following is most likely to undergo the widest cyclical fluctuation over the years? Why?

    (a) Electric and gas companies
    (b) Electronics companies
    (c) Retail food stores
    (d) Banks

7. Xerox Corporation, Polaroid and International Business Machine are companies whose stocks pay very small dividends. Why do investors purchase these issues and others like them when their money can earn from $4\frac{1}{2}$ to $5\frac{1}{2}$ percent in a bank?
8. Since it is acknowledged that U. S. Government Savings Bonds are absolutely safe, shouldn't a person invest all his money in them so that he'll have no worries at all?
9. Can you distinguish between an investment and a speculation? Which of the following appear to be speculations?

    (a) Consolidated Edison preferred stock
    (b) A uranium stock selling at $1.50 per share
    (c) The common stock of American Telephone and Telegraph Company
    (d) The stock of a new company beginning to manufacture fire-proof paints

10. Why do many savings and loan associations pay higher interest on funds on deposit in their banks than do other banks?

13. taxpayers all

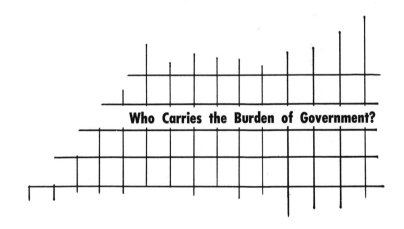

Who Carries the Burden of Government?

TAXPAYERS ALL

Taxes are to government what the weekly pay check is to the consumer. Though people have rebelled and spoken out against taxes through the ages, the fact remains that like Death they have stayed with us. Taxes represent a necessary item of expense—they are required to support the operations of the three levels of government—federal, state and local. As citizens we are required to contribute our share for the support of all governmental agencies that provide the services and protection so necessary for the continued welfare of society.

Primitive man was concerned solely with survival. He provided his own food, shelter and clothing. He took care of all of his own needs and protected himself without outside assistance. In fact, he feared all outside forces. As man progressed through the years, however, he developed a need for companionship as well as some degree of dependency upon others. Soon man became used to living among others and began to accept prescribed patterns of behavior that were set down by the group which acted for the benefit of all its members.

As the governing body expanded its activities it wasn't long before the need for some kind of tangible support manifested itself. Man was called upon to contribute his labor to build fortifications to defend the group against its enemies, to hunt and fish for food not only for himself but for those in his group who were unable to provide for themselves, and to fight to preserve the group.

With the growing complexity of these early social units or groups, individual efforts became specialized. Some members became skilled hunters, others concentrated upon agriculture, making crude weapons, tools and implements and a select few acquired the basic responsibility of governing. Unquestionably, the factors of strength, wisdom, maturity and heredity played important roles in the choice of those few upon whom the group depended for leadership. As this specialization and division of labor increased, a system of barter developed whereby individuals exchanged goods for services. Further social development made barter too difficult since it was not always possible for an individual to find someone else willing to make a direct exchange. The man who had the carcass of an animal, for example, could not readily locate another man with spears or clay bowls who wanted to exchange them for meat. Thus, the need for a medium of exchange developed. In this way it became possible to place a value on various goods and services so as to dispose of them without difficulty. Money is the current means of exchange which evolved over the centuries from such diverse forms of exchange as pelts, stones, animal teeth, beads, precious gems, gold, silver and many other items. Even today in certain remote areas of the world people still use slabs of stone, whale teeth and similar primitive articles as a medium of exchange.

As early social groups increased services their need for revenue grew in proportion. Therefore, the compulsory contributions or taxes of the individual members took a larger portion of the members' wealth. It became apparent that individuals had to pay for the privilege of belonging to the group. As governments grew through the ages, taxes kept pace and became the established method whereby the cost of providing services for the good of society was spread among all its members. Taxes became a necessary obligation divided among all members so that, theoretically at least, no one member became too heavily burdened. The willingness of individuals to be taxed is based on the realization that government functions in behalf of all members of society.

WHAT ARE THE BASIC PRINCIPLES OF TAXATION?

As has already been shown, taxation is based on the government's need for money. Taxes constitute the main source of revenue and the types of taxes vary with the level of government. A local government depends primarily on property taxes to obtain its revenue whereas the federal government depends primarily on income taxes. The Constitution of the United States established the right of all levels of government to levy and collect taxes.

Every citizen is obliged to pay his share in return for which he can avail himself of the many and varied services that government provides. Traditionally, there have been two theories of taxation. One is called the *benefit* theory and the other the *ability to pay* theory. The *benefit* theory holds that the taxpayer should pay taxes in proportion to the benefits he receives from government. However, it is difficult to utilize this theory because it would involve untold numbers of taxes to include the various groups and interests that go to make up the country. From the government's point of view it is impossible to achieve a satisfactory tax based on the benefit theory that will produce sufficient revenue. The kind of tax that comes closest to beng a *benefit* theory tax is the gasoline tax. The tax the motorist pays when he purchases gasoline is in many areas utilized primarily to build and maintain roads and highways. Thus the motorist receives a direct return from his tax dollar.

The *ability to pay* theory is one that is used universally and is justifiable in that it does not place too heavy a burden on any one individual. The best example of the *ability to pay* theory is the graduated income tax. As the amount of income increases, the amount of tax obligation increases.

Regardless of the tax theory employed, a tax must have certain characteristics to be of benefit to a government. The ingredients of a good tax are as follows:

◆ It must be economical to collect. Government should not have to spend too much money to obtain every tax dollar.

◆ It must provide sufficient revenue. It is not difficult to see the merit in a tax on cigarettes and the corresponding weakness of a tax levy on such items as harmonicas and toothpicks.

◆ It should not place too heavy a burden on any one group.

◆ It should be easily regulated but not easily evaded.

◆ It should permit taxpayers to pay their taxes in a fashion that is as painless as possible. For example, the federal income tax provides a withholding feature which enables the taxpayer to pay as he works. Prior to July 1, 1943 he was required to pay his tax in one lump sum on or before March 15. It is interesting to note that this relatively recent concern for the taxpayer was not the issue which brought about the change in payment method. The real causes were the urgent need for money to support the war effort and the desire of the government to decrease the inflationary tendencies of the war economy which was providing the people with large incomes and profits.

◆ It should be levied with the full knowledge and understanding of all citizens as to purposes and need. The taxpaying public certainly deserves full information concerning the need for a sales tax that is being imposed upon it.

WHAT ARE THE TAXES WE PAY?

It is possible to pay a tax and yet not have to bear the cost of paying it. This sounds strange, yet it is a fact. Take the tax on cigarettes and tobacco, for instance. The manufacturer pays the tax to the government, but the amount of the tax is then added to the selling price of the various products that are included by that particular type of tax—cigars, cigarettes, smoking tobacco, etc. So all consumers who buy tobacco products shoulder this tax burden when they pay higher prices for the goods they desire. The manufacturer is the taxpayer in name only. Actually he's the tax collector of a hidden tax, or one that is also known as an *indirect* tax.

Any tax like the one just described that can be shifted so that the burden moves from one group to another is an example of *indirect* taxation. The personal income tax, on the other hand, cannot be shifted. Therefore, such a tax is called a *direct* tax. All levels of government make use of both direct and indirect taxes to meet their operating costs. Each government sets up a tax system that is most suitable to its needs and most acceptable to its citizens. It can be safely stated that indirect taxes are ultimately paid by the consumer. He is at the end of the line—he cannot shift his burden elsewhere. Needless to say, he must also shoulder his portion of the burden imposed by all direct taxes to which he is subject. It has been estimated that an individual with a gross annual income of

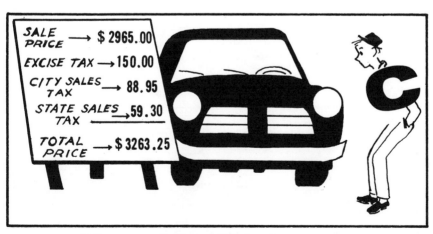

Indirect taxes are always shifted to the consumer.

$12,000 pays out $4,000 *in direct taxes alone.* It is impossible to compute how large the total would be for the hundreds of indirect taxes that are included in the sales price of goods and services. Bear in mind that when you buy a loaf of bread you are paying some 27 different taxes. This illustration will serve to emphasize forcefully the enormous effect that hidden taxes have on the level of prices.

In the remaining portion of this section we shall discuss the various forms of taxes that are levied on the American consumer by local, state and federal levels of government. From the consumer's point of view, the most important one is the income tax because it takes the biggest slice from his pay check. The federal government holds this tax in equal rank since it provides 40 percent of its income (corporate income taxes provide an additional 20 percent). Many state governments levy personal income taxes as well. The income tax rate on the state level is lower than those imposed by the federal government.

THE GOVERNMENT DOLLAR

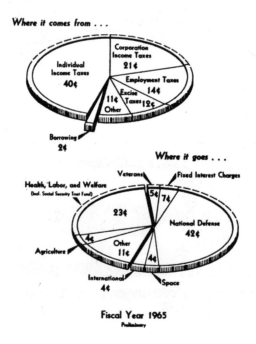

Where it comes from . . .

Individual Income Taxes 40¢

Corporation Income Taxes 21¢

Employment Taxes 14¢

Excise Taxes 12¢

11¢ Other

Borrowing 2¢

Where it goes . . .

Veterans 5¢

Fixed Interest Charges 7¢

Health, Labor, and Welfare (Incl. Social Security Trust Fund) 23¢

National Defense 42¢

Agriculture 4¢

Other 11¢

International 4¢

Space 4¢

Fiscal Year 1965
Preliminary

Federal Individual Income Tax at Selected Income Levels

Income Year 1965

Adjusted gross income(a)	Single person with no dependents		Married person with no dependents(b)		Married person with two dependents(b)		Adjusted gross income(a)
	Tax	Effective rate (percent)	Tax	Effective rate (percent)	Tax	Effective rate (percent)	
$ 1,000	$ 14	1.4	—	—	—	—	$ 1,000
1,500	85	5.7	—	—	—	—	1,500
2,000	161	8.0	$ 56	2.8	—	—	2,000
3,000	329	11.0	200	6.7	—	—	3,000
4,000	500	12.5	354	8.8	$ 140	3.5	4,000
5,000	671	13.4	501	10.0	290	5.8	5,000
6,000	866	14.4	658	11.0	450	7.5	6,000
7,500	1,168	15.6	915	12.2	686	9.1	7,500
10,000	1,742	17.4	1,342	13.4	1,114	11.1	10,000
15,000	3,154	21.0	2,335	15.6	2,062	13.7	15,000
20,000	4,918	24.6	3,484	17.4	3,160	15.8	20,000
25,000	6,982	27.9	4,796	19.2	4,412	17.6	25,000
50,000	19,230	38.5	13,964	27.9	13,388	26.8	50,000
100,000	48,182	48.2	38,460	38.5	37,748	37.7	100,000
250,000	142,570	57.0	127,640	51.1	126,800	50.7	250,000
500,000	300,070	60.0	285,140	57.0	284,300	56.9	500,000
750,000	457,570	61.0	442,640	59.0	441,800	58.9	750,000
1,000,000	615,070	61.5	600,140	60.0	599,300	59.9	1,000,000

(a) For income levels of $10,000 or less the optional standard deduction was used. For income levels above $10,000 deductions were assumed to amount to 10% of adjusted gross income.

(b) Filing joint returns.

Source: Computed by Tax Foundation from Treasury Department data.

Facts and Figures on Government Finance, Tax Foundation, Inc., Prentice-Hall Incorporated, Thirteenth Edition, 1964-1965, p. 104.

PERSONAL INCOME TAX

In 1965 approximately $50 billion was received by the federal government from personal income taxes. The income tax system is constructed to take a proportionate amount of the individual's income. The percentage increases as one's income increases. In 1966 the range was from 14 percent to 71 percent. This progressive type of taxation assures us that the individual is assessed only for that income which is not allocated for certain deductible items such as medical costs, dependents, casualty losses and contributions.

Every citizen or resident of the United States whose gross income throughout the year amounts to $600 or more must file a federal income tax return. Since income taxes represent obligations that affect virtually every person earning an income, it is vital that we learn all we can about income tax procedures. Included are: proper record keeping, itemization of allowable expenses including medical costs and contributions, and sources of income that are not subject to taxes.

Even though the thought of making out an income tax form frightens many people as the year draws to a close, there is no valid reason for such fear. Adequate assistance is available at all income tax offices, and every year the Treasury Department issues full instructions for all taxpayers. If you know how to read, the task is not too difficult.

PROPERTY TAX

Next to the income tax the second largest producer of revenue for the government is the property tax. Local governments are most likely to take advantage of this type of tax. Contrary to what most people seem to believe, property taxes are not exclusively confined to real estate. In various areas of the country personal items such as stocks and bonds, automobiles, clothing, furniture and jewelry are taxed in order to obtain revenue. In reality, any personal property that has value and that can be bought and sold is subject to taxation. The tax on real estate is not considered to be just because it is not really based on the ability-to-pay theory. Ownership of property alone is not a true indication of ability to pay. The owner of a small private home pays at the same rate as the owners of a large office building. Moreover, the property tax fails on a number of other points as well. Property as one form of wealth is easier to conceal than income. Therefore, the property tax is much more vulnerable to tax evasion. In addition, it is often difficult if not impossible to assess properly the value of property. Fair valuation is a very subjective process and will vary between one assessor and another.

SALES TAX

This form of taxation is one that affects the consumer directly. In many states and localities the sales tax is levied against every item that is placed on the market for sale. Some areas exempt certain items such as foods and drugs from taxation. From the consumer's point of view the sales tax is the most inequitable tax since it is regressive by nature. By this we mean that the consumer with the lowest income bears the greatest burden. A small tube of toothpaste costing 49 cents may have a tax of 2 cents levied against it on its purchase. The effect of this sales tax on a person with a $50 a week gross income is far greater than upon a person who earns $250 or $300 a week. Once again, we see in a form of taxation a complete disregard for the ability-to-pay factor. It is unfortunate that the sales tax is increasing in popularity.

In addition to the sales tax, the consumer is confronted with excise taxes at the point of purchase. These taxes are levied by the federal government against a group of so-called luxury items such as furs, cameras, jewelry, leather goods, appliances, automobiles, and even tickets to theatrical, motion picture and sports presentations. Gasoline, tobacco, and liquor are perhaps the greatest income producers for the excise tax levies. In 1963 excise tax revenues from the sale of alcoholic beverages amounted to $3,442,000,000. Consider also that if you traveled from New York to San Francisco by automobile, you would have to pay $20 in excise taxes for gasoline exclusive of the local sales taxes. In New York City in 1966 the taxes on a pack of cigarettes amounted to 22 cents—8 cents federal excise tax, 10 cents state excise tax and 4 cents for the city excise and sales tax. In other words, well over half the cost of the pack of cigarettes went for taxes.

SCHOOL TAX

Schools are big business in America and therefore require great revenue to keep them properly staffed and maintained. School costs are zooming without cessation and the nation's taxpayers are feeling the effects of these mounting expenses. While in some communities, cities for the most part, school expenses are defrayed by income received from all tax revenues, in most localities there are special school taxes levied for the purpose of meeting school budget costs. Property owners bear the burden of school taxes.

ESTATE AND INHERITANCE TAX

All states except Nevada and the federal government place a tax on the value of an estate before the property is legally given to the rightful heirs. Such a tax is frequently called an *estate* tax. The *inheritance* tax is paid by the person who inherits the property and is based on his share of the estate.

TARIFFS

A tariff is a tax or duty imposed on products brought in from foreign countries. Tariffs serve two purposes: (a) to provide revenue for government, and (b) to protect domestic products from competition with foreign goods. Unfortunately, however, the consumer bears the burden regardless of which purpose is served. He pays the higher price, which includes the hidden tax, and is also prevented from taking advantage of full competition and the economies that follow naturally in a competitive climate.

MISCELLANEOUS TAXES

Government derives considerable income from licenses, fees and special assessments. Licensing is primarily of concern to producers, but fees are of interest to the consuming public since by paying a fee people receive special services from governmental agencies. When a deed is recorded, for example, a fee must be paid.

Payroll taxes, as they affect social welfare, have already been treated in detail in section 11 dealing with insurance and social legislation. They also have a direct effect upon the consumer as they nibble away some more of his vulnerable dollar.

EXCLUDING UNEMPLOYMENT TAX COLLECTIONS

Fiscal Year 1964(a)

(Thousands)

State	Total	General sales use, or gross receipts	Selective sales(b)	Licenses	Individual income	Corporation income	Property	Death and gift	Severance	Other taxes
States using tax	50	37	50	50	36(c)	38(d)	45	49	29	26
Total	$24,244,333	$6,133,761	$7,869,733	$3,060,474	$3,363,439	$1,698,732	$727,307	$657,786	$489,428	$243,673
Alabama	384,054	141,179	140,137	27,929	36,591	15,766	16,858	1,530	1,856	2,208
Alaska	39,034	—	11,902	7,948	13,931	1,764	11(e)	89	2,637	752
Arizona	221,118	84,785	59,083	17,176	14,053	9,174	35,350	1,497	—	—
Arkansas	203,912	72,891	72,210	25,894	15,616	11,059	473	801	4,968	—
California	2,930,188	882,872	760,136	224,573	391,853	404,757	163,328	101,479	1,190	90
Colorado	247,112	60,724	61,928	31,329	52,521	24,735	6,674	7,654	1,477	—
Connecticut	357,382	109,918	136,503	34,073	—	51,081	10	25,797	—	—
Delaware	100,553	—	23,489	25,152	35,354	9,997	224	6,337	—	—
Florida	708,637	228,449	291,142	124,860	—	—	21,885	15,399	45	26,857
Georgia	490,915	185,424	170,852	32,986	56,018	41,049	1,658	2,928	—	—
Hawaii	142,104	70,956	26,335	1,915	34,680	7,053	—	1,165	—	—
Idaho	83,180	—	28,433	17,789	25,292	6,071	4,337	1,098	160	—
Illinois	1,122,335	558,584	382,041	144,677	—	—	1,250	35,783	—	—
Indiana	556,899	236,007	164,746	56,531	74,750	5,500	10,193	8,216	343	613
Iowa	311,285	88,215	94,039	61,718	48,524	5,017	4,256	9,516	—	—
Kansas	248,632	86,140	71,197	35,855	29,433	10,765	9,325	5,234	683	904
Kentucky	353,512	109,455	122,185	24,762	46,067	23,255	19,594	7,024	266	—
Louisiana	542,627	104,748	155,218	47,066	18,697	22,144	17,150	4,291	173,313	—
Maine	109,667	40,780	44,929	17,238	—	—	2,148	4,569	—	3
Maryland	474,729	104,496	158,230	42,095	123,266	23,829	14,230	7,373	—	1,210
Massachusetts	631,953	—	204,260	151,922(f)	202,541	41,820	434	29,342	—	1,634
Michigan	1,220,153	537,524	326,950	187,506	—	—	62,177	14,998	1,060	89,938
Minnesota	479,939	—	163,858	62,147	149,505	40,286	31,882	15,963	14,956	1,342
Mississippi	235,333	89,003	87,133	20,052	7,962	12,990	4,414	1,270	12,502	7
Missouri	463,681	173,785	132,787	66,878	63,726	10,750	5,866	9,884	5	—
Montana	75,872	—	34,615	10,101	14,691	5,051	6,415	2,263	2,736	—
Nebraska	111,206	—	61,759	13,879	—	—	33,591	794	1,183	—
Nevada	73,430	25,244	33,416	11,722	—	—	2,878	—	12	158

Facts and Figures on Government Finance, Tax Foundation, Inc., Prentice-Hall Incorporated, Thirteenth Edition, 1964-1965, pp. 176-177.

State Tax Collections by Source and State—Continued

EXCLUDING UNEMPLOYMENT TAX COLLECTIONS

Fiscal Year 1964(a)

(Thousands)

State	Total	General sales use, or gross receipts	Selective sales(b)	Licenses	Individual income	Corporation income	Property	Death and gift	Severance	Other taxes
New Hampshire	$ 50,114	—	$ 30,819	$ 11,177	$ 1,893		$ 2,201	$ 2,551	$ 86	$ 1,387
New Jersey	517,224	—	291,671	136,810	6,962	$ 31,733	2,392	47,656	—	
New Mexico	172,782	$ 57,836	45,499	18,183	13,138	(g)	11,051	865	26,193	17
New York	2,712,907	—	711,700	250,086	1,136,263	421,700	5,435	111,097	—	76,626
North Carolina	623,835	156,731	190,975	68,467	115,920	66,218	14,550	10,886	—	88
North Dakota	76,187	21,115	24,063	15,109	7,263	2,028	2,720	406	3,483	—
Ohio	1,006,929	296,353	455,842	193,853			45,510	15,371	—	—
Oklahoma	332,257	66,397	123,373	56,334	21,773	16,863		9,554	37,963	—
Oregon	255,123	—	54,285	45,723	122,876	23,325	1,181	7,065	668	—
Pennsylvania	1,407,465	507,569	472,164	197,182		155,457	1,827	51,774	—	21,492
Rhode Island	109,531	30,179	49,391	13,848		10,804		5,309	—	—
South Carolina	279,529	85,481	114,075	21,024	35,083	19,021	1,107	1,928	—	1,810
South Dakota	64,289	18,206	31,007	12,893		537	(h)	1,156	490	—
Tennessee	407,710	147,289	144,190	70,369	6,541	28,392	6(e)	8,323	—	2,600
Texas	1,122,553	204,735	468,964	188,932			43,876	16,474	196,360	3,212
Utah	136,005	47,739	33,074	11,751	20,055	6,696	11,058	1,603	4,029	
Vermont	56,273	—	25,823	10,669	14,539	2,568	388	1,491	—	795
Virginia	437,666	—	180,368	64,562	128,460	34,233	14,775	7,434	326	7,508
Washington	561,660	304,920	153,294	47,359			42,264	12,858	—	965
West Virginia	231,341	104,684	78,072	25,763	18,061		342	3,174	—	1,245
Wisconsin	715,979	80,274	158,702	62,502	259,541	95,244	41,291	17,812	381	212
Wyoming	47,522	13,074	12,849	12,105		—	8,722	705	67	—

(a) Preliminary; unemployment tax collections shown in Table 160.

(b) Includes collections of motor fuels, alcoholic beverages, tobacco products, insurance, public utilities, parimutuels, amusements, and other selective sales or gross receipts taxes.

(c) Includes New Hampshire and Tennessee where tax is limited to dividend and interest income; and New Jersey where tax is limited to earnings of New York residents employed in New Jersey.

(d) Includes South Dakota where tax is limited to banks and financial corporations.

(e) Back taxes only; not included with number of states using tax.

(f) Amount for licenses includes $92,225 thousand, corporation taxes measured in part by net income.

(g) Combined corporation and individual income taxes are tabulated with individual income taxes.

(h) Less than $500.

Source: Department of Commerce, Bureau of the Census.

The consumer's disposable income is sharply reduced by the great variety of taxes with which he must contend. He cannot avoid them and in the vast majority of instances does not seek to do so. The average consumer is well aware that government requires his tax dollar in order to provide the services and protection that all of us require. In our democratic system the people form the government to protect their inalienable rights. To accomplish this goal it is evident that money must be provided. At the same time, however, the taxpayer has an obligation to himself and his country—he should see to it that his tax dollars are spent wisely to provide the services that he desires. He should be alert to recognize the presence of new needs for tax revenue and should support required legislation that will produce social improvements at costs that will be fairly and comfortably distributed among many citizens. Perhaps it is in this area where effective economic citizenship is put to its most demanding test.

TAXES AS AN ECONOMIC STABILIZER

Since the acceptance of John Maynard Keynes' theories regarding the role of government in the economy, taxes have been utilized to influence the level of economic growth. Taxes have become a major tool of government fiscal policy. In a period of declining production and consumption the federal government can give impetus by decreasing income and excise taxes. The result will be an increase in the amount of money in consumers' hands. Therefore, purchasing power will stimulate the demand for goods and services which in turn will cause increased productivity. In effect, this may be likened to a beneficial dose of iron tonic to the nation's economic blood stream.

On the other hand, an increase in federal income and excise taxes can serve to brake an economy that threatens to get out of hand. This type of "overheated" economy is very vulnerable to the dangers inherent in inflation. But it can be slowed down by decreasing purchasing power on all fronts through an increase in taxation. The manipulation of tax rates must be accomplished with extreme care since our economy is a delicate mechanism. Inaccurate tampering can produce disastrous results. A partner to taxes in this role is the amount of government spending that is carried on during a given period in our national economy. To increase goverment spending is the same as decreasing taxes. To decrease government spending is the same as increasing taxes.

When taxes are altered for fiscal purposes, many consumers find it difficult to appreciate the reasoning behind such alterations. In such cases the consumer must recognize the basic need and should place the public's welfare before his own. In effect, his interests are tied in with those of the general public, and what is good for the nation is good for him.

CONSUMER UNDERSTANDING CHECK

1. What are the social purposes of taxation?
2. List six or more services that each level of government provides for the benefit of its taxpayers.
3. Is the tax on cigarettes and tobacco products an example of benefit theory taxation? Explain.
4. It has been said that the graduated personal income tax provides for redistribution of income. Discuss the validity of this statement.
5. Why is it that the state and federal governments do not use general property taxes to raise revenue?
6. How does a decrease in income taxes increase industrial production?
7. Why does government use so many indirect taxes as a way of obtaining revenue?
8. The state of Nevada does not have an individual income tax, a corporation tax or a death and gift tax. Why?
9. Why are sales taxes used with increasing frequency as important sources of revenue even though it is admitted they are not equitable for all income groups?
10. Since the consumer almost always bears the final tax burden, why is he likely to accept the responsibilities that taxes produce? Why was the familiar criticism so widespread during the Revolutionary War era—"Taxation without representation"?

14. frauds, quackery and deception

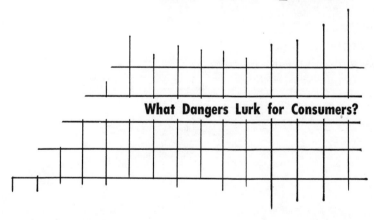

What Dangers Lurk for Consumers?

FRAUDS, QUACKERY AND DECEPTION

WHAT DANGERS LURK FOR CONSUMERS?
WHAT ARE THE FACTS?

We've said it before and we emphasize again the basic truth that the overwhelming majority of business men are honest and ethical. The public gets a square deal in most instances from American business establishments. Yet there are some sharp operators who, through the promotion of unfair schemes, prey on the public and smear honest business people.

It is estimated that over 800 different schemes are operating at this writing—schemes that thrive on human weaknesses and ignorance of the economic facts of life. Every one of the schemes we shall expose in this section relies on these human goals: the desire to become rich, to stay healthy, to get something for nothing or to get a lot for a little. Greed breeds fraud, quackery, gyps and deception. The consumer becomes the victim of his own overpowering desire to get a "good deal." When he starts out by wanting so much for so little, he very often winds up getting nothing for a lot of money.

No segment of our society is immune. Regardless of station in life, level of education or environment, American consumers are susceptible to being fleeced by unscrupulous operators who employ a wide assortment of tricks, devices, schemes and campaigns.

Health quackery alone is responsible for the staggering figure of a $1 billion yearly swindle involving almost $70 per buyer because each year some 15,000,000 Americans fall for the sales promotions conducted under the guise of "nutritional science." Doesn't almost everyone feel tired, pepless or tense at one time or another? Why of course! That's why it is so simple to swindle people simply by convincing them that they are being robbed of energy because they consume foods lacking nutrients, vitamins and minerals. Every health huckster has the *cure*—a unique preparation chuck full of "special ingredients" available at a bargain price.

This gyp is but one in a long parade. Now we shall take the reader on a quick tour of many frauds and schemes that deserve close scrutiny by all who seek to become informed consumers.

HEALTH QUACKERY

One of the most fertile fields of operations for sharp dealers with a rich amount of larceny in their blood is that of health aids. As was stated previously, the quacks with their phony cures and worthless potions, tablets and pills bilk American consumers of about a billion dollars a year. Even though the figure of the frontier medicine peddler has long since disappeared, along with his magic snake oil and mixtures compounded from fox milk smuggled from the tombs of ancient Egypt, he has been replaced by another type of medicine man who uses lectures, advertisements and the mail to brainwash gullible people into believing that they are getting old before their time, have "subclinical deficiencies" and are starving to death by eating devitalized foods. The American Medical Association refers to these quacks as *merchants of menace*—dangerous to the consumer and his health. In its pamphlet entitled "The Merchants of Menace"[18] the AMA states the following: "Unless your doctor recommends 'tonics,' 'supplements,' vitamins or minerals in concentrate form, no one need take them if he follows a fairly well-balanced daily diet. Yet pseudo-health lecturers, advertisements, and salesmen may suggest that standard foods are inadequate because of 'overprocessing,' 'worn-out soil,' 'poisonous combinations,' and other such nutrition nonsense.

"They pretend that their exotic products—made from sea kelp, yogurt, yeast, iodine, blackstrap molasses, and herbs of an infinite variety—will fortify your diet, steady your nerves, strengthen your bones, enliven your blood, evacuate your bladder, and roll back the stones from the graves of your dying kidneys!

"Beware of these blandishments—there are no shortcuts to health."

To be sure, many of the phony products are harmful. Some others are harmless, but of no value to anyone. The greatest danger lies in the fact that the quacks and the products they sell often make a really sick person waste valuable time in obtaining the professional help he really requires. Older people, in particular, are easy prey for the health hucksters. Many senior citizens suffering from chronic diseases are swindled by those who offer quack treatments and products. Recent statistics show that over $250 million a year is spent on worthless remedies for arthritis. The following are a few of the areas in which quacks have been doing a thriving business offering phony treatments and cures: air purifiers advertised to treat virus conditions, colds, pneumonia, etc.; anemia or "tired blood" preparations; baldness cures, cancer treatments, cough and cold remedies; diagnostic machines, cosmetic fakes; diabetes treatments; geriatric foods (to meet the needs of the aged); health books; hearing aids; reducing products and sea water remedies. This is but a partial listing; the parade could spread over many pages.

Beware of the quack! The American Medical Association warns that you're in the hands of one if:

---

[18] *The Merchants of Menace*, American Medical Association, 1966.

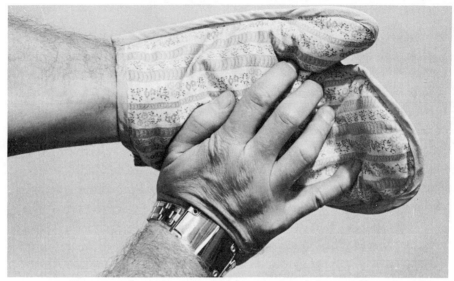

Phenomenal results have been guaranteed by vendors of such worthless items as magic copper bracelets and uranium mittens. Arthritic diseases, growths and even paralysis are alleged to have been cured   FDA photo

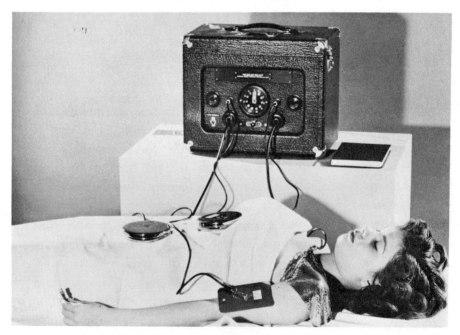

A worthless therapeutic device, the "Oscillotron." This fake was banned by Federal Court order. It was advertised as being effective for diagnosis and treatment of all diseases

◆ A "doctor" offers a treatment that he claims is available only from himself.

◆ His treatment bears his own name, or is offered in the name of his research organization whose other members, if any, are not listed.

◆ He claims he is being persecuted by the "medical trusts."

◆ He says his "cure" is being sabotaged by the medical profession.

◆ He refuses or discourages consultations with specialists in the medical profession.

◆ His "cured" patients and most ardent supports have only his word to support the fact that they were sick when they first came to him.

HOME IMPROVEMENT SWINDLES

Believe it or not, Americans are "relieved" of over $500 million a year by dishonest contractors in the fields of painting, building, roofing, siding and related trades. A typical "con job" goes like this: a corporation advertising itself as a specialist in aluminum siding sends a representative to speak to a homeowner. He convincingly proposes that because of its ideal location, the company has chosen his home to be photographed to show the before-and-after appearance. He promises that the company will reimburse the homeowner for use of the illustrative photograph and, in addition, will pay a special bonus to every homeowner in the area who places an order for aluminum siding as a result of the advertisement. Very often he goes so far as to offer a further inducement such as 10,000 trading stamps in order to soften the potential victim right there on the spot. If he falls for the scheme, the salesman then produces a large pack of papers which he mentions in an offhand way as being just "authorization forms" and nothing more. In reality the packet consists of an installment sales contract, with many carbon copies as well as a blank Trust Deed. The sad ending reveals that the company never took any pictures and the homeowner was hoodwinked into signing a retail installment contract obligating him to pay $4,000. The comfortable, romantic cottage becomes a paradise for gyps.

Another favorite trick used very frequently with housewives is the "scare" approach. This method has been used with great success by nomadic groups of oil burner repairmen. "Lady, your oil burner is in sorry shape. It might blow up any day. It's so bad that we really should report it to the fire department. But if you let us fix it right now, we'll forget about it. How about it?"

One crooked oil burner "specialist" finished his repair job in 25 minutes and made out a bill for $105. The same day, the burner broke down again and had to be replaced at a much higher cost. The reputable repairman who installed the new burner pointed out that the old burner had been tampered with and actually damaged —not repaired.

In 1965 the New York State Bureau of Consumer Frauds and Protection found home improvement schemes to be the highest single area for fraudulent operations. During the spring and the fall the homeowner is literally beseiged by salesmen, advertisements and telephone calls offering a wide range of services and products. It is unfortunate that many legitimate business men are placed in the same category along with the shady operators. The State of Massachusetts in 1966 enacted a law which calls for a 24 hour "cooling off" period to allow homeowners time to reconsider any contract which they sign. This eliminates a good deal of the pressure which swindlers always use as part of their stock and trade.

The homeowner can protect himself against gyps by: (a) doing business with persons who are well-known in the community, (b) having a lawyer read all agreements that involve considerable amounts of money, (c) never permitting himself to be pressured into signing a contract, (d) not falling for promises of a lot for a little, and (e) checking the reputation and work of the contractor with other homeowners for whom he has done work in the past.

BAIT ADVERTISING

Bait advertising, also known as "bait and switch" advertising, is another big consumer fraud in this country. It is the practice of offering at a spectacularly low price a brand-name product or service which the dealer never intends to sell if he is allowed to get his own way about it. The gyp might properly be termed bait for suckers. Here's how it works. A business establishment will lure customers to it by advertising well-known merchandise at very low prices. When the customers begin to arrive they are apt to find that the merchandise on sale is not fit for use, or in shabby condition. In addition, they may discover that the salesmen are most eager to point out the weaknesses of the products rather than the virtues. Another strong possibility is that even at the minute when the doors of the store open for business the supply of merchandise on sale is limited to a very few items. When customers complain, the salesmen promptly reply that the advertised bargains are sold out. Such operators take advantage of customers' frustration and disappointment and immediately try to persuade them to buy other merchandise at much higher prices. The persuasive salesman uncorks every known selling

device when a wary customer insists that he or she wishes to buy
only the sewing machine or the washing machine advertised at the
special sale price. He may tell the customer that he's too ethical
to sell such poor quality merchandise, or that replacement parts are
no longer available. But he does have the kind of product that he's
sure the customer wants (he or she, according to the salesman, is
a person of education and good taste capable of recognizing superior merchandise)—and the price is a mere $80.95 more. From that
point he's off and running. In many case he scores well and another customer is "taken."

The description above should not be interpreted as a blanket in-
dictment of all merchants who advertise their products at special
discount prices. Honest stores and business establishments frequently offer "loss leaders" as inducements to increase sales volume.
The alert consumer should learn to distinguish between those honest merchants who conduct ethical sales and the shady pitch men
whose stores are traps for the unwary and unsuspecting shopper.

THE REFERRAL RACKET

The many referral schemes that are in operation in all sections of the country have one major objective—to get the customer to buy a product at a highly inflated price through the dishonest approach whereby the customer is promised reductions in the total price if he supplies "leads" for additional sales.

For example, a salesman will call at a home and offer a "free" electric sewing machine. He states the proposition in these terms: all you are asked to pay is $395.49. However, if you supply the salesman with a list of 20 or 25 names of people you know, who might also be interested in buying a sewing machine, you will receive a $20 commission for every sale that is made from your list. Therefore, if the salesman sold 20 sewing machines from your list you would actually be getting your machine at no cost at all. And if all 25 purchased a machine, you would be over a $100 ahead in addition to owning a beautiful machine of your own free and clear.

The deal sounds too good to be true. You're right, because the

salesman knows it isn't true at all. It's an out and out swindle just as was the well-known chain-letter racket* that was popular some twenty-five or thirty years ago. In the first place, the basic price of the merchandise is always pumped up drastically. Then, too, the pitch made by the salesman hardly ever bears any resemblance to the actual truth.

A "boiler room" operation in a suburb of a large city had succeeded in skinning several hundred people before the law forced the masterminds behind the scheme to close shop. Specifically, they sold TV-stereo combinations at $1,500 to $1,700 along with offers to pay $150 commissions for each additional combination set sold. The Attorney General's office, after receiving several complaints from customers who said that the sets were defective when received and that the seller refused to give them any satisfaction, brought criminal charges against the schemers. It was shown that a $390 selling price would have yielded a nice profit.

The referral schemes are particularly insidious because the customers are high-pressured into putting their names on papers that promise to make them "buyer representatives." The tempting credit terms may be stated on a certificate, to be sure. However, along with the sweet goes the sour—a contract, which is a chattel mortgage and a promissory note. The buyer agrees to make regular payments over a specified period of time on merchandise that is inflated in price. The sales contract is then sold in a real hurry to a finance company who has no interest whatever in the agreement between the seller and the buyer. If the customer fails to meet his payment obligations he runs the risk of having the merchandise taken away from him as repossessed goods. The seller has washed his hands and the hard-hearted finance company becomes the menacing demon. What happened to the credit that the unhappy purchaser was supposed to have received? It was just a lot of empty sales talk. The

---

* The chain letter scheme promised fortune and good luck to those who kept up the chain. The person would buy a letter by sending money or sometimes a bond to the ten people listed. He would remove the top name and add his name to the bottom of ten more letters. The only ones who profited were the promoters. For this reason the endless chain scheme has been ruled illegal and in violation of the Postal Fraud Statute, 18 USC 1341, when use of the mails is made by the promoters of the rackets.

company that produced the product as well as the finance company shrug their shoulders—they know nothing of such promises. So they are in the clear.

All referral sales are based on fraud, deceit and misrepresentation. Those who have been duped readily admit that they never realized that they were being approached as potential customers. They actually were fooled into believing that they had been selected to participate in a very special program whereby they could earn handsome amounts of money by acting as company "representatives." Won't people ever learn?

CHARITY GYPS

In the last few years the mails have been flooded with toiletries, household products, jewelry, stationery and other goods sent by private companies to citizens with a "hearts and flowers" charitable appeal. In the majority of cases the charities receive only a very small portion of the proceeds whereas the promoters take the largest

cut for themselves. The mail is not the only method of distribution, of course. Charitable solicitations take many forms and one should never give money until all the facts are known. If charities employ professional solicitors, it certainly pays to examine their structure and method of operation before you make a donation. Be wary also of those who seek to collect for phony causes—small children, people with serious physical handicaps, and people who misrepresent themselves as clergymen and public officials. They are artists in arousing your sympathy.

It is not too difficult to identify the phony collector—he's usually dramatic in his style and in a hurry. He appears at your home with a request that you give him money on the spot. Since he is in reality a con man, he finds it easy to make up names for charities that sound plausible (The Fund for the Support of War Veterans of the Galapagos Campaign). Hundreds of thousands of dollars are extracted from gullible persons for just such nonexistent charities.

DEBT CONSOLIDATION SCHEMES

Why fret over ten, twelve or fifteen outstanding bills when just by walking into any of the 21 conveniently located offices of *Friendly Frank, Your Financial Pal* you can clear them all up by receiving one loan? That's the familiar come-on of the debt consolidation sharper. By promising to provide a painless way of pooling or adjusting people's debts the tricky loan companies that operate just barely inside the legal edge succeed in accomplishing only one thing—their victims are plunged further into debt. There is no method whereby debts can be pooled without adding more debt.

While there are honest finance companies, legitimate bank officials, counselors and lawyers who do manage to find a way to spread out outstanding indebtedness by means of honest-to-goodness debt-consolidation loans, the fact remains that the field has been invaded by some hungry gyp artists.

"One is a breed of unlicensed second mortgage brokers who promise that they can reduce monthly payments on outstanding debts

by as much as 50% with a tricky loan agreement. A big loan to the debtor, calling for monthly installments over three to five years, is secured by a second mortgage and the older debts are paid with the loan proceeds. Everything looks rosy. The interest rate on the loan seems fair—6% to 8%. Then the first installment notice is received in the mail, calling for a much larger payment than was expected. There is a list of fees which the broker neglected to mention. A 'placement' fee, say, of $500 on a $1,000 loan. Often there is a second broker who also gets a fee. There are fees for appraisal, photographs, searches, recordings, etc. Even if the loan is paid off in advance, these fees are not pro-rated or refunded.

"An Ohio woman who consolidated her debts found herself obligated to pay back $5,850 over a five-year period on an original loan of $3,000. One New Jersey man who borrowed $4,800 became indebted for $9,600!"[19]

[19] "The Top Ten Consumer Gyps in the U.S.A.," Jack Pearl, *The American Legion Magazine*, April 1966, p. 46.

BUSINESS OPPORTUNITY SCHEMES

The daily papers everywhere contain ads describing glowing opportunities for those who would like to go into business for themselves. To be sure, many of the listed opportunities are legitimate business propositions. Yet among the sheep there are wolves—fraudulent operators who concoct elaborate schemes to fleece trusting souls eager to make their investments grow.

The frauds advertise for partners, promising that those who are ready to recognize a "good thing" when it is handed to them on a silver platter will become full partners as soon as they produce the required amount of money. The business enterprises are always described as thriving growth propositions. Growth is so rapid that new funds are required AT ONCE to finance the much needed plant expansion. The really wary reader might as well ask himself this question: "If the business is so good, why aren't the local banks and investors fighting to get into the act?" Why advertise?

These claims deserve very close scrutiny. Remember, as a partner you assume obligations. You can be held liable for the company's debts as well as those of the other partner.

Another variation involves the offer of franchises, territorial rights, vending machines or merchandise possessing the potential for fabulous, quick profits. They are made to appear as short cuts to wealth. After the sales pitch has found its mark, the investor is then informed that he naturally will have to buy certain equipment or make a series of payments in order to gain full possession of the rights, franchises or merchandise he assumed he'd receive with no strings attached.

Beware of such get-rich-quick offers. Be cautious and investigate thoroughly before entering into any agreement. Have an accountant and an attorney look into the matter before making any commitment.

The list of frauds is practically without an end. Unscrupulous operators are constantly scheming to devise new ways to extract hard-earned dollars from the unthinking public. Unfortunately, in many cases people help to perpetuate these frauds because they are embarrassed at having been taken and are shamed into silence. For this reason the same schemes are tried over and over again. The consumer owes it to himself to become acquainted with the many variations that exist so that he will be able to act intelligently when an attempt to "take him" is made. In sections 2 and 3 of this book you were informed of a great many agencies whose purpose is that of assisting and protecting consumers. Once again we emphasize the value in learning all you can about those consumer safeguards. Armed with knowledge you are in a better position to stand up and be counted as one of the citizens who refuse to sit idly on the sidelines while the dishonest merchants grow fat on their ill gotten gains.

SOME DECEPTIVE PRACTICES

How soothing to the ear is the sweet news that the rugs and the piano you want can be obtained at between 46 to 50 percent below retail price. There always seems to be someone around who just happens to know "a fellow who can get everything wholesale." He either is in league with a shady retailer who falsely advertises himself as a wholesaler (he gets a percent of the take), or else is a front for a professional wholesale broker. Very often the latter has an attractive office in an imposing building and gives every appearance of being legitimate. The unsuspecting customers are always assured by the broker that he is more than happy to save them 45, 50, or even 60 percent on any purchase they want to make. He knows just where to go to get the "hottest deal in the city." Do you want a best buy in a piano? Of course, you do. So off you go to a warehouse well stocked with pianos. Each instrument has a tag with a code—no prices. You are told to select the model you want and the broker will do the rest. To be sure the quoted price is reduced by 46 to 50 percent. What you do not realize is that the original price has been puffed up 150 percent or more to start with. But the best is yet to come. When the piano is delivered it may be a beat up model, scratched, with a faded finish—not at all like the floor model you liked so much. So you hasten to look at your receipt only to find that the scribbling on it tells an incomplete story of a piano bought for such and such a price. But you do have one consolation—you get it wholesale!

Since by the very definition of the word, wholesale means the sale of goods in large quantity, it should be quite apparent to any thoughtful person that an individual cannot really buy merchandise at wholesale prices. A company that sells merchandise to a department store in lots of hundreds or even thousands can afford to accept a lower price. But when it comes to selling a single item that is another matter. The price must be higher because the cost is higher. One may obtain a bargain in a retail establishment when the proprietor decides to cut the price. However, he is not selling at wholesale prices regardless of what the claim may be.

PACKAGING DECEPTIONS

HIDDEN PRICE INCREASES

Everybody is aware that manufacturing costs are mounting. As a result, it is natural to expect retail prices to rise also. And rise they do. Almost every product you can think of has gone up in price lately, and few persons try to hide this bare fact. The food industry, however, seems to attempt to mask price increases. Nobody questions the right of producers to increase prices when their costs increase. What people do object to is the deliberate attempt to make them believe that they are getting the same products for the same old price. One of the ways this deceit is accomplished is to mask price increases behind reductions in the net contents of packages. Even more flagrant is the practice of increasing the size of a container in order to create the illusion of an increase in contents.

The consumer is easily deceived by these tricks because he finds it difficult to remember the net weight of the great variety of food products he buys each week. Bear in mind that there are about 8,000 items for sale in the average American supermarket.

DECEPTIVE SIZES

Who hasn't become aware of the commonly used size descriptions: "Family," "Economy," "Jumbo," and "King"? Each word intends to convey the impression of quantity and economy. But the connotation is false in many instances. In order to determine the validity of the claims you would need time, pen, pencil, slide rule and a magnifying glass.

For that matter, it is equally dishonest to parade before the public such designations as "Giant half-quart,' "Full quart," and "Jumbo pint." All three terms can be said to be absolutely meaningless and concocted only to make the shopper feel that he is getting more than there really is. Whenever an advertisement is read and the product is placed in a special category, certain consumers are fooled. After all, how different is a full quart from a regular quart? How does a giant half quart differ from an ordinary half quart or a jumbo pint from a regular pint?

PRICE COMPARISONS

The food shopper's task is made even more difficult by the odd weights and measures that are used for similar products. There are 71 different ways of packaging potato chips in weights up to 3½ pounds. And when we speak of detergents, the problem really gets complex. The supermarket shelves contain any number of "giant size" detergent containers. Included among them are at least 8 different weight valuations varying from 2 pounds 8 ounces to 3 pounds 7 ounces—almost a one pound spread. Yet they are all advertised as being "giant size."

How can the average shopper make valid price comparisons so that he can purchase the lowest priced product? As matters stand at present he would need an electric computer to come out ahead of the game. For this very reason the Truth-in-Packaging legislation, which was introduced by Senator Philip A. Hart of Michigan, has placed the problem in focus. If passed, it should go far toward correcting these abuses.

One supermarket, the Hyde Park Cooperative Society of Chicago, has removed this obstacle—shoppers can buy there honestly informed. Every product on the shelves not only carries the unit price, but the cost *per ounce,* as well. There's no need to go groping in the dark in this store.

STEPS TO BE TAKEN

Persons knowledgeable in this area have found the range of deception and fraud in the sale of consumer goods and services to be as long as it is wide and that it even filters through to the activities of legitimate business. In order to keep the public informed of the areas in which the fringe operators and gyps are or can be operating in, the various protective agencies conscientiously issue public warnings in the form of releases to the newspaper, radio and television. These warnings have exposed dozens of flagrant attempts to fleece consumers: the sale of wigs that failed to meet the specifications contained in the glowing ads; the purchase of tickets for charter flights and cruises that could never be conducted because of failure to comply with federal regulations; the air conditioning repair racket, in which the owners had to pay exorbitant service charges before they could get their appliances back from the repair shops; the approach of the seasonal door-to-door gyps who, with great cunning, unload assorted junk on defenseless victims; and other frauds so numerous that a volume could be compiled about them.

In many instances these warnings reach interested and alert consumers. However, many less educated, elderly and low income citizens who, to date, have appeared to be less sensitive to the dangers that exist, have not been very successful in developing an immunity to false advertising and misleading and deceptive trade practices. Their buying power continues to be drained away year after year by gyp artists and out and out swindlers.

Happily, the tide is now turning. The American consumer is feeling his strength—he's flexing his muscles at long last. The federal and state governments are working feverishly to enact laws to protect their citizens and to assist them in making purchasing decisions. Our increasingly well-informed society is now demanding more protection and government is heeding this request. It is to be regretted that some businessmen still harbor a misguided fear of consumer protection, although it does not mean oppressive government interference in business decisions. They appear to ignore the important fact that any practice which deceives consumers also harms the honest businessman. Where fraud abounds, the consumer's basic confidence in advertising and business ethics tends to be destroyed. And last but not least, to have continued prosperity and economic growth we must keep a healthy climate within which consumers are not afraid to buy—consumers who trust businessmen.

Let us hope that in the not too distant future our nation's consumers will be able to concentrate upon the positive aspects of transacting business rather than expending their energies in order to save themselves from being gypped.

CONSUMER UNDERSTANDING CHECK

1. How can the consumer protect himself against frauds and deception?
2. Do you think it is possible to eliminate all frauds, quackery and deception? If your answer is yes, how can it be done? If your answer is no, why can't it be done?
3. What is the effect on the honest businessman when a consumer falls prey to a fraudulent promoter?
4. Select a common product on the shelves of your local supermarket. List the net weight and price of all the various brands that are available. Which is the most economical? What is the range of prices?
5. Housewives today are beginning to look with suspicion on door-to-door salesmen but permit certain legitimate salesmen like the Fuller Brush man to enter their homes and sell them various products. Why?
6. Check with your library for the meaning of the "Pigeon Drop Hoax" and read your daily paper to locate a news item about this particular type of fraud.
7. Why is it that certain states have declared debt consolidation loans and referral sales illegal while other states have taken no action?
8. In 1966 Massachusetts passed a law requiring a 24 hour "cooling-off" period before a credit contract becomes valid, stipulating that either party may void the contract within that time. Discuss the effects of this law on unscrupulous promoters.
9. Select from the want ad section of your newspaper two business opportunity advertisements—one which looks legitimate and another which appears to be a "come-on." Explain how you made the distinction and the difference in the wording between the two.
10. Why is it impossible for retail merchants to sell at wholesale prices?

15. the consumer and the law

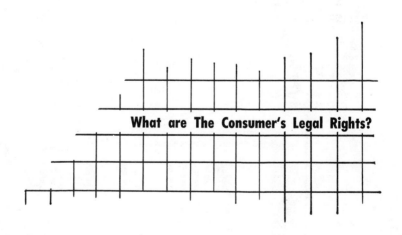

What are The Consumer's Legal Rights?

These legal documents are not of the do-it-yourself variety.

THE CONSUMER AND THE LAW

WHAT ARE THE CONSUMER'S LEGAL RIGHTS?
DOES THE CONSUMER NEED SOME LEGAL KNOWLEDGE?

A lawyer stated some years ago that the cardinal sin of America's schools was that of having taught people to write their own names. That lawyer was not a foe of education, naturally. What he meant was that as consumers Americans too frequently sign documents that obligate them to meet conditions which they do not understand. The thousands of consumers who sign installment contracts without stopping to read the conditions printed in small type are examples of amateur buying, born of ignorance and pitiful indifference. Their helpless cries may be heart rending, but in the final analysis they have no one to blame but themselves. Safeguards for

MAKE SURE YOU READ A CONTRACT BEFORE YOU SIGN.

the consumer do exist and government on all levels provides a good measure of protection for him. Violation of established laws are civil or criminal offenses and the proper legal agencies do their utmost to prosecute known offenders. However, if consumers desire to be protected by these laws they must do two things:

1. They must be willing to reports violations to the proper authorities.

2. They must acquire at least a familiarity with the important legislation that has been passed for their protection.

In this section we wish to emphasize strongly the fact that by taking the time to understand the many laws already on the books for the protection of consumers, people who enter the marketplace may avoid difficulties. It is hoped that people will act ethically because it is the right way to behave and not because there are statutes that prescribe penalties for their violation. Happily, the majority of people, whether they are buyers or sellers, will abide by the Golden Rule. But there's always a black sheep in the pack. So we must watch out for that creature.

When the shady dealer, the huckster and the shyster show their hand and it becomes crystal clear that they are out to exploit the consumer, there is only one course of action that can be taken. When a person's rights are endangered it becomes his duty and his right to call the matter to the attention of the proper authorities. Action to correct abuses will only result when the person who is wronged assumes some initiative. Bear in mind that the government never prosecutes civil suits; the only time it will act is when it is aware that the law has been broken. It will prosecute whenever criminal intent is involved, however.

The consumer who rushes headlong into business transactions armed only with hunches, amateurish information and a faint hope that all will go well is courting disaster. He requires basic understandings that will lead to immunization against unscrupulous business practices as well as an awareness that will enable him to distinguish between honest dealings and fraud. The wise consumer will soon learn to respect the knowledge possessed by the expert in

YOUR LAWYER CAN ROLL BACK THIS FOG OF CONFUSION.

legal matters—the lawyer. He will avoid difficulties by consulting the expert *before* he signs a sales contract or makes a financial commitment. If it is considered prudent to consult a physician before we become ill, it is just as logical to consult a lawyer before we make a legal mistake. A lawyer should not be thought of only in time of distress. He stands ready to be of service to defend your rights and to assure you that justice prevails.

But the lawyer is not the only defender of consumers' legal rights. There are a number of agencies to which the consumer may have recourse in order to clarify his rights and obligations. In fact, they stand ready to aid the consumer at little or no cost. Several outstanding resources are mentioned here.

The Better Business Bureau. The consumer may avail himself of the services of a Better Business Bureau in order to determine whether a particular firm or dealer is considered reputable in its dealings. In addition, in the event of a report of a transaction which has been accomplished under questionable circumstances, the Bureau will exert influence to correct the inequity. Better Business Bureaus cannot prosecute cases, however. On occasion they will refer flagrant violations to the proper legal authorities for action.

Legal Aid Societies. Many cities have a legal aid bureau which gives legal advice to persons too poor to engage the services of a lawyer. People who have problems concerning debts, consumer credit and breach of contract will find legal aid societies or bureaus very helpful. Even though they may not be able to afford a lawyer, needy citizens do not have to forego justice. These bureaus stand ready to protect their rights and opportunities.

Small Claims Courts. Very often wronged consumers fail to press their just claims because they are aware of the length of time it frequently takes for their prosecution as well as the great cost. To make it convenient for people to present small claims for adjudication, many states and cities have established small claims courts. These courts generally try cases where the claims involve small sums, frequently less than $50. While it is possible to be represented by an attorney, a lawyer is not needed. The plaintiff and the defendant present their arguments and the presiding judge decides according to the law involved. The proceedings are simple and efficient.

City or County Attorney. It is the duty of the city or county attorney to represent the consumer and his interest. Throughout the nation it has been through municipal attorneys that consumers have received important protection, especially in cases involving unfair prices. In fact, it was the unified effort of the Kansas City District Attorney and the municipal attorneys of neighboring cities that successfully opposed the rate increase sought by the Cities Service Gas Company some years ago.

State Attorneys General. Since 1957 when the Attorney General for the State of New York, Louis J. Lefkowitz, first established the Consumer Frauds and Protection Bureau, many other states have followed suit. As of 1966, 24 states have effective bureaus that operate to drive unscrupulous operators out of business and to recover losses suffered by those who have been cheated. In 1965 the New York Bureau recovered over $1,200,000 in goods and money for consumers who had been victimized by dishonest businessmen. In many instances the mere threat by a consumer that he intends to expose a shady transaction to a state attorney general will suffice to bring about a quick settlement.

Let it not be assumed that in the introduction to this section a case has been made for having a lawyer at one's side at all times. Nor has the intent been one of encouraging recourse to the various courts of law. What has been forcefully suggested is that consumers everywhere become alert to the danger of remaining indifferent, fearful and ignorant in the face of the threat of fraud, misrepresentation, deception and outright thievery in the marketplace. Bear in mind that the gypsters, the hit and run merchants, the sharp dealers and common run-of-the-mill crooks thrive in an atmosphere where the wronged are reluctant to expose them. They are encouraged to ply their shabby trade where the victims are fearful of disclosing their crimes either because of shame or because they are ignorant of what procedures to follow in order to see that justice prevails.

WHAT COMMON LEGAL PROBLEMS DO CONSUMERS ENCOUNTER?

In the vast majority of business transactions that take place every day it is highly probable that both buyer and seller conduct themselves in a businesslike way. Honest intent is apparent on each side and for the most part each party achieves a comfortable and satisfying feeling—the American way of doing business isn't so bad after all. But the marketplace is also the breeding ground of discord and legal entanglements. We might properly refer to these as the harmful fallout of business. It may be small, yet the effect is strong and certain.

Every time a transfer of a good or a service takes place a legal transaction is effected. An agreement is involved when one individual in order to obtain a commodity consents to a specific arrangement to accomplish the transfer. Each party to this agreement assumes certain responsibilities and obligations to the other. In most cases these are legally enforceable. The businessman selling goods or services is normally quite expert in his understanding of the legal implications of his actions. On the other hand, the buyer is very frequently acting without legal knowledge when he trusts that the seller is acting in good faith. Even though this is generally justified, the consumer should develop a storehouse of basic legal information in order to be able to participate in the marketplace with confidence. He must protect his rights and his hard-earned dollars. Action of this type eliminates complications later on.

The *contract* is the most common form of agreement we encounter. Virtually every one of our normal daily activities involves either a formal or an informal contract. Let us take a look at a few familiar illustrations of contracts that apply to the lives of every individual or family:

◆ Buying gasoline for your car.

◆ Having a suit of clothes dry cleaned.

◆ Having your TV set repaired.

- Going to the dentist.

- Buying a ticket for a basketball game.

- Obtaining a credit card.

- Buying a car with the use of credit.

- Engaging the services of a lawyer.

- Agreeing to play bridge with your neighbors.

- Agreeing to going to the senior prom with "that certain young lady."

Some of the above are illustrations of informal contracts and cannot be enforced under the law. But formal transactions which represent contracts of a truly legal nature because of certain special features are legally binding upon those individuals who make them. These special features are:

Legal capacity. Under the law only certain individuals may enter into contracts. These individuals are called *competent.* For example, a boy of 14 is considered a legal infant and is therefore not a *competent* person. Likewise, a person who is senile or mentally ill cannot enter into an enforceable agreement.

Offer and acceptance. This is sometimes called *mutual assent* or agreement. That means that one party offers something and the other party agrees to accept that same thing. They must both enter into this agreement freely and with full understanding of what the offer and acceptance entail. If you hire a cabinetmaker to install a bookcase in your home, the contract is his offer to build the bookcase and your agreement to accept his services and the particular bookcase he promises to build.

Price or consideration. A contract cannot be considered legal unless there is a transfer of money or something of value. An agreement to give someone something without charge is not legally binding. In other words, a price tag must be attached to the bookcase mentioned above. The party receiving the bookcase agrees ahead of time to pay for it.

EVERY DAY WE MAKE CONTRACTS

Transfer. A contract must specify the method by which the commodity will pass from one party's hands to the other. This may include time, place and procedure to accomplish the transfer. Referring once more to the illustration of the bookcase, the contract would indicate when the cabinetmaker is to deliver the finished product, where he will install it and some particulars concerning the method of installation which must be done to the purchaser's satisfaction.

Form. Although some contracts are made in the course of conversation, an enforceable contract must be made in the manner prescribed by law. For example, the transfer of title to a house must be accompanied by a deed as well as a written contract.

Legality. A contract must not be opposed to existing law. A contract which would be harmful to others or would have criminal intent would not be legally binding. An agreement to purposely damage someone else's property for a specified fee would be an illustration of invalid contract. Another illustration of an invalid contract is an agreement to build a factory in an area zoned for residential purposes only.

Contractual difficulties almost always involve one or more of the elements or features we have just defined. To emphasize this point a few actual cases are cited so that the reader can more clearly understand how the consumer can become involved through either misunderstanding or purposeful intent to not live up to the terms of the contract.

A. Mrs. C_____ was 82 years old and senile. A neighbor who had an antique shop prevailed upon her to sell a valuable antique chest worth at least $1,500 for $20. The elderly lady's daughter brought the matter to the attention of the family lawyer who promptly instituted steps to prevent the sale of the antique to the dealer in question. Mrs. C_____ was legally incompetent to enter into a contract.

B. John L_____, a 17 year old high school boy, visited a used car lot and contracted to buy a used car for $50 a month over a year's period of time. The state in which John resided required that a person had to be at least

21 years of age in order to be legally capable of entering into a contract. John was unable to meet his payments after the fourth month, so the dealer sued him for the balance due him. The court refused to accept the dealer's claims because the contract was invalid.

C. Arthur J_____ signed a contract to sell his house to Thomas T_____. The day following the signing of the contract, Arthur's employer informed him that he would not be transferred as originally planned. Upon receiving this news Arthur called Thomas and informed him that the "deal is off." Since all of the elements of the contract were included, Arthur J_____ was forced to fulfill his part of the transaction. The house had to be sold to Thomas T_____.

D. Mr. and Mrs. Harold B_____ purchased a new washing machine on the installment plan and signed a retail conditional sales contract. On delivery of the machine as promised, they discovered, much to their dismay, that it did not fit into the space in which their old washer had been kept. Since the dealer had lived up to all conditions in the contract, Mr. and Mrs. B_____ were forced to accept the washing machine they had purchased. They could not void the legally binding agreement.

From the illustrations above it becomes painfully clear that when a signature is carelessly or indifferently written on a contract much unhappiness and actual loss can result. It is extremely important that before agreeing to sign any contract you become completely familiar with all the terms and that you read it thoroughly. Keep in mind the following—by considering them you can avoid difficulties:

◆ Don't sign a contract until you thoroughly understand the contents.

◆ Make sure that all the terms to which you agree are included, in writing.

◆ Likewise, have terms to which you do not agree removed.

◆ Insist that the terms of payment and delivery are very clearly stated.

◆ Don't be shy. Demand explanation of any terms you do not understand.

◆ Make sure that the other party to the contract signs at the same time that you do and that each party receives a copy of the contract containing *both* signatures.

◆ If a contract for a major transaction, such as buying or selling a house, is contemplated, be sure to have your lawyer read it before signing.

◆ Before signing a retail conditional sales contract (installment purchases involve such contracts), be sure that you are fully aware of the credit terms and your responsibilities.

◆ Never sign a contract containing blank spaces.

SOME LEGAL ASPECTS OF CONTRACTS

Even though a contract may contain the required signatures of both parties it may not be binding if certain conditions exist. The reader should find it well worthwhile if he carefully analyzes the following examples of contracts that cannot be legally enforced.

1. *A contract which is signed under pressure or threat.* Such a contract is not binding. However, you would have the burden of proving before a court of law that you were pressured into entering into the agreement and thereby being deprived of your free will.

2. *A contract that is contrary to law.* Any contract containing any provision which could lead to the commission of a crime or violation of existing laws is illegal.

3. *A contract where one of the parties is a minor.* Most states hold that any person below the age of 21 is a legal minor. Some states have lower ages for girls. A minor can choose to ignore the terms of a contract he has signed. Therefore, anyone who makes a contract with a minor does so at his own risk. There are some exceptions to this, however, especially when agreements concerning shelter, food and clothing are involved.

4. *A contract in which misrepresentations are made.* Misrepresentation that can be substantiated is grounds for having a contract voided.

5. *A contract which combines both written and oral agreements.* In such cases only the written agreement is enforceable.

6. *There is no obligation to pay for merchandise that has not been requested.* There is no contract, hence no obligation to pay. In fact, the State of Illinois passed a law in 1965 called the *Unsolicited Merchandise Act* providing for retention by the receiver of all merchandise that he has not requested. Such merchandise is to be treated as a gift.

So much for contracts that cannot be enforced. The majority of contracts that people sign are very much enforceable. In fact, a contract doesn't even have to be in writing to be valid. To claim that you signed an agreement without reading it is not a cause for having the contract voided. Once you have placed your signature on the contract it signifies that you have read it and that you understand all the terms and conditions.

There are many cases on record involving claims that even though the contracts had been signed there were other promises or provisions which were not written into the agreement. Unfortunately, such provisions cannot be enforced because they were not written into the contract in the first place. It is always presumed that when signatures are fixed to an agreement the parties have written down everything that was agreed upon. It is very difficult to enforce oral provisions or promises.

A housewife in California refused to meet the terms of a contract she claims she signed only to get rid of an annoying vacuum cleaner salesman. A judge ruled that the woman was obligated to the agreement she had signed and she had to pay for the vacuum cleaner. The reason she had advanced was termed irrelevant by the judge.

Another consumer complained that the reason for not keeping up payments on his TV set was his inability to read English. He felt that since he was not able to read the contract he signed, he was not bound by that written agreement. Here again, the court ruled against the defendant. It was made clear that at the time of signature all the terms were read aloud and that they were readily understood by the buyer before he signed the sales contract.

The bulk of business law concerns itself with phases of contracts of all kinds. Business thrives only because of the generally accepted knowledge that unless certain promises are kept they will be enforced by the courts. Thus conduct in many areas is shaped by contracts. People enter into contracts and assume the requisite obligations because they feel that benefits to be received outweigh the obligations assumed. No one enters into a contract with the object of losing money. In the fullest sense the making of a contract symbolizes our free market system—every individual is free to act according to his own will provided in so doing no law is violated. The parties to a contract come together to exchange goods or services to meet their individual objectives.

SOME LEGAL ASPECTS OF WARRANTIES

A warranty is a promise or representation of performance or quality of goods or services. It is not legally necessary to state this promise as a guaranty or warranty—the intent is sufficient. If the manufacturer of a particular brand of shirts uses printed matter stating that under normal conditions the shirts will not tear or fray within the first year of use, he is offering a warranty for those shirts even though the word itself is not included. The basic ingredient of a warranty is the promise of representation.

Since in most cases warranties are expressed by the seller orally or in written fashion, such warranties are called *expressed warranties*. They include a specific promise or representation (as illustrated above). However, even if a seller makes no promise or representation, the law imposes certain warranty obligations upon him. Since these are not expressly stated by the seller, they are called *implied warranties*.

In most cases these warranties, that are legally enforceable, are built-in devices for the protection of the buyer. They also obligate the seller by law in the following areas:

1. *Title.* The law holds that every seller must warrant that he has the right to sell the commodities and that the buyer shall have

the right to possession of them. For example, if Mr. "X" sold Mr. "Y" a fur coat without legal title to that coat (Mr. "X" had illegally acquired the coat), Mr. "Y" would have the right to take legal action against Mr. "X." In technical terms it would be called a breach of an implied warranty of title. Needless to say, Mr. "X" would also be exposed to criminal prosecution for theft.

2. *Fitness for purpose.* If a buyer relies on the skill and judgment of the seller to select goods which are best suited for the purpose the buyer has in mind, the seller is legally obligated to a warranty that the goods are reasonably fit for that purpose. To illustrate: Mr. "X" goes to Mr. "Y," a hardware store operator, in order to obtain non-rusting roofing nails. Mr. "Y" sells nails to the buyer, but after the first rain, Mr. "X" notices that all the nails have become coated with rust. Clearly there is a breach of warranty of fitness for purpose in this transaction. Mr. "X" would get satisfaction in any court were the matter to go to trial. Most sellers are eager to make good in cases involving merchandise that fails to fit the purpose in reasonable fashion. Therefore, not too many cases of this kind reach the courts.

3. *Fitness for human consumption.* The law holds that anything sold for human consumption must be wholesome and fit for use. This does not place any responsibility on the buyer's request for information about the product's fitness. If a person enters a restaurant and orders a dinner he naturally expects food that is fit for him to eat. If, however, he gets a splinter of wood in his tongue as the result of a sharp piece of wood having been mixed with sausage meat, he will be able to collect for damages for the injury suffered. There would be evident in this case a breach of the implied warranty that the food was fit to eat. The customer could even sue for negligence, if he so desired.

4. *Conformity to description.* Merchandise that is sold must be exactly as described to the buyer. It must be the same trade name, model, size, color, etc., as agreed to by the buyer in contracting for the purchase. Any deviation makes it possible for the buyer to refuse to accept the merchandise. The most frequent situation which

results in a breach of warranty of this type is the mail order or catalogue transaction.

5. *Corresponding to a sample.* Merchandise selected after seeing a sample or a demonstration model must be of the same quality and, in effect, identical in every respect with the sample or demonstration model. Many transactions therefore involve warranties of conformity to description as well as corresponding to a sample.

6. *Merchantability.* Merchantable goods are goods that are fit for the use for which similar goods are usually employed. For example, a sporting goods store has a display of baseball bats in the window. They have been in the window for several years. A boy purchases a bat which the salesman removes from the window (it's the last one left). The first time the boy uses the bat, it cracks in half as it makes contact with the baseball. That bat was clearly not merchantable, nor was it fit for use.

Very often consumer-buyers become confused and find it difficult to distinguish between the high-sounding claims made by the seller and actual representations of fact. When a seller makes representations of fact regarding goods and the buyer depends upon them, the seller becomes responsible for these representations and they become express warranties. A contract and a warranty made at the same time become one and tie a contract. If the contract is a written one, the warranty must also be in writing. It should be noted at this point that no seller is liable for any express warranties made by an unauthorized dealer or agent. However, the wise consumer can receive additional protection by requiring the seller to include in the contract express warranties with regard to quality or performance of the product. If you ever are in doubt ask the dealer to warrant his goods. Should he refuse to do so, flee from his establishment at once. Honest people always stand behind the products they sell.

The express warranty is the method by which the consumer may avoid the responsibility of *caveat emptor,* which means "let the buyer beware." This principle serves to make the individual reliant on his own judgment and responsible for his actions. It is important for the buyer to inspect carefully any merchandise that he proposes to purchase. If the transaction has been concluded without fraud on the seller's part, the buyer can blame no one but himself if he gets the worst of the deal. The express warranty does serve to increase the responsibility that falls to the seller.

REDRESS FOR THE CONSUMER

The philosophy that has colored American legal thinking with regard to the consumer over the years has been the belief that since buyers and sellers bargain on equal terms, the person who goes out to make a purchase ought to take care of himself. This principle is contained in the common law and, as previously stated, means "let the buyer beware," or in Latin, *caveat emptor*. However, historically that principle has almost always favored the producer or the seller. The buyer or consumer, as has been repeatedly stated elsewhere in this book, knows little compared to the fund of knowledge at the disposal of the producer or seller.

Even in these times when the government is concerned with consumer protection and assistance to a degree never equaled in this country's history, the Uniform Sales Act and the Uniform Commercial Code, which are in effect in most states (the other states follow the common law), seem to support and affirm this age-old attitude. Undoubtedly the time-tested and widely heralded American virtues of rugged individualism, self reliance and independence of action formed the platform for the opinion that man should rely on his own judgment and protect his interests without interference from any source. In fact, this principle is the foundation of *laissez-faire*, which means to let people do as they choose; and it characterized America's economic system until the end of the nineteenth century.

In order to maintain full free competition, the change in attitude that has resulted in government participation in buyer-seller conduct has produced an atmosphere in which consumers may now obtain assistance and protection. Contracts commonly include express warranties which go a long way toward making up for the uncertainty of consumers regarding their participation in the marketplace.

◆In the event of a breach of warranty, the consumer can do one of three things:

1. He may cancel the contract and refuse to receive the goods, or if the merchandise has already been delivered, he can return it to the seller and demand the return of the purchase price.
2. He can keep the merchandise and sue the seller for damages.
3. He can claim a deduction from the original purchase price.

◆ If a buyer believes that he has just cause and can prove fraud, he may sue the seller and attempt to collect damages for breach of contract.

◆ When a buyer selects, orders and deposits money on the purchase of an article, the seller is obliged to deliver the article in accordance with the terms of the sales contract. The buyer, likewise, is obliged to accept the article and to pay the remaining portion of the purchase price. If the buyer refuses to accept the article or pay the remainder of the purchase price, the seller can take legal action against him.

◆ If a person receives merchandise which he has not ordered he is not obligated to pay for it and he is not obliged to return it. However, the merchandise should not be used.

◆ Specific statements of important facts made about merchandise such as ingredients, performance, tested strength, quality, etc., if proven untrue can become the basis for the buyer to break a contract. Such statements must be included in the contract, of course.

◆ The best course of action for every consumer-buyer is to be alert, informed and questioning in order to guarantee that he will receive the product he wants, that it will perform as desired and that all terms contained in the contract are clearly stated and fully understood. Moreover, the buyer must never rely upon the seller's interpretation of any portion of the contract that may seem unclear to him.

◆ Buyer and seller should stand ready to live up to the terms of the contract upon which they have reached agreement. A contract is only as good as the people who enter into it. Good faith is important on the part of both parties.

A contract is only as good as the people who enter into it.

In conclusion, a strong case should be made for avoiding legal difficulties and controversies in connection with business transactions because even if one has the law on his side the tremendous legal costs involved in the quest for justice may make legal remedies too expensive for most consumer-buyers. Moreover, the technicalities of the law make it difficult to prove just claims. The law imposes a severe burden of proof on consumers who bring suits in courts of law. It's not easy to claim breach of contract or fraud.

Protect yourself! Don't sign any contract before you read it, understand it and agree to every provision it contains. Understand what you're getting and get what you want.

CONSUMER UNDERSTANDING CHECK

1. Mr. B. bought a rug for $1,200 from Mr. C. which the latter had expressly warranted to be a genuine Oriental rug. Later Mr. B. discovered that the rug was a cheap imitation of an Oriental rug. What courses of action are open to Mr. B.?

2. What is the basic difference between an express warranty and an implied warranty? Give specific illustrations of each type as applied to the sale of a washing machine.

3. Why is it that most states have established consumer frauds and protection agencies under the State attorneys general?

4. John K. bought a radio at a local appliance store. On the way out of the store John asked the dealer whether the set would give good service because it seemed to him that the price was very low. The dealer stated that he guaranteed that the radio would function without need for service for a minimum of one year. Within three weeks the radio ceased to operate though it had not been misused in any way. John stated that this constituted breach of warranty. Discuss the validity of his claim.

5. Mary W. purchased a TV set by making a $50 down payment and signing a contract to pay the balance over the period of 12 months. After making the first two payments she discovered that the interest rate was illegally high. What recourse does Mary have?

6. A man you do not know approaches you and attempts to sell you a gold ring for what seems to be a really low price. What factors should you consider before making your decision?

7. At what point does title actually pass to the buyer when he purchases an automobile?

8. One day before the warranty on a new car expires a noise develops in the transmission. You immediately take the car for repair to the dealer from whom you purchased the car. He informs you that he cannot peform the service you require that day and that you should return the following week. Realizing that the warranty will expire the following day what can you do to protect yourself?

9. Robert T., a boy of seventeen years of age, purchased a second-hand car from a local dealer for $125. He paid $50 as a down payment but then found that he could not pay the balance due. Is Robert liable on this contract?

10. You attend a country auction and make a bid on an oil painting. Does your bid constitute a legally enforceable contract?

16. the case for consumer education

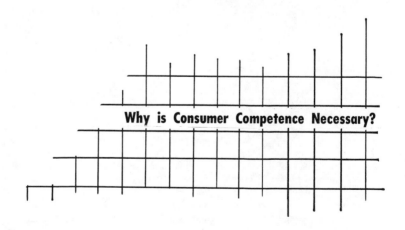

Why is Consumer Competence Necessary?

THE CASE FOR CONSUMER EDUCATION

WHY IS CONSUMER COMPETENCE NECESSARY?

By the very definition of the word, we are all consumers and as such, we comprise the largest group in the American economy. Over two-thirds of all money spent comes from consumers. And yet consumers are the only group on the economic scene that lack effective organization and whose feelings and wishes appear to fall on deaf ears.

Unfortunately, the development of economic citizenship has not received in our schools the emphasis that its importance merits. It was only some thirty years ago that educators in this country began to focus attention upon consumer education. Even at that, they were forced to do so because of economic conditions of the time. The Great Depression had created record unemployment. Since there were no jobs available, young people looked to the schools for guidance. There seemed to be no solution for the most serious problems with which they were being confronted. Schools, therefore, began to adapt their courses of study to meet the important problems of life itself. There was an almost spontaneous admission of the apparent deficiency that characterized the "traditional" nature of the curriculum—it was not in tune with the interests and needs of many of the young people in school at the time.

As with all systems or programs, the measure of success of an educational program is the degree to which it fully offers preparation for life. The proof of the pudding is in the eating. Education which fails to equip citizens with the knowledge required to live successfully in a society beset with problems more complex than those of any other era in history would be deficient and inadequate.

Consumer education must become an integral part of the training offered to all young people and adults alike. The time has come when all who are concerned with economic, social and educational improvements will have to provide meaningful, practical training so that consumers will be able to make informed decisions.

Consumers operate in a kind of vacuum because their choices in the marketplace are not based on rational information. The market is simply too complex for the average consumer—he is not trained to cope successfully with it. Ignorance of the marketplace is not confined to any one group in our society. It is a known fact that lawyers, teachers, doctors, dentists and engineers have been "taken" with monotonous regularity despite their high level of education. The education represented by these professions, it is sad to note, does not include training for the art of everyday economic living.

Education in our society seems to concentrate on two areas: (1) the so-called producer-type education which stresses the acquisition of skills that are needed for an individual who will eventually become a producer. From very basic and elementary skills this learning is developed by the student along lines that most appeal to him as he progresses. This in itself involves free choice; (2) cultural education which emphasizes the development of an appreciation of the various arts which tend to enrich our lives. Both of these areas are vital, one from the point of earning income and the other to reap the benefits of a life which takes full advantage of leisure time. But a third area is currently in a state of neglect. This is the area of education for preparation of the individual's life as a consumer. In effect, education is accomplishing only part of the job. We teach a person how to earn his livelihood, but we fall short of showing him how best to utilize his income when he goes to spend or save it.

Consumer education is vital not only for the individual but for the economy as a whole. If we are to enjoy an economy in which the consumer is king, he should have the capability of acting with intelligence so that he casts his economic vote for those producers who can best satisfy his wants and needs.

The individual is confronted with a basic economic problem of scarcity. Therefore, it is necessary for him to allocate his limited resources to achieve the maximum good. A society which develops intelligent consumption will necessarily achieve maximum efficiency of production. Producers must be responsive to consumers, and if consumers will buy only the best, producers will only produce the best. This would result in tremendous savings because of the redirection of producer activity. Wasteful production would be eliminated and producers would be able to concentrate on the production of those goods which would most benefit all sectors of the economy.

It should be made very clear that consumer education does not have as one of its purposes that of directing consumer choices. Purely and simply, it involves the exposure of all possible alternatives and opportunities for the consideration of the consumer. The individual consumer then assumes the responsibility for making a decision after having given full consideration to his particular needs and to the product that will best meet those needs. Consumer education tells the consumer what the possible alternatives are and how he can make an intelligent choice. Its responsibilities end there. The consumer who still acts impulsively but is fully conscious that he is doing so, becomes in reality a free agent. Consumer education will only be as good as the use to which it will be put.

Regardless of whether you call it economic citizenship or economic literacy, its basic relevance and importance remain the same—all citizens young or old require it in order to live effectively in our democratic American society. All of us have become keenly aware of the increased envy with which other nations of the world view Americans. Our high living standard which causes such envy is not a level that can afford to become a plateau—it must continue to grow. But continued growth will be possible only if our citizens receive the necessary economic education to enable them to make sound, mature decisions. Our economic life affects our social life and both have changed drastically within a short period of time. A few illustrations will serve to underscore the importance of this fact:

1. The consumer's skill as a buyer determines to a large extent the quality of living that an individual or family can anticipate. Whereas people made the things they needed years ago, today we buy most of the goods and services we use. Never before have people bought so large a portion of what is needed for their living. Consequently, never has good buymanship been so essential to successful living as it is these days.

2. The quantity and variety of goods and services offered for

sale have increased in phenomenal fashion. This in itself poses a great threat to the uninformed consumer. He becomes easily confused and unwittingly wastes his hard earned money by making the wrong decision. Consumer education is the only effective bulwark against incompetent spending of money.

3. The complexity of the problem of selecting from particular lines of goods or services places demands upon consumers that require increased knowledge. People must know much more not only about purchasing but also about proper use and maintenance of goods.

4. In America's free and competitive economic system the basic motivating force of producers is the aim to make a profit. The consumer, on the other hand, hopes to get the most for his money. While both aims seem to be at odds with one another, they somehow do manage to mesh and result in a workable economy—the American way of doing business. Within this favorable framework there still lurk several dangers for the uninformed consumer. Whether through carelessness or lack of sound judgment, when he does business with unethical dealers who make extravagant claims and enhance their own welfare through fraud and deceit, the ignorant consumer actually encourages such undesirable practices. Society becomes the gainer when consumers, through valid, effective programs of education build a solid defense against those who are prone to engage in shady practices. Within 50 years the United States weathered two major wars and a disastrous depression that lasted for more than a decade. Shortages of food, fuel and manufactured goods, rationing, restrictions of one type or another, unemployment, relief lines, the WPA, OPA, etc., had a profound effect upon all Americans. They were urged to avoid waste, not to patronize black marketeers, to battle inflation, to buy only what was absolutely necessary and to act as loyal patriots. In half a century so many consumer problems developed that the average man was left dizzy with confusion. He certainly needed consumer help.

After World War II consumers in this country were beset by a new wave of uncertainties. "When he speculated on the post-war world, the consumer thought not only in terms of world organization. He had lived through a period of failure in our economic system, so depression was one menace he wanted to banish. But he had seen the disasters in Europe growing out of authoritarian government, and he had been irritated by war-time governmental controls in his own land, so he was not altogether kindly disposed toward proposals to gain economic security by integrated national planning. The intellectual air was full of social-economic proposals and counter-proposals for America. Looming on the horizon was the major domestic issue: Can Americans, through the use of intelligence, distribute and consume the plenty they can produce? For when confronted with the traditional war-time choice between guns and butter, having matter-of-factly produced both, they knew beyond the shadow of a doubt that they could produce plenty. But would the level of effective demand permit production for peace to stay near the record production of war years? Or were we to experience again the ironic paradox of poverty in the midst of plenty?

"Perhaps the greatest of all the factors which led an increasing number of Americans toward a concern for consumer problems was a growing impatience with the gap between actual living conditions and what they believed to be pragmatically possible. If they had been living in an economy physically incapable of satisfying their wants, they might stoically have drawn in their belts and lived on a low standard without much complaint. But they believed that an 'economy of abundance' was possible; they meant to have it in their own lives; and they were impatient of delay.

"Corollary to the major issue were allied problems, enough of them to make the American restless as he thought of the days to come. The woods ahead were shadow-filled. Would the threat of inflation be followed by the reality of deflation? Would the savings of war-time years move rapidly enough into peace-time spending? Or, perhaps, *too* rapidly? Should we attain full employment—or unprecedented relief rolls? Would war-time consumption controls stay on or be released? Would the mammoth new physical plant be utilized for production of goods or permitted to rust away? Would surpluses and government plants go to strengthen monopoly, pass into the hands of small, competitive business, or remain the property of the state? Was the towering national debt a menace to national stability or a matter of no great concern if interest charges were steadily met? Should government control and regulation be extended, or minimized, in the interests of full employment and full consumption?"[20]

ARE THERE NEW GOALS FOR CONSUMER EDUCATION?

Let's first answer by saying, "No." Then we should qualify that answer by saying that the kind of program that we feel should be offered to consumers should be considered new. A meaningful, effective program of consumer education should emphasize not one major purpose, but many. It should not be a recitation of the do's and don't's of shopping, or for that matter be a watered down version of basic economics with a sprinkling here and there of a few catch phrases referring to consumer problems. No, consumer education is neither the one nor the other.

A sensible educational program designed for young people of junior and senior high school age or older people who may be attending evening or extension division courses on the secondary or college level, should focus upon providing opportunities for learning ways to get more and better satisfaction for the time, energy, and money that we all have at our disposal. Whether the program takes the form of a separate one-semester or full year course in consumer economics, or is integrated into such courses as home economics, the social studies, business education, science, mathematics, industrial arts and others the essential goal should be the same. Valid goals should include the following:

1. *Every consumer should be taught how to make intelligent choices.* We cannot afford to make too many mistakes. In the first place, we don't have an unlimited amount of time or money. We cannot possibly examine samples of all the merchan-

---

[20] *Consumer Education and the Social Studies,* The Consumer Education Study, Washington, D.C., 1945, pp. 2-3.

dise and services that exist. Therefore, we must learn how to plan effectively before we spend.

2. *Every consumer should develop the art of becoming a skilled buyer.* After choices have been made, one has to actually purchase the item or service he requires. That is when know-how in the marketplace enters into the picture. The consumer education program should deal in thoroughly realistic fashion with such problems as: where to buy, how to analyze advertising material, how to evaluate merchandise and how to avoid being fleeced.

3. *Every consumer should learn the importance of being an efficient user of goods and services.* Choosing and buying wisely are of scant value if, as consumers, we do not show intelligence and concern for the way in which we use and care for goods and services. Greater satisfaction will result from the proper use and maintenance of what we buy.

4. *Every consumer should learn how to manage his personal financial affairs.* Who can do without useful training for living in businesslike fashion? Every person should learn to appreciate the value of making and keeping within a budget, to save with a specific purpose in mind and to put surplus funds to work so that they will grow and be safe at the same time. Moreover, everyone should become thoroughly familiar with the purposes and forms of insurance, the kinds of investment possibilities that are available and how to select from among them according to individual circumstances.

5. *Every consumer should be conscious of his wider social and economic responsibilities.* Like every area of the curriculum designed to make students conscious of their responsibilities as citizens in our democracy, consumer education has an important role to play in this area.

Consumer education does not have an axe to grind, though there are those who believe otherwise. While it is true that any program in this area will naturally favor the consumer, it does not follow that such education is opposed to or attempts to downgrade business, labor, agriculture or government. Every segment of society has organized groups with vested interests. Consumers can point to no major organized group with sufficient strength to effectively espouse their cause. In fact, there is no common cause or movement that reflects the concern and interests of all consumers. Consumers are society's largest group, yet their role as consumers still plays second fiddle to the individual's primary role as a producer. And it's the latter which becomes the nucleus of social concern. Do you know why? The prevalent feeling is that it is easy to spend money. The difficult task is to earn and save it. Not enough of us realize that production and consumption are complementary. More efficient consumption will reap added benefits from the producer's income just as effectively as an increase in wages or salary. Likewise, an increase in production leads to increased potential for consumption. Basically, the realization of this fact leads to changes in attitude and behavior in one's role as a consumer.

Consumer education should not be treated as a "how to" subject. The consumer should develop an appreciation for the interests and needs of all elements of society and should shoulder equal responsibility along with them for increasing the level of living. The building of new attitudes on the part of the consumer requires that he develop an awareness of the economic and moral truism that one does not get anything for nothing. But at the same time he must not permit himself to be deluded into thinking that every item or service has value consistent with the price tag.

A positive approach to useful consumer training is to emphasize the importance of developing a thoroughly practical consumer viewpoint—he should strive to obtain maximum value at the minimum cost in a framework that is consistent with the understanding that (1) every seller must have a margin of profit, and (2) value and cost cannot be opposing forces. In other words, the consumer must be certain that he receives value consistent with the money he spends.

All of us must learn that what we do when we act as consumers not only has importance for us but for others as well. We must not just expect to take. We have to do our share to promote the general welfare of the nation. We cannot vote intelligently unless we understand the social and economic issues at stake. Almost every political question is related to economics in one way or another. We must delve into such problems as taxes, advertising, labeling, credit, prices, cooperatives, social legislation and housing. And we must understand how the government attempts to assist consumers since these topics are of great social importance.

IS THERE SUPPORT FOR CONSUMER EDUCATION?

Because consumer education is a term of fairly recent origin, it has not been thoroughly understood by all segments of the business world or for that matter, by the general public. Frankly speaking, the very fact that the nature of consumer education demands that an honest, unbiased picture of all phases of existing business practices be unfolded, there has been some opposition from influential community and organized business pressure groups. Objection to the inclusion of consumer education in the curricula of our nation's schools has been slight compared with the warm and enthusiastic support demonstrated by educators, economists and the vast majority of substantial businessmen of the nation. Business men who are engaged in legitimate enterprises and who deal with the consumer in honest fashion are more than anxious to see consumer education spread and grow. They know that intelligent consumers make for more satisfactory buyer-seller relationships. There will be less likelihood of friction and misunderstanding. For every criticism of consumer education that makes its way into print, at least four to five laudatory retorts will follow in rapid succession. The advocates are becoming vocal and no longer reluctant to remain on the side lines. Whenever an explosive attack is made in one sector of the country there rallies to its defense an enthused army of supporters who see the value of this kind of education in the development of social responsibility and economic citizenship.

Consumer education in no way aims to discredit business; it applauds the healthy recent trend whereby consumers and businessmen have gotten together to work toward the elimination of unsavory practices that had been vexing both camps.

A wise old man once defined education as "what a man remembers after he has forgotten what he's learned." If there is merit in that definition (and there certainly appears to be plenty), then consumer education deserves an A+ rating as top-flight education. Such knowledge has present value and future application as well. It's like learning to swim. You never forget how to cut through the water once you've mastered the fundamentals.

GLOSSARY OF IMPORTANT TERMS

A

Add-on: A method of computing interest charges whereby the interest is added to the amount and payments including interest, are made on the larger amount (on a $100 loan at 6%, you repay $106 having received $100).

Administered Price: A price which is set outside the competitive market.

Amortization: Payment reduction of the principal, or the amount of a mortgage through regular payments.

Annuity: A form of insurance whereby the individual pays a larger sum of money over a relatively short period of time in order to receive periodic payments at a future date. (Ex. at 50 years of age). Often used as retirement income.

Assess: To estimate the value of goods or property for purposes of placing a tax on them.

Assets: Items that are owned.

Automation: The process whereby human labor is eliminated or reduced and replaced by machines in order to increase production and decrease costs.

B

Beneficiary: The person to whom an insurance policy is payable.

Blue Chip Stocks: Securities of the soundest corporations.

Boiler Room: The name given to fraudulent promotions of stocks and bonds which most often have little or no value.

Budget: A statement of expected income and a plan for expenditures over a period of time.

Business Cycle: A period of time during which the level of economic activity fluctuates—normally divided into 4 phases: prosperity, recession, depression, recovery.

C

Capital Growth: Increase in the value of money invested.

Cash Value (cash surrender value): The value of the insurance policy at maturity or commodity at market price.

Charge Account: A special arrangement between a buyer and a seller which permits the buyer to receive goods without making full payment. Payment is made at a later date.

Choice: The selection of one commodity means that you have rejected one or more alternatives.

Co-insurance: Situation in which the insured and the insurer share the risk—normally associated with fire insurance.

Commodity: A tangible good that is bought and sold.

Common Stock: A share of ownership in a corporation that generally gives the holder the right to a voice in the company's management. However, the holder is not entitled to the preferential treatment that holders of bonds and preferred stock receive.

Condominium: A form of cooperative housing in which the people involved have individual mortgages rather than one large mortgage. Thus, the responsibility of each is limited.

Conspicuous Consumption: The purchase and use of goods and services to impress others rather than to meet the direct needs of the buyer (keeping up with the Joneses).

Consumer: anyone that uses goods and/or services.

Consumer Co-operatives: Associations of purchasers of consumer goods who organize a distributing organization and share the profits on the basis of the total value of what is bought. Elimination of the middleman decreases costs.

Consumer Credit: Financing used by persons to buy consumer goods that are not paid for at the time of purchase.

Consumer-Directed: The producer is completely responsive to the wishes of consumers.

Consumer Finance Company (also known as a small loan company) A lending institution which normally charges a high rate of interest because it assumes large risks and lends out only small amounts of money.

Consumer Price Index: An index showing fluctuations in the cost of living published by the Bureau of Labor Statistics.

Constant Dollars: The value of the dollar has been adjusted to eliminate the inroads of inflation or deflation as related to a base year (in order to demonstrate changes in purchasing power over the years).

Consumption-Directed: The consumer has little voice in determining what is to be produced. Producers make available what they would like to sell.

Cost of Living: The amount of money a person must have to buy all the goods and services that he requires in order to maintain a certain level of living.

Credit: A promise to pay at a future date in exchange for immediate receipt of goods or money.

Credit Card: A system whereby the individual holding the card receives 30 day credit—usually associated with hotels, restaurants, gas stations, etc.

D

Debt: The liability or obligation to repay.

Defensive Stocks: Securties of companies whose business varies little regardless of changes in the nation's business conditions.

Demand: The quantity of goods that consumers are willing to buy.

Discount: (a) A portion of the selling price that is deducted. (b) Interest is deducted first and you are charged the face amount of the loan. (Ex.—on a $100 loan at 6% you receive $94 but pay interest on $100).

Discretionary Income: Income which remains after all necessities and obligations have been paid for.

Disposable Income: The total amount received by consumers, less the total amount of their income and social security taxes (take-home pay).

Distribution: The physical procedure of moving goods from production areas to consumers.

Diversification: Generally used in relation to investments. It means varying or spreading the funds to be invested among a number of investments.

Dividends: Financial returns received by stockholders on their investments. Stockholders are owners and share in the profits of the corporation.

Down Payment: The amount of money paid to the seller at the time of purchase. It is only a portion of the total purchase since the balance is paid in subsequent installments.

Durable Consumers' Goods: Consumers' goods that may be used time and again over a long period of time. A refrigerator is an example.

E

Economic System: The method by which a country provides its needs and wants—provides for production and consumption of goods and services.

Economic Vote: When an item is purchased in the market, it, and the producer, receive a vote of approval.

Economy: The entire process of production, distribution and consumption.

Endowment Policy: An insurance policy on which the insured party pays a stated premium for a set number of years. After that time he receives the amount of the policy.

Equity: The amount of net ownership of property. In other words, it is the amount that a property is worth beyond what is owed on it.

Expertise: Expert appraisal of a situation (French). Used in English to mean expertness of a very high degree.

F

Face Value: The amount written into a credit instrument.

Fixed Income: Return from invested funds which does not change.

Free Enterprise: A form of economic system in which productive capital (wealth) is privately owned. The motivation is profit.

G

Goods: Material objects that are desired by consumers. (Ex.—T.V., Refrigerator)

Gross Income: The salary or wage for which a person is hired.

Gross National Product: The total dollar value at market price, of all the goods and services produced in the nation in one year.

I

Impulse Shopper: A consumer who buys irrationally without consideration for need or alternatives.

Inflation: An excessive amount of money and/or credit in circulation with a corresponding decrease in the supply of goods and services. This results in increased prices and decreased purchasing power (too many dollars chasing too few goods).

Insurance: The pooling or shifting of probabe loss among a group. Spreading of risk—larger the group, smaller the cost.

Installment Buying: Acquiring goods or services first and then paying for them at regular intervals later.

Installment Credit: The unpaid balance of purchases made under a plan of installment buying.

Interest: Payment received by lender and charge paid by borrower for the use of credit.

Intermediate-term Credit: Credit which extends for a period of from one to five years.

Intrinsic Value: The price established on the commercial value for the material of which an item is made; for example, the market price of the gold in a gold coin.

Investment Trust: A financial corporation that sells shares of the trust and then invests the funds it obtains in the stocks and bonds of other companies.

L

Landlord: A person who owns buildings or land that he rents to others.

Lease: A contract, usually in written form, giving the right to use property for a stated length of time under specified conditions, usually by paying rent.

Limited Payment: Payments are made on a life insurance policy for a specified period of time (20, 30 years), after which time the policy is completely paid for and remains in force.

Loan: Money that is given to an individual contingent on his promise to re-pay, usually with interest.

Loan Shark: A person who lends money at a very high, illegal rate of interest.

Long-term Credit: Credit that will remain outstanding for a period of five years or longer.

Luxuries: Commodities which are not needed to maintain life (other than food, clothing, shelter).

M

Major Medical: A form of health insurance to protect against large expenses resulting from hospital and medical costs over and above the prescribed amount.

Marketing: The process by which producers make their products available to consumers.

Marketplace: Any place where producers and consumers meet to exchange goods and services.

Mass Production: Production of large quantities of standardized goods by the assembly-line method. The workers perform specialized tasks.

Money: Is the medium of exchange—the individual receives it as income for his labor and in turn uses it to buy in the marketplace.

Mortgage: A credit arrangement whereby the individual obtains conditional possession of a piece of property.

Mutual Funds (investment trusts): Organizations that invest funds of their members in a number of corporations. By investing in these funds, the small saver and investor can benefit from the diversified investments and the experience of the experts who manage the funds.

Mutual Savings Bank: Savings banks whose depositors are the actual shareholders. These banks offer all banking services with the exception of checking accounts.

N

Needs: Items necessary for every-day life.

Nondurable Consumers' Goods: Consumers' goods that are quickly used up. Food would be an example.

O

Obsolence: The quality of passing out of use or tending to become outdated.

O P A (Office of Price Administration): Congress established the O P A in April, 1941 for the purpose of controlling prices by means of rationing and price ceilings.

Opportunity Cost (alternative cost): The purchase of one product involves the cost of that product plus the cost of an alternative which was not purchased. This is justified in that you are denying yourself the use of the alternative in favor of the purchased product.

P

Per Capita: For each person.

Perfect Competition: A situation in which no one individual or group of individuals exercises a controlling influence over market price, supply, or demand.

Preferred Stock: Stock that entitles the holder to a fixed rate dividend which is apportioned before common stockholders receive their dividend.

Premium: The amount of money paid for insurance protection.

Private Enterprise: Individuals and companies engage in economic activities for the purpose of profit and at the same time must contend with the possible risk of loss.

Producer: Anyone or an organization that provides goods and/or services for consumers.

Profit: Financial return for investment and risk of economic activity.

Progressive Tax: A tax that grows proportionately greater as the base increases. For exampe, the income tax—the higher the income, the higher the tax.

Policy: A written insurance contract.

Prospectus: Information given about a corporation in order to attract potential investors.

Purchasing Power: The amount of goods and/or services that can be obtained by the individual with his disposable income.

R

Real Estate: Land, including buildings and other improvements.

Real Income: The amount of goods and/or services that can be purchased —the effective purchasing power.

Recession: That period of the business cycle between prosperity and depression when business activity slows down.

Redemption Value: The value of a bond or security when it is delivered by the owner for payment .

Regressive Tax: A tax that grows proportionally less as the ability to pay

taxes increases. Example, a 2c tax on a tube of toothpaste.

Re-Possession: The lender or his agent takes the good which has been obtained through the use of credit because the individual has not been able to make payments.

Revolving Charge Account: A form of credit offered by department stores whereby the customer is granted a specific amount of credit. As repayment is made, the difference between the maximum and the balance is available to the shopper in the form of additional credit. Usually a charge of 1½% per month (18% per year) is made on the outstanding balance.

Risk: The chance of or potential for loss.

S

Salary: Fixed pay for regular work.

Security: (a) A contract which can be easily bought and sold. It gives its owner the right to income or control over some kind of property, such as a bond or stock. (b) Physical property put up by a borrower to assure the lender that he will be repaid.

Services: Results of labor that do not produce material items. (Ex.—barber, airline pilot)

Short-term Credit: Credit which must be repaid in less than a year.

Simple Interest: Interest which is charged on the unpaid balance of a loan (i.e., interest on a mortgage).

Social Insurance: A program administered by the government and financed by employer and employees to protect workers' income and health.

Solvent: Able to pay all that a person or a group owes. The amount (things) owned outweigh the things or amount owed.

Speculative Stocks: Securities whose prices fluctuate sharply depending upon a variety of factors.

Straight-life Insurance (also known as ordinary or whole-life): Insurance on which premiums are paid over an entire lifetime. The premiums are not determined by age.

Standard of Living: The way we live. Also used to express our hopes for a future way of life.

Supply: The quantity of goods that producers are willing to offer for sale.

Supply and Demand: The interaction of the amount of goods producers are willing to offer for sale at different prices, and the amount of goods consumers are willing to buy at different prices, results in an equilibrium at a **market price.**

T

Tenant: A person who pays rent for the temporary use of the land or the building that belongs to another person.

Term Life Insurance: Insurance protection for a limited number of years —no savings or cash surrender value.

Trademark: The mark, picture, name or letters owned and used by a manufacturer or seller to distinguish his products from others.

True Interest: The actual rate of interest paid by an individual when using credit. A good rule of thumb is to double the stated rate of interest.

U

Underwrite: To assume risk of loss in return for premium payments.

Unsecured Loan: A loan based solely upon a person's capacity or ability to pay.

W

Wages: Specific rates of pay for work of any kind, usually production work.

Wants: Items which we would like to have—i.e.—luxury items.

Wealth: Material economic goods that are subject to ownership.

W P A (Works Progress Administration): Set up in 1935, the federal government made it possible for unemployed persons to be put to work in a wide variety of useful projects—an anti-depression measure.

SELECTED BIBLIOGRAPHY

Ackerman, L. J. and Ivry, D. A.
Fundamentals of the Federal Old-Age, Survivors, and Disability Insurance System. American College of Life Underwriters. c1962.

Adams, E. Sherman.
You, Money, and Prosperity. Banking Education Committee. The American Bankers Association. c1964.

AFL-CIO Department of Publications:
Consumer, Beware! AFL-CIO Department of Publications. c1962.

American Association of University Women.
Money Management Portfolio. American Association of University Women. c1960.

American Home Economics Association.
Working with Low Income Families. c1965.

American Security and Trust Company.
Your Bank and How it Can Serve You. American Security and Trust Company.

Angell, F.
Health Insurance. Ronald. c1963.

Bagdikian, Ben H.
In the Midst of Plenty—The Poor in America. Beacon Press. c1964.

Banking Education Committee.
Banking from the Stone Age to the Atomic Age. American Bankers Association. c1962.

Banking Education Committee.
Personal Money Management. American Bankers Association. c1962.

Banking Education Committee.
Using Bank Services. The American Bankers Association. c1961.

Banking Education Committee.
Using Bank Services. The American Bankers Association.

Barach, A. B.
Kiplinger's Family Buying Guide. Prentice-Hall Inc. c1959.

Better Business Bureau of Metropolitan Boston.
Accident and Health Insurance. Better Business Bureau of Metropolitan Boston. c1962.

Better Business Bureau of Metropolitan Boston.
Borrowing. Better Business Bureau of Metropolitan Boston c1957.

Better Business Bureau of Metropolitan Boston.
Buying New or Used Cars. Better Business Bureau of Metropolitan Boston. c1956.

Better Business Bureau of Metropolitan Boston.
Buying or Building a Home. Better Business Bureau of Metropolitan Boston. c1956.

Better Business Bureau of Metropolitan Boston.
Fact Booklets Series. Better Business Bureau of Metropolitan Boston.

Better Business Bureau of Metropolitan Boston, Inc.
Facts You Should Know About Your Credit. Better Business Bureau of Metropolitan Boston, Inc. c1962.

Better Business Bureau of Metropolitan Boston.
Life Insurance. Better Business Bureau of Metropolitan Boston. c1959.

Better Business Bureau of Metropolitan Boston.
Savings. Better Business Bureau of Metropolitan Boston. c1957.

Better Business Bureau of Metropolitan Boston.
Securities. Better Business Bureau of Metropolitan Boston. c1958.

Black, Hillel.
Buy now, pay later. William Morrow and Company, c1961.

Boston Better Business Bureau.
Facts You Should Know About. (Series includes: Accident and Health Insurance; Savings; Rugs and Carpeting; Securities and Commodity Exchanges; Earn Money at Home Schemes; Home Appliances; Buying or Building a Home; etc.). Boston Better Business Bureau.

Bridewell, D. A.
Credit Unions. Bender. c1962.

Britt, Stewart Henderson—Editor.
Consumer Behavior and the Behavioral Sciences: Theories and Appli-

cation. John Wiley and Sons, Inc. c1966.

Britt, S. H.
The Spenders. McGraw-Hill and Company. c1960.

Bureau of Labor Statistics.
Estimating Equivalent Incomes or Budget Costs by Family Type. U. S. Department of Labor. c1960.

Burg, Robert.
The Buyers Guide to Nearly Everything. McFadden-Hartell Corporation. c1965.

Campbell, M.
Cash and Credit. Vantage Press. c1965.

Campbell, Persia C.
The Consumer Interest: A Study of Consumer Economics. Harper and Brothers. c1949.

Caplovitz, David.
The Poor Pay More; Consumer Practices of Low-Income Families. Free Press of Glencoe. c1963.

Changing Times.
Kiplinger's Family Buying Guide. Prentice-Hall Inc. c1959.

Changing Times.
All About Credit. Changing Times Reprint Service. c1963.

Changing Times.
Your Health, Your Doctor, and Your Pocketbook. Changing Times Reprint Service. c1961.

Changing Times.
Your Personal Money Plan and Family Finance Diary. Changing Times Reprint Service. c1959.

Channing L. Bete Co.
About Health Insurance. Channing L. Bete Co. c1962.

Channing L. Bete Co.
Consumer Credit and You. Channing L. Bete Co. c1962.

Channing L. Bete Co.
Going to Buy a Car? Channing L. Bete Co. c1962.

Channing L. Bete Co.
Savings and Loan Way to Save Money. Channing L. Bete Co. c1958.

Channing L. Bete Co.
Scriptographic Booklets. Channing L. Bete Co.

Channing L. Bete Co.
The ABC's of Home Furnishing. Channing L. Bete Co. c1961.

Channing L. Bete Co.
You and Your Money. Channing L. Bete Co. c1961.

Channing L. Bete Co.
Your Best Years. Channing L. Bete Co. c1962.

Cheyney, William J.
Using Our Credit Intelligently. National Foundation for Consumer Credit. c1963.

Clark, Lincoln H.
Consumer Behavior. Harper and Brothers. c1958.

Cohen and Hanson.
Personal Finance, Principles and Case Problems. (Revised Edition) Richard D. Irwin, Inc. c1964.

Cohen, Jerome B.
Personal and Money Management. The American Bankers Association. Savings Division. c1962.

Coles, Jessie V.
Consumers Look at Labels. Council on Consumer Information. c1964.

Committee for Economic Development.
Committee for Economic Development (CED) Publications: List and Order Form. CED Distribution Division. c1965.

Committee for Economic Development.
Economic Education in the Schools. Committee for Economic Development. c1961.

Consumer Education Division.
Hidden Values. Consumer Education Division. Sears, Roebuck and Company.

Consumers Union.
1966 Buying Guide Issue of *Consumer Reports*. Consumers Union of United States, Inc. c1965.

Consumer Education Study.
Consumer Education Series. National Association of Secondary Schools Principals.

Consumers' Research, Inc.
Consumers Bulletin. Consumers' Research, Inc.

Council on Consumer Information.
A Guide for Family Financial Counseling. Council on Consumer Information. c1962.

Council on Consumer Information.
Bringing the Consumer Point of View

into Government. Council on Consumer Information. c1958.

Council on Consumer Information.
Consumer Look at Burial Practices. Council on Consumer Information. c1956.

Council on Consumer Information.
Consumers Look at Discount Houses. Council on Consumer Information. c1963.

Council on Consumer Information.
Consumer Look at "Fair Trade." Council on Consumer Information. c1955.

Council on Consumer Information.
Consumers Look at Federal Protective Services. Council on Consumer Information. c1959.

Council on Consumer Information.
How to Choose Your Doctor, Hospital, Health Insurance. Council on Consumer Information. c1961.

Council on Consumer Information.
The Consumer Looks at Deceptive Packaging. Council on Consumer Information. c1961.

Cox, Reavis.
Consumers' Credit and Wealth; A Study in Consumer Credit. National Foundation for Consumer Credit. c1965.

Crabbe, Ernest H., Enterline, Herman G., and DeBrum, S. Joseph.
General Business for Economic Understanding. South-Western Publishing Company. c1961.

Crabtree, A. P.
You and the Law. Holt, Rinehart, and Winston. c1964.

Credit Union National Association.
Credit Union Yearbook. Credit Union National Association.

Credit Union National Association.
What are Credit Unions and How Can We Use Them? Credit Union National Association.

Cross, Arlene.
Tips for Teaching Life and Health Insurance. Educational Division, Institute of Life Insurance. c1962.

Crown, Paul.
Legal Protection for the Consumer. Oceana Publications. c1963.

Cruikshank, Nelson H.
The Consumer's Stake in Medical Care. Reprint Series Number 28. Sidney Hillman Foundation. c1965.

Dichter, Ernest.
Handbook of Consumer Motivations. McGraw-Hill. c1964.

Dodd, James Harvey, Kennedy, John W., and Olsen, Arthur R.
Applied Economics; Introductory Principles applied to Everyday Problems. South-Western Publishing Company. c1962.

Dolphin, Robert J.
An Analysis of Economic and Personal Factors Leading to *Consumer Bankruptcy*. Michigan State University. c1965.

Donaldson and Pfahl.
Personal Finance. (Third Edition). Ronald Press. c1961.

E. I. DuPont de Nemours and Company.
The Story of Competition in the American Market. E. I. DuPont de Nemours and Company. c1959.

E. I. DuPont de Nemours and Company.
The Story of Prices. E. I. DuPont de Nemours and Company. c1960.

East, Dr. Marjorie.
Consumer Education for Family Life. National Education Association. Department of Home Economics. c1962.

Educational Affairs Department.
1965 Business: Trends and Progress. Ford Motor Co. c1965.

Educational Services Division.
Selected and Annotated Bibliography of Reference Material in Consumer Finance. National Consumer Finance Association. c1961-62.

Educational Services Division.
Teacher's Kit—A One Week Teaching Unit on Consumer Finance. National Consumer Finance Association, c1962.

Engel, Louis.
How to Buy Stocks; A guide to Making More Money in the Market. Bantam Books. c1962.

Farnsworth, C. H.
No Money Down. McFadden. c1963.

Faulkner, E. J.
Health Insurance. McGraw-Hill, c1960.

Federal Housing Administration.
Estimating Ability to Pay for a Home.

Director of Public Information. Federal Housing Administration. c1962.

Federal Reserve Bank of New York.
Money: Master or Servant. Federal Reserve Bank of New York. c1955.

Federal Reserve Bank of New York.
The Story of Checks. Federal Reserve Bank of New York. c1958.

Feinberg, Daniel.
Consumer economics. Holt, Rinehart and Winston, Inc., c1964.

Fisk, McKee, and Snapp, James C.
Applied Business Law; Business Law Applied to the Problems of the Individual as Citizen, Consumer, and Employee. South-Western Publishing Company. c1960.

Fitzsimmons, Cleo.
Consumer Buying for Better Living. Wiley. c1961.

Follman, J. F.
Medical Care and Health Insurance. Irwin. c1963.

Francis I. duPont and Company.
10 Common Mistakes in Investing—10 Common Sense Rules for Successful Investing. Francis I. DuPont and Company. c1965.

Galbraith, J. K.
The Affluent Society. Houghton, Mifflin Co. c1958.

Gale, Ella.
Dollars and Sense. Fleet Publishing Company. n.d.

Geier, A.
Life Insurance; How to Get Your Money's Worth. Collier. c1965.

Good Housekeeping Bulletin Service.
Good Housekeeping's Guide to Life Insurance. Good Housekeeping Bulletin Service. c1962.

Goodman, Kennard E. and Harriss, C. Lowell
Economics. Ginn and Co. c1963.

Gordon, Leland J.
Economics for Consumers. American Book Co. Fourth Edition. c1961.

Grocery Manufacturers of America, Inc.
The Label Tells the Story. Grocery Manufacturers of America, Inc. c1964.

Hamilton, David.
The Consumer in our Economy. Houghton, Mifflin Co. c1962.

Harrington, Michael.
The Other America.

Hathaway, Barbar H.
Your Life Insurance. Doubleday and Co. n.d.

Health Insurance Institute.
ABC's of Health Insurance. Health Insurance Institute. c1962.

Health Insurance Institute.
Source Book of Health Insurance Data, 1965. Health Insurance Institute. c1965.

Holbrook, S. H.
The Golden Age of Quackery. Macmillan Co. n.d.

Household Finance Corp.
Children's Spending. Household Finance Corp. c1961.

Household Finance Corporation.
Money Management. Edited by Sally Ralph Campbell. Money Management Institute of Household Finance Corporation. c1963. (Series includes: Your budget; Children's spending; For young moderns; Your food dollar; Your clothing dollar; Your shelter dollar; Your home furnishing dollar; Your shopping dollar; Your equipment dollar; Your automobile dollar; Your health and recreation dollar; and Your savings and investment dollar.)

Household Finance Corp.
Your Health and Recreation Dollar. Household Finance Corp. c1961.

Household Finance Corporation.
Your Savings and Investment Dollar. Household Finance Corporation. c1963.

Money Management Institute of Household Finance Corp.
H. F. C.'s Money Management Program. Money Management Institute of Household Finance Corp. c1965.

Industrial Union Department.
It's What's Inside that Counts. AFL-CIO.

Institute of Life Insurance.
A List of Worthwhile Life Insurance Books. Institute of Life Insurance.

Institute of Life Insurance.
Catalog of Teaching Aids. Institute of Life Insurance. c1962.

Institute of Life Insurance.
Decade of Decision. Institute of Life Insurance. c1961.

Institute of Life Insurance.
Dollars and Sense for Young Couples. Institute of Life Insurance. c1962.

Institute of Life Insurance.
Family Finance Topics for Teachers.
Institute of Life Insurance (with the
cooperation of the Health Insurance Institute).

Institute of Life Insurance.
Family Needs for Life Insurance.
Institute of Life Insurance. c1960.

Institute of Life Insurance.
Four Basic Life Insurance Policies.
Institute of Life Insurance. c1960.

Institute of Life Insurance.
Life Insurance Fact book, 1965. Institute of Life Insurance. c1965.

Institute of Life Insurance.
Sharing the Risk. Institute of Life
Insurance. c1960.

Institute of Life Insurance.
The Family Money Manager. Institute of Life Insurance.

Institute of Life Insurance.
The Search for Economic Security;
America's Evolving Pattern of Family
Security form Colonial Times to the
Present. Institute of Life Insurance.
c1965.

Institute of Life Insurance.
Tips for Teaching Life and Health
Insurance. Institute of Life Insurance.
c1962.

Insurance Information Institute.
A Family Guide to Property and Lia-
bility Insurance. Insurance Information
Institute. c1962.

Insurance Information Institute.
Automobile Insurance. Insurance Information Institute. c1961.

Insurance Information Institute.
Basic Insurance Books — Casualty,
Fire, Marine, Surety. Insurance Infor-
mation Institute.

**International Consumer Credit
Association.**
How to Use Consumer Credit Wisely.
International Consumer Credit Asso-
ciation. c1962.

**Katona, George, Lininger, Charles
A., and Mueller, Eva.**
1964 Survey of Consumer Finances.
Monograph No. 39 Survey Research
Center, Institute for Social Research,
The University of Michigan. c1965.

Katona, George.
The Mass Consumption Society. Mc-
Graw-Hill. c1964.

Katona, George.
The Powerful Consumer. McGraw-
Hill. c1960.

**Kelsey, R. Wilfred and Daniels,
Arthur C.**
Handbook of Life Insurance. Insti-
tute of Life Insurance. c1961.

Kiplinger Washington Editors.
Changing Times Classroom Program.
Kiplinger Magazine School Services.

Kiplinger Washington Editors.
Family Success Book. Changing
Times.

Kiplinger Washington Editors.
Murder of the Highways—Who Cares?
Reprint Services.

Kiplinger Washington Editors.
What Other People Spend. Reprint
Services. c1959.

Kling, Samuel.
Guide to Everyday Law. Follett.
c1965.

Lasagna, L.
Doctors Dilemmas. Harper. c1962.

Lasser, Jacob K. and Porter, Sylvia.
Managing Your Money. Henry Holt.
c1961.

Lasser, J. K.
Your Social Security—Medicare Guide.
Simon and Schuster. c1965.

Leavitt, G. L. and Hanson, Carl O.
Personal Finance. McGraw Hill Co.
c1950.

Lee, Baldwin, Editor.
American Capitalism. Council for
Advancement of Secondary Education.
c1958.

Lee, Baldwin.
Capitalism and Other Economic Sys-
tems. Council for the Advancement of
Economic Education.

Liblit, J.
Housing — The Cooperative Way.
Twayne Publishers. c1964.

**Lindholm, Richard W., and
Driscoll, Paul.**
Our American Economy. Harcourt,
Brace and World, Inc. c1962.

Margolius, Sidney.
The Consumer's Guide for Better
Buying. Pocket Books, Inc. c1963.

Margolius, Sidney.
How to Finance Your Home. (Public
Affairs Pamphlet No. 360.) Public Af-
fairs Committee. c1964.

Masteller, Kenneth C.
How to Avoid Financial Tangles. (In *Economic Education Bulletin*, vol. V, no. 1, February 1965.)

Masters, Dexter.
The Intelligent Buyer's Guide to Sellers. Consumers Union of the United States. c1966.

Mayer, Martin.
Madison Avenue, U.S.A. Harper and Brothers. c1958.

McCracken, Paul W.
Consumer Installment Credit and Public Policy. Bureau of Business Research, University of Michigan. c1965.

McEwen, Robert J., Editor.
New Frontiers in Consumer Economics; Selections from the 11th Annual Conference of the Council on Consumer Information, Berkeley, California, April, 1965. Council on Consumer Information. c1966.

McNeal, James V.
Dimension of Consumer Behavior. Appleton-Century Crofts. c1965.

Merrill, Lynch, Pierce, Fenner, and Smith, Inc.
About this Stock and Bond Business. Merrill, Lynch, Pierce, Fenner, and Smith, Inc.

Merrill, Lynch, Pierce, Fenner, and Smith.
How to Invest in Stocks and Bonds. Merrill, Lynch, Pierce, Fenner, and Smith. c1962.

Merrill, Lynch, Pierce, Fenner, and Smith.
How to Read a Financial Report. Merrill, Lynch, Pierce, Fenner, and Smith. c1962.

Merrill, Lynch, Pierce, Fenner, and Smith, Inc.
Questions and Answers About the Stock Market. Merrill, Lynch, Pierce, Fenner, and Smith, Inc. c1962.

Merrill, Lynch, Pierce, Fenner, and Smith, Inc.
What Everybody Ought to Know About this Stock and Bond Business. Merrill, Lynch, Pierce, Fenner, and Smith, Inc. c1963.

Milton, A.
How to Get a Dollar's Value for a Dollar Spent. Citadel. c1964.

Mintz, Morton.
The Therapeutic Nightmare. Hough-

ton, Mifflin. c1965.

Morse, Richard L. D. and Umberger, Marguerite H.
Student Financial Management Records. Kansas State University. Department of Family Economics. c1961.

Morse, Richard L. D.
What Are You Worth? A Guide for Family Money Management. Kansas State University. Department of Family Economics. c1957.

Myers, Samuel L.
Oeconomia; A Family Life Series. (Series includes: Housing, c1964; Foods, c1962; Clothing, c1963.) Baltimore Urban League.

National Association of Secondary Principals.
Consumer and the Law. National Association of Secondary School Principals. c1958.

National Association of Secondary-School Principals. The Consumer Education Study.
Consumer Education and Home Economics in the Secondary Schools, by a Committee of the American Home Economics of the National Education Association. National Association for Secondary-School Principals. c1945.

National Association of Secondary-School Principals. The Consumer Education Study.
Buying Insurance. National Association of Secondary-School Principals. c1946.

National Association of Secondary-School Principals. The Consumer Education Study.
The Consumer and the Law, by S. George Getz. National Association of Secondary-School Principals. c1958.

National Association of Secondary-School Principals. The Consumer Education Study.
Investing in Yourself, by Ruth Strang. National Association of Secondary-School Principals. c1945.

National Association of Secondary-School Principals. The Consumer Education Study.
Learning to Use Advertising; A Problem of the Modern American Consumer. National Association of Secondary-School Principals. c1960.

National Association of Secondary-School Principals. The Consumer Education Study.
Managing Your Money. National Association of Secondary-School Principals. c1947.

National Association of Secondary-School Principals. The Consumer Education Study.
The Modern American Consumer; His Problems and His Opportunities. National Association of Secondary-School Principals. c1945.

National Association of Secondary-School Principals. The Consumer Education Study.
The Place of Science in the Education of the Consumer, by The National Science Teachers Association. National Association of Secondary-School Principals. c1945.

National Association of Secondary-School Principals. The Consumer Education Study.
The Relation of Business Education to Consumer Education, by the National Council for Business Education. National Association for Secondary-School Principals. c1945.

National Association of Secondary-School Principals. The Consumer Education Study.
Time on Your Hands; Choosing and Using Recreation. National Association of Secondary-School Principals. c1945.

National Association of Secondary-School Principals. The Consumer Education Study.
Using Consumer Credit. National Association of Secondary-School Principals. c1947.

National Association of Secondary-School Principals. The Consumer Education Study.
Using Standards and Labels; A Problem of the Modern Consumer. National Association of Secondary-School Principals. c1953.

National Committee for Education in Family Finance.
Free and Inexpensive Materials for Teaching Family Finance. National Committee for Education in Family Finance.

National Consumer Finance Association.
Consumer Credit and You. National Consumer Finance Association. c1961.

National Consumer Finance Association.
Consumer Finance Catalog of Educational Aids for Classroom Teachers. Educational Services Division, National Consumer Finance Association. c1963.

National Consumer Finance Association.
Finance Facts.

National Thrift Committee.
Budgets Are What You Make Them. National Thrift Committee. c1953.

National Thrift Committee.
Budget Ideas for Youth. National Thrift Committee. c1954.

National Education Association.
The Teaching of Consumer Education. National Education Association. Department of Home Economics. c1962.

National Education Association. Dept. of Home Economics.
Youth and Money. National Education Association.

National Underwriter Company.
Handbook of Health Insurance. National Underwriter Company. c1962.

Neal, Charles.
Dollars With Sense. Doubleday and Co. c1965.

Nelson, Walter Henry.
The Great Discount Delusion. David McKay Company, Inc. c1965.

New York State Department of Law.
Your A B C's of Careful Buying.

New York State Department of Law.

New York Stock Exchange.
Bibliography. New York Stock Exchange. c1962.

New York Stock Exchange.
How an Order is Executed on the New York Stock Exchange. New York Stock Exchange. c1961.

New York Stock Exchange.
How to Understand Financial Statements. New York Stock Exchange. c1961.

New York Stock Exchange.
The Language of Investing: A Glossary. New York Stock Exchange. c1960.

New York Stock Exchange.
The World of Investing: A Test. New York Stock Exchange. c1961.

New York Stock Exchange.
Understanding the New York Stock

Exchange. New York Stock Exchange. c1962.
New York Stock Exchange.
You and the Investment World. New York Stock Exchange. c1963.
New York State Extension Service.
Do You Know Food Labels? (Food Marketing Leaflet no. 15.) New York State Colleges of Agriculture and Home Economics, c1960.
Office of Information.
Packet for the Bride. United States Department of Agriculture.
Olgilvy, D.
Confessions of An Advertising Man. Atheneum Press. c1963.
Oppenheim, Irene.
The Family as Consumers. Macmillan Company, c1965.
Pacific Finance Corporation.
Some Odd Facts About Money. Pacific Finance Corporation.
Packard, Vance.
The Hidden Persuaders. David McKay. c1958.
Pescow, J. K.
Getting More Out of Your Social Security. Grosset. c1965.
Phelps, Clyde William.
Financing the Instalment Purchases of the American Family; The Major Function of the Sales Finance Company. (Studies in Consumer Credit, no. 3.) Commercial Credit Company, c1954.
Phelps, Clyde William.
Using Instalment Credit. (Studies in Consumer Credit no. 4.) Commercial Credit Company. c1955.
Philips, E. B.
Consumer Economic Problems. Henry Holt and Co. c1957.
Phillips, E. and Lane, S.
Personal Finance. Wiley. c1963.
Porter, Sylvia.
How to Get More for Your Money. World Publishing Company. c1961.
Price, Ray G., Musselman, Vernon A., Hale, J. C. and Weeks, E. E.
General Business for Everyday. McGraw-Hill. c1966.
Public Relations Committee.
A.B.A. Film Guide. The American Bankers Association. c1961.
Ratchford, B. U., and Monhollon, Jimmie R.
Notes on Central Banks. Federal Re-

serve Bank of Richmond. c1963.
Rodda, W. U. and Nelson, E. A.
Managing Personal Finance. Prentice-Hall. c1965.
Rogers, Charles E. and Burk, Marguerite C.
Helping You Plan Your Life Insurance Program. Council on Consumer Information. c1956.
Roy, Ewell P.
Cooperatives: Today and Tomorrow. Interstate. c1964.
Smith, Augustus H.
Economics for Our Times. McGraw-Hill Book Company. c1963.
Smith, Paul F.
Consumer Credit Costs 1949-59. Princton University Press. c1964.
Smith, Paul.
Cost of Providing Consumer Credit. National Bureau of Economic Research. c1962.
Smith, Ralph Lee.
The Bargain Hucksters. Thomas Y. Crowell Company. c1962.
Smith, Ralph Lee.
The Health Hucksters. Thomas Y. Crowell Company. c1960.
Social Security Administration.
Essentials of Social Security in the United States. U. S. Government Printing Office. c1964.
Springer, J. L.
Make the Most of Your Income. Prentice-Hall. c1961.
Staab, Josephine, Heywood, Eunice, and De Vivo, Anita.
Improving Economic Literacy Through Family Economics. American Home Economics Association. c1963.
Stewart, Maxwell S.
Investing for Income and Security. (Public Affairs Pamphlet no. 317.) Public Affairs Committee. c1961.
Tax Foundation, Inc.
Facts and Figures on Government Finance. Prentice-Hall, Inc. c1965.
Tax Foundation.
State Retail Sales and Personal Income Taxes. Tax Foundation. c1963.
Texas. Bureau of Business Research.
An Analysis of the Teen-Age Market, by Philip R. Cateora. (Studies in Marketing, no. 7.) The University of Texas. c1963.

Time Inc.
Life Study of Consumer Expenditures. Time Inc.

Towle, J. W., Editor.
Ethics and Standards in American Business. Houghton, Mifflin. c1964.

Toyer, Aurelia.
Get Your Money's Worth. Holt, Rinehart, Winston, Inc. c1965.

Trilling, Mabel.
Design Your Home for Living, by Mabel B. Trilling and Florence Williams Nicholas. J. B. Lppincott Company. c1953.

Troelstrup, Arch W.
Consumer Problems and Personal Finance. McGraw-Hill Co. c1957.

Trump, Fred.
Buyer Beware. Abingdon. c1965.

Tyler, Poyntz, Editor.
Advertising in America. (Reference Shelf, vol. 31, no. 5.) H. W. Wilson Company. c1959.

Unger, M. A. & Wolf, H. A.
Personal Finance. Allyn. c1964.

Union Dime Savings Bank.
Budget and Expense Record. Union Dime Savings Bank.

U.S. Congress.
Economic Report of the President, transmitted to the Congress, January 1966, together with the Annual Report of the Council of Economic Advisers. U.S. Government Printing Office. 1966.

U.S. Congress. Joint Economic Committee.
1964 Supplement to Economic Indicators. U.S. Government Printing Office. c1964.

U.S. Department of Agriculture.
Consumers All; The Yearbook of Agriculture, 1965. U.S. Government Printing Office. c1965.

U.S. Department of Agriculture. Division of Home Economics.
Understanding Life Insurance for the Family. U.S. Government Printing Office. c1964.

United States Department of Health, Education and Welfare.
Free Social Security Teaching Aids. Social Security Administration.

United States Food and Drug Administration.
Read the Label. United States Department of Health, Education and Welfare. c1962.

United States Food and Drug Administration.
What Consumers Should Know About Food Standards. Superintendent of Documents. United States Government Printing Office. c1963.

U.S. Internal Revenue Service.
Teaching Taxes Program Materials. U.S. Treasury Department. c1963.

U.S. Internal Revenue Service.
Your Federal Income Tax. U.S. Treasury Department.

U.S. Department of Labor. Bureau of Labor Statistics.
Spending and Saving in Urban and Rural Areas; Survey of Consumer Expenditures, 1960-61. BLS report no. 238-14. U.S. Government Printing Office. c1965.

United States Savings and Loan League.
Home Buyer's Check List. United States Savings and Loan League.

U.S. Securities and Exchange Commission.
Investigate Before You Invest. U.S. Securities and Exchange Commission. c1959.

U.S. Senate. Special Committee on Aging—Hearings.
Health Frauds and Quackery. U.S. Govt. Printing Office. c1964.

U.S. Social Security Administration.
Essentials of Social Security in the United States. U.S. Dept. of Health, Education, and Welfare.

U.S. Social Security Administration.
Financing Your Social Security Benefits. U.S. Dept. of Health, Education, and Welfare. c1962.

U.S. Social Security Administration.
Social Security Benefits—How You Earn Them. U.S. Dept. of Health, Education, and Welfare. c1961.

U.S. Social Security Administration.
The Social Security Disability Program—Facts and Figures. U.S. Dept. of Health, Education, and Welfare. c1962.

U.S. Social Security Administration.
Social Security Teaching Aids. U.S.

U.S. Social Security Administration.
Three Who Came Back. U.S. Dept.

of Health, Education and Welfare. c1961.

U.S. Social Security Administration.
Your Social Security, U.S. Dept. of Health, Education, and Welfare. c1961.

U.S. Treasury Department.
Shareholders in America. U.S. Treasury Department. Savings Bond Division. c1961.

U.S. Treasury Department.
Internal Revenue Service.
Your federal income tax; 1966 edition for individual. (Publication no. 17.) U.S. Government Printing Office, 1966.

United States Treasury Department.
Teaching Federal Income Taxes. United States Treasury Department. Internal Revenue Service.

University of Wisconsin. Center for Consumer Affairs.
The spender syndrome; case studies of 68 families and their consumer problems. The University of Wisconsin, c1965.

Voorhis, J.
American Cooperatives: Where They Came From What They Do, Where They Are Going. Harper and Bros.,

N.Y. 1961. 738.

Waage, Thomas O.
Teachers Guide to Money, Banking and Credit. Joint Council on Economic Education. c1955.

Weir, Walter
Truth in Advertising. McGraw-Hill 1963. Do advertisers tell the truth? An attempt at an objective assessment of what goes on in the field. 738

Willet, E. R.
Personal Finance. Merrill, 1964, 550 p. $11.35. A 550 page book of 18 chapters for the college trained adult dealing with earning a living, budgeting, savings, banking, borrowing, buying a car, education, housing insurance, securities starting a business and estate planning. 738-572-731

Welfling Weldon.
Money and Banking in the American Economy. Council for the Advancement of Secondary Education Economic Literacy Series. No. 3. McGraw-Hill Book Co. c1962.

Wilson, Charles M.
Common Sense Credit. Devin Press, 1962. N. Y. 10011   738-572-731

INDEX

Advertising, 25, 61-82, 92
aims of, 61-63
goals for, 67-70
pros and cons of, 71-81
techniques of, 64, 67, 73-77
American Dental Association (ADA),
55, 74
American Gas Association (AGA), 53
American Home Economics Association,
55-56
American Institute of Lanudering, 54
American Medical Association (AMA),
55
on health frauds, 293-295
American Stock Exchange, 265
American Telephone and Telegraph,
258-260, 266
American Tobacco Company, 266
Antitrust Division of Department of
Justice, 30
Appliances, buying of, 142-144
Automation, effects of, 85, 239-240
Automobiles, buying of, 125-138
financing of, 137-138
new versus used, 126-133, 137-138
selection of, 125-129
used car buying guide, 133-137

"Bait and switch" advertising (see Deceptive advertising)
Banks, commercial, 253-254
loans from, 137-138, 181-184, 213-
215, 254
savings banks, 253-254
Better Business Bureaus, 50-53, 316
Boeing, 266
Borrowing money (see Credit, consumer)
Boston Stock Exchange, 265
Brand names and trademarks, 61, 63,
67-69
Bristol-Myers, 74
Budgeting, 149-165
goals, 150-151
need for, 158-159
a plan for spending, 149-158
as record, 164
saving by, 161-164
Bureau of Consumer Frauds and Protection (New York), 32-33, 296, 317
Bureau of International Business Operations (see Department of Commerce)

Bureau of Labor Statistics (see De-
partment of Labor)
Bureau of Narcotics, 22
Bureau of Public Roads (see Depart-
ment of Commerce)
Buyer (see Consumer)
Buyer beware, let the (see caveat
emptor)
Buying, motivation for, 75-76
Buying guides, 44, 46
American Home Economics Associa-
tion, 56
use of, 98, 143
(see also Consumer Bulletin, Con-
sumer Reports)
Buying on Time (see Credit, consumer)

California, 33
Car (see Automobile)
caveat emptor (philosophy), 3, 327-328
Census Bureau, The (see Department
of Commerce)
Charge accounts, 179
Charity gyps, 301-302
Cities Service Gas Company, 317
Clothing, buying of, 115-120
care of, 119-120
needs, 115-117
shopping guide for, 117-118
value of labels, 118-119
Coast and Geodetic Survey, The (see
Department of Commerce)
Collier's magazine, 19
Committee on Consumer Interests, 21
Consolidated Edison, 266
Consumer(s), 1, 80, 93-97, 101
effect on economy, 5-12
importance of, 1-2
income expectancy of, 85-86
legal problems of, 318-323
protection, 17-21, 32-35, 73, 307-310,
328-330
protection agencies, 316-317
(see also Consumer protection)
purchasing power of, 3-4, 85
rights of, 313-317
role of, 11-12
Consumer Advisory Council, 21
Consumer Bulletin magazine, 46, 143,
162
Consumer cooperatives, 48-50

· 361

Federal Communications Commission (FCC), 31
Federal Consumer protection (*see* Consumer protection, Federal)
Federal Deposit Insurance Corporation (FDIC), 254
Federal Hazardous Substances Labeling Act, 23
Federal Housing Administration (FHA), 213, 215
Federal Maritime Board (*see* Department of Commerce)
Federal Power Commission (FPC), 31
Federal Reserve System, 189
Federal Trade Commission (FTC), 21-22, 25, 76-77, 97
Fixed-income investments, 256
Food and Drug Administration (FDA), 22-23, 74
Food, buying of, 105-115
  daily food guide, 105-109
  government grades, 112
  guide for shopping, 110-115
  inspection stamps, 113
Food, Drug, and Cosmetic Act (1938), 22-23
Food, standards (*see* Standards)
Food, store's own brands, 113
Ford, Henry, II
Fraud, mail, 28-29
  (*see* Post Office Department)
Fraud, protection against, 51-52
  (*see also* Better Business Bureaus)
Frauds and deceptions, 291-310
Freeman, Orville L., 26
Furniture, guides to construction, 140-142
  hints for buying, 139-142

General Motors, 258-260, 264, 266
General Telephone and Electronics, 266
"get-rich-quick" schemes, 304-305
Gimbel's, 54
Government, interest in consumer, 18-35
  as a regulatory agency, 6
  "watch-dog" agencies, 22-32
Government agencies (*see* specific agency)
Government bonds, 263
Government Life Insurance (G.I.), 230
Grading, food, 28
  meat, 27
  (*see also* Meat Inspection Act, Department of Agriculture, Department of Commerce)
Group Life Insurance, 230

Guaranty (*see* Warranty)
Gulf, Mobile and Ohio Railroad, 260-261

Hart, Senator Philip A., 307
Health frauds, 291-295
Home Delivery Food Service, 76
Home improvement swindles, 295-297
Household Finance Corporation, 140
Housing, 195-222
  apartments, 201-202
  cooperatives and condominiums, 202-204
  cost of buying, 206-208, 213, 215
  determining factors in choice, 208-213
  financing, 213-215
  as investment, 215-217
  mobile homes, 204-205
  ownership, costs of, 217-219
    financial advantages of, 219
    pros and cons, 201-205
  selection of, 196-205, 208-213
Hyde Park Cooperative Society of Chicago, 307

Income, 85-103
  expectancy, 85-86
  purchasing power of, 85-90
  real, 9, 97-98
  use of, 90-101
Income tax (*see* Taxes)
Industrial insurance, 230
Inflation, 10
  effect on income, 89-90
  effect on purchasing power, 88-92
Information Service publication, 29
Installment credit (*see* Credit, consumer)
"in-store" comparative pricing, 97
Insurance, 227-238
  how to buy, 243-244
  purpose of, 225-226
  types of, automobile, 235-237
    credit, 238
    fire, 233-234
    health and accident, 232
  home owners, 234
    inland marine, 238
    liability, 234-235
    life (*see also* Life Insurance), 227-230
    theft, 234
    title, 217, 237
Interest, earning of, 253-254

Safeway Stores, 266
Salary (*see* Income)
Savings (*see* Investments)
Savings and Loan Associations, 253-254
Savings bank life insurance, 230
Seals of approval, value of, 53-54, 56, 144
   (*see also* Consumer protection)
Searle, 266
Sears, Roebuck and Company, 54
Securities and Exchange Commission (SEC), 30
Seller, 93-97
Sherman Anti-Trust Act, 5
Shopping, for appliances, 142-144
   for automobiles, 125-138
   for clothing, 115-120
   for food, 105-115
   for furniture, 139-142
Sinclair, Upton, 19-20
Small Claims Courts, 316-317
Small-loan companies, 183
Smith, Adam, 5-6
Social insurance and legislation, 238-242
Social Security Administration, 29-30
   (*see also* Department of Health, Education and Welfare)
Speculative investments, 256
Standard of living, 93
Standard Oil of New Jersey, 258-260, 266
State consumer protection (*see* Consumer protection, state)
Steffens, Lincoln, 19
Sterling Drugs, 266
Supply and demand, 3-4, 85, 153, 170

"take-home" pay (*see* Income)
Taxes, 275-288
   direct, 278-280
   indirect, 278-280
   influence on economy, 286-287

need for, 275-276
   as revenue source, 282-284
   types of, estate, 284
      excise, 283
      income, 282
      personal property, 282-283
      sales, 283
      school, 284
      tariffs, 284
Ted Bates and Company, 68
Testing consumer goods, 28, 41-47
The Jungle, 19-20
The Merchants of Menace (AMA), 293
Today's Health, 55
Treasury Department, U.S., 282
"Truth-in-Packaging" legislation bill, 307

Underwriters' Laboratories, Inc. (UL), 53
Unemployment, 239
Unemployment insurance, 238, 242
Uniform Sales Act and the Uniform Commercial Code, 328
Unsolicited Merchandise Act, 324

Veterans Administration, guaranteed loans), 213, 215

Wage or wages (*see* Income)
Warranty (ies), 325-330
Weather Bureau, U.S. (*see* Department of Commerce)
Weiss and Geller, 75
Wheeler-Tea Act (1938), 25
Wiley, Dr. H. W., 19
Woolworth, F. W., 266
Workmen's compensation, 238, 242-243

Xerox Corporation, 261